$40 MILLION SLAVES

$40 MILLION SLAVES

The Rise, Fall, and Redemption of the Black Athlete

WILLIAM C. RHODEN

Crown Publishers | *New York*

The poem on page xv is by William C. Rhoden.

Library of Congress Cataloging-in-Publication Data

Rhoden, William C.
$40 million slaves : the rise, fall, and redemption of the black athlete /
William Rhoden.—1st ed.
p. cm.
Includes bibliographical references and index.
1. African American athletes—History. 2. Sports—United States—History.
3. Discrimination in sports—United States—History. 4. African American
athletes—Social conditions. I. Title: Forty million dollar slaves. II. Title.

GV583.R46 2006
796'.08996073–dc22   2005034952

ISBN-13: 978-0-609-60120-4
ISBN-10: 0-609-60120-2

Printed in the United States of America

Design by Leonard Henderson

10 9 8 7 6 5

First Edition

To Sharon and Raisa: the other half of my heartbeat
My guiding lights, Bill and Janet Rhoden
My pillars of support, George and Mary Lopez

Contents

Prologue

THE TITLE OF THIS BOOK comes from a remark made by a white spectator during a professional basketball game in Los Angeles. The comment was aimed at Larry Johnson, then a player with the New York Knicks. The previous season, Johnson had referred to some of his Knicks teammates as "rebel slaves," unleashing a storm of controversy. That night in Los Angeles, as his team headed toward the bench during a time-out, a heckler yelled out: "Johnson, you're nothing but a $40 million slave."

★   ★   ★

When I began writing this book in the spring of 1997, the title that initially came to mind was *Lost Tribe Wandering,* an idea inspired by the biblical book of Exodus, which tells the story of the Israelites' flight from bondage in Egypt to the Promised Land. It seemed like an apt comparison: Virtually from the moment enslaved Africans came face-to-face with Christianity, Exodus became emblematic of our journey from Africa to the New World, though with a paradoxical twist. For generations of European immigrants, the United States was the Promised Land, the land of milk and honey. For enslaved African Americans, America became that Egypt from the book of Exodus. The quest to find the Promised Land in this New Egypt has been for many a never-ending journey through a succession of ostensible Promised Lands, none of which has turned out to be the final destination. This has certainly been the case for black athletes, who've journeyed from slavery to segregation to an exploitative integrated sports world, never finding a true Promised Land.

The image of a tribe of athletes crossing a dusty, desolate wilderness, sustained by the faith that there is an ultimate destination, remained my inspiration as I wrote this book: Black athletes appeared to me to be a multifaceted tribe whose march across time and against tremendous odds put an indelible stamp on the culture and psyche of this country.

Eight years later, *Lost Tribe Wandering* has become *$40 Million Slaves.* How did the book's title make such a jarring leap from the impressionistic *Lost Tribe Wandering* to a much more provocative one? This new title cuts to the chase in describing the white wealth–black labor★ condition that has merely changed forms from generation to generation. Even in 2005, with African American athletes making up a so-called majority in professional football and basketball and a significant minority in Major League Baseball, access to power and control has been choked off. The power relationship that had been established on the plantation has not changed, even if the circumstances around it have.

The use of the language of slavery in any variation always strikes an exposed nerve in the United States, the result of guilt, denial, and deep-rooted anger and frustration over the inescapable reality that our country's foundations are buried in the fields of slave plantations.

So the inevitable question will be asked: How can you use "slavery" and "$40 million" in the same breath? Even Bob Johnson, the owner of the Charlotte Bobcats and an African American, raised the question during an interview for this book.

After I told Johnson the title of my book, he said, "I'm not quite sure making $12 million a year playing 82 basketball games is called a plantation. If it is, I know a whole lot of folks who want to be on that plantation."

Johnson added: "I'm not sure the plantation-to-plantation metaphor works . . . because you have to explain how a guy gets paid that much money for doing basically what people do in the street every day."

Later, though, during the same interview, Johnson conceded that,

---

★See Claude Anderson's book *White Wealth, Black Labor.*

from an athlete's perspective, professional sports might be a plantation of sorts.

"Do the players see themselves on a plantation? I think they do, in that all of the owners are white. That creates the dynamic: The owners are white, the coaches work for the white owners, and the industry is run by white commissioners. Anyone who exercises power over them is white, and they feel or believe that the owners are taking more value out of them than what the owners are putting in."

To the general public, athletes have achieved the Promised Land. And their salaries are always a part of the discussion; the inference never far from the surface is that they should be grateful—more grateful than their white peers—for the money they make.

David Falk, the sports attorney who helped make Michael Jordan into a global icon, recalled a negotiation session with the Knicks in 1991. After Falk and player Patrick Ewing made an offer, the general manager looked at Ewing and asked, "How much money is enough?" Falk said he knew that Ewing was offended, and so was he.

"I knew that in [Ewing's] mind that wasn't an economic statement, it wasn't a negotiation statement. It was a racist statement saying, 'You're a young black man, how much is enough?' "

The celebrity of African American athletes is still used to make the case that discrimination has disappeared and that integration in the West has created equal opportunity. For many, African American athletes embody the freedom and expanded opportunities that are there for everybody, provided they work hard.

The elevated compensation of some players obscures the reality of exploitation and contemporary colonization. Black players have become a significant presence in major team sports, but the sports establishment has tenaciously resisted that presence percolating in equal numbers throughout the industry in positions of authority and control.

In 1988, the late Jimmy "The Greek" Snyder created a firestorm when he said African American athletes were physically superior because they had been bred for the role. Black athletes, he said, "can jump higher and run faster because of their bigger thighs. I'm telling you that the black is the better athlete and he practices to be the better athlete and he's bred to be the better athlete, because this goes all the way to the Civil War when, during the slave trading, the owner, the slave owner, would breed his big woman so that he would have a big black kid, you see."

Snyder's comments created a knee-jerk reaction and dredged up silly arguments about the merits (and lack thereof) of black athletes' so-called physical superiority.

Those debates for me are like play-action passes designed to suck you into the line, pump fakes designed to entice you to leave your feet.

The more interesting part of Snyder's comment reflects a more substantial concern. He said that the only place white people dominate sports is in coaching, and if blacks "take coaching, as I think everyone wants them to, there is not going to be anything left for the white people."

★　　★　　★

This book is a map, a look back at roads crossed, a glimpse forward at roads not yet traveled.

It's difficult for professional athletes to focus on anything historical beyond yesterday's game. They are so focused on the here and now—the next game, the next season, the next contract—that many have no sense of what came before, and none at all of what is coming around the bend. History suggests that African American athletes should be ever on the lookout. Their predecessors were excluded, blocked, persecuted, and eased out when white owners and management decided they weren't needed or wanted. Today's generation of pro athletes may be wealthy, but they are simultaneously cheered and resented—a tension that cannot last forever.

The community of black athletes, like the black community at large, is wealthier and in some ways more powerful than ever before, but in many other ways it resembles that wandering lost tribe, a fragmented remnant unable to organize itself to project the collective power it embodies but is afraid to use.

Isolated in summer camps and prestigious universities and pampered as the budding millionaires that many of them will become, today's big-time college and professional players are far less prepared to deal with the racial realities that exist in America than any previous generation of athletes.

Yet today's racial realities are more complex—less black and white, if you will—than they've ever been before. Tragically, in this their wandering mirrors that of the larger black community, illustrating once again, as if it needed to be, how closely black sporting life reflects the main currents of black life in America. At this unprecedented crossroads, the question is, Which way forward? Have we strayed too far from the road our ancestors paved for us, the road we tread as young men and women?

Or does the future demand that we strike out on a new path? In either case, we need to have a clearer understanding of how we got here before we can even begin to set a new course.

Like the bounty hunter who tracked escaped slaves during America's period of slavery, another bounty hunter of sorts is still on the trail. A century later, pursuing from one Promised Land to another, this hunter is trying to catch, to replace, and to eliminate those costly $40 million slaves. This is the story of the chase so far.

Glistening black bodies
on
fields of dreams
on battlefields, scoring,
between
defense's seams.
Tight muscles
bulging,
ferocious bucks
who scratch and claw,
say,
"Aw shucks, wasn't much."
Cream-colored spectators
cheer and roar
for conquering heroes
who conquer
no more.

Family Collage

Introduction

IN 1895, CHARLES DANA, the editor of the *New York Sun,* warned his readers, "We are in the midst of a growing menace. The black man is rapidly forging to the front ranks in athletics especially in the field of fisticuffs. We are in the midst of a black rise against white supremacy."

Dana would be astounded by the completeness of his prediction.

The contemporary tribe of African American athletes has become one of the defining social and cultural forces of the United States' most unique invention: the multibillion-dollar sports industry.

Black athletes are running faster and jumping higher than ever before. They earn more money in one season than their predecessors earned during their entire careers. Such contemporary African American athletes as LeBron James, Michael Vick, and Tiger Woods are worshiped almost as gods. At a time when the number of black males attending college is increasing at a slower rate than the number being incarcerated, young black men with stellar athletic ability are still hotly pursued, coddled, and showered with gifts for a promise to attend major colleges and universities.

Black faces and black bodies are used to sell everything from clothing to deodorant and soft drinks. Their gestures, colorful language, and overall style are used by Madison Avenue to project the feel and fashion of inner-city America to an eager global marketplace—they're the stealth ambassadors of hip-hop culture and capitalism, bridges between the "street" and the mainstream. No longer with hat in hand, the contemporary black athlete, represented by an impressive, mostly white armada of advisers, demands rather than asks. Many are showered with gifts and favors without even having to ask. Who could possibly call these powerful, globe-straddling icons failures?

I do. Today, perhaps more than at any other juncture of their long, rich journey, black athletes are lost.

Despite their fifty-year rise to prominence on the fields of integrated sports, African American athletes—male and female—still find themselves on the periphery of true power in the industry their talent built. In the public mind, the black athlete is still largely feared and despised, in keeping with the history of black Americans, whose success is often seen as an imminent danger. Every African American accomplishment in sports has—for more than two centuries now—triggered a knee-jerk backlash from forces within the white majority. The strategies of the white reactionaries have become predictable: to take back, dilute, divide, and push back any black achievement, in an effort to restore the same balance of power that has existed in this country since slavery, one in which the bulk of the rewards reaped from black talent and labor are distributed to and serve to perpetuate white power. And, just as predictably, black athletes have been slow to see the backlash coming until they have been swamped by it, finding themselves struggling just to survive. In their failure to heed the lessons of history, today's black athletes are squandering the best opportunities yet for acquiring real power in the sports industry.

This is not the heartwarming and triumphant narrative to which many of us have become accustomed—the inspirational reel that goes from victory to victory, from Jackie Robinson breaking into the major leagues to Arthur Ashe winning at Wimbledon to Muhammad Ali lighting the Olympic torch. This, in truth, is a more complicated tale of continuous struggle, a narrative of victory and defeat, advance and retreat, the story of an inspiring rise, an unnecessary fall, and an uncertain future.

★   ★   ★

Why are today's athletes so lost? The answer lies mainly in the succession of devastating spiritual losses black athletes have sustained since they began participating in integrated sports. The most significant of these has been the loss of mission, a mission informed by a sense of connection to the larger African American community and a sense of responsibility to the legacy of struggle that made possible this generation's phenomenal material success.

This sense of mission has been a cornerstone of African American survival, a source of strength and inspiration. A sense of being part of a larger cause has historically permeated nearly every action of the black athlete. For many of our most prominent athletes of every race, their victories were fueled in part by the notion that they represented something larger than themselves, that they embodied the values and aspirations of a people. Black athletes have symbolically carried the weight of a race's eternal burden of proof; their performances were among the most visible evidences that blacks, as a community, were good enough, smart enough, strong enough, brave enough—indeed, *human* enough—to share in the fruits of this nation with full citizenship and humanity. For much of this century the black athlete has, for the most part, carried that burden in public and before the world with style, grace, power, and nobility. The black physical presence in the United States has become part of our collective folklore; the physical feats of our athletes are metaphors for what African Americans might do on level playing fields in other aspects of society.

But today, when so many black athletes have little or no sense of who or what came before, there is no sense of mission, no sense of the athlete as part of a larger community, as a foot soldier in a larger struggle.

Young athletes, and many older ones, have dropped the thread that joins them to that struggle. They often have little or no understanding that they are part of a long and rich tradition. Black athletes attend some of the nation's most prestigious universities, but many are largely unaware of the depth and significance of their athletic roots. Many of their coaches aren't familiar with the history, either. If they are, many of them fail to encourage athletes to explore their roots, lest they become distracted from the task at hand: shooting, jumping, running fast and hard.

A number of years ago I was standing on the Seton Hall University campus talking with Mike Brown, at the time an assistant basketball coach. Tchaka Shipp, then a talented freshman player, was walking across campus wearing an Ethiopian Clowns baseball cap from the Negro Leagues. Mike complimented Shipp on his cap and asked him whether he knew anything about the Clowns. Shipp said he didn't; he'd bought the cap because it looked sharp. Brown asked, "Do you know about the Negro Leagues?" Shipp shook his head. Brown continued, "You know there was a time that blacks couldn't play major-league baseball, don't you?" Shipp looked at Brown incredulously and said, "Coach, get the fuck outta here!"

Shipp's stunned reaction was rooted in ignorance of history, not in contempt. But that doesn't make it any less shocking or excusable. Shortly after his encounter with Tchaka Shipp, Mike Brown went out and bought Negro League baseball caps for the entire team and had them each write a brief essay on the teams and their star players. Other coaches have also attempted to remedy the historical blind spot of contemporary players. John Thompson, for instance, when he was still head basketball coach at Georgetown University, in an effort to paint a wider historical context for their life journeys, took his players to the Civil Rights Museum in Memphis, Tennessee, on the site of the Lorraine Motel, where Dr. King was murdered, and to the Baptist church in Birmingham, Alabama, where in 1963 four little girls were killed when a bomb exploded during Sunday school.

If anyone should know the value of history, athletes should. They spend most of their time studying the past. Athletes watch game film incessantly. No responsible coach would think of sending a team into battle without having had his or her team spend hours studying game film. Film allows the viewer to study an opponent's trends and to assess strengths, weaknesses, and tendencies in order to devise strategies for the future. Film provides a means of studying the past to prepare for the future. Coaches do not, as a rule, demand that their black athletes study their historical past, and this has created a vacuum. The magnitude of the vacuum was articulated a few years ago by a young girl at Joan of Arc Elementary School in New York (since renamed), who asked me, "Who was the first white player to integrate the NBA?"

For many of us over fifty who were born in the United States, the idea of a player—any player—not knowing the story of Jackie Robinson is blasphemous. It's like not knowing about Rosa Parks, the Black Panthers, Martin Luther King, or the Montgomery, Alabama, bus boycotts. For people of my generation, the wide spectrum of black resistance and conflict are carved into our hearts. Those events remain so vivid, and represent such powerful emotional benchmarks in the ongoing struggle, that it is inconceivable to us that anyone could forget. We remember the history of struggle, we recall the terms on which liberation was won. We understand how much distance has been covered, but we also know how much more distance remains. I have to remind myself that, for athletes born after 1970, these memories are like outtakes from a grainy newsreel or epic myths from a long-lost era. For the young black athlete, the mere idea that African Americans could not play professional baseball, basketball, or football is beyond comprehension. After all, far from remembering a time of segregated leagues, this generation cannot recall a time when African American athletes were not the dominant force in the mainstream sports landscape.

Black athletes of an earlier era were forced by upbringing—and circumstance—to see themselves as part of a national community. They grew up at a time when the black community could still be said to be more or less united in common cause, a cause that transcended class, educational level, and other secondary social categories. For hundreds of years, athletes as diverse as Jack Johnson, Jackie Robinson, Joe Louis, Wilma Rudolph, and Althea Gibson were part of that larger community, a community linked by a common struggle for human rights in the world's greatest democracy. The goals of that community were clear: to attain power. The nature of that power evolved over time. In the days of chattel slavery, power meant literal freedom, as in the case of Tom Molineaux, a former slave who freed himself to become a champion boxer in England. In the uncertain period after the end of slavery, power meant using freedom to carve out individual success, as in the case of the black jockeys who dominated horse racing in the late nineteenth century. In the early years of Jim Crow, power meant defying growing white supremacy, as Jack Johnson did in his individualistic way. When segregation became the law of the land, power meant creating our own institutions, like Rube Foster's Negro Leagues, which created economies around sport and allowed for the development of a uniquely black athletic style. In the Civil Rights era, power meant representing a force for change, both practically and symbolically, in the manner of Muhammad Ali, Jim Brown, or John Carlos and Tommie Smith, the two American runners who raised their fists in protest at the 1968 Mexico City Olympics. In the era of integration, power often meant finding a way to avoid the exploitation of the sports-industrial complex and maintain a link to the larger black community, a goal that many black athletes, to their shame, failed to achieve or even attempt.

And what defines the quest for power today, in our post-integration era, when black athletes have become rich and famous, and in some cases have achieved positions in management, or, in the case of Bob Johnson of the Charlotte Bobcats, even ownership?

The quest today is to remember. Black athletic culture, like the rest of African American culture, evolved under the pressure of oppression. At every stage, that oppression—from slavery to segregation—has been struggled against, and in some cases vanquished. But at every turn, lessons were learned, weapons formed, a legacy created. Black athletes have historically struggled against the great problems of

American life—in fact, the great problems facing humanity. They have fought dehumanization, an unfair playing field, economic exploitation, and inequalities in power. The legacy of black athletic culture is a fighting spirit, as embodied in fiery characters from Jack Johnson to Curt Flood. The legacy of the black athlete is an elegant style, developed by physical artists from Willie Mays to Allen Iverson, as a way of showcasing the humanity, creativity, and improvisatory spirit of its practitioners. And the legacy of the black athlete is an acceptance of a larger mission, as displayed by Muhammad Ali's stands of conscience, Tommie Smith's raised fist, or Rube Foster's goal of creating an economically viable, independent black baseball league. Each of these legacies was initiated and refined as a response to a specific historical barrier, but the responsibility of black athletes today—and of all of us, really—is to understand how those legacies can also shape the future.

Ignorance of the past makes it difficult for black athletes today to unite and confront the issues of the present. This contemporary tribe, with access to unprecedented wealth, is lost, precisely because it has failed to complete what New York Sun editor Charles Dana described as the black athlete's "rise against white supremacy." On the contrary, African American athletes, blinded by a lack of history of what preceded them, have played a major role in helping maintain an unfair, corrupt, destructive system.

Today, the black athlete, while potentially more powerful than ever, is at a historical nadir. When the face of black sports is Kobe Bryant or Mike Tyson or even a raging capitalist like Bob Johnson, it's clear that the sense of larger mission has collapsed. A once-dominant cultural icon, the inheritor of an outsized legacy of glory and struggle, has become a spectacle that exists at the pleasure of its white owners. African American athletes today have the potential to be so much more than that—and God knows we need them to be more than that. More than politicians or clergy, contemporary black athletes have unfettered access to young minds, even when at times they seem to have lost their own. They exercise phenomenal influence on styles and tastes, but their reach could potentially extend so much wider, and deeper. For instance, there is growing and persistent poverty in our communities and less access to, or even hope for, a substantially better life among many in the so-called underclass. The divide between the haves and have-nots is greater than ever, but the diminishing of hope among the poorest of the poor is even more troubling. Who better than black athletes to bridge this divide? Many athletes come out of the most economically disadvantaged communities in the nation and have used sports to catapult themselves from poverty to wealth. Occupants of two worlds—the world of the streets and the world of wealth—these athletes can speak from a perch of power and influence, while holding the kind of "keep it real" pedigree that makes them relevant to the core black community. But now that they occupy a position where they can be more than mere symbols of black achievement, where they can actually serve their communities in vital and tangible ways, while also addressing the power imbalance within their own industry from a position of greater strength, they seem most at a loss, lacking purpose and drive. Given the journey that has led to this point, contemporary black athletes have abdicated their responsibility to the community with treasonous vigor. They stand as living, active proof that it does not necessarily follow that if you make a man rich, you make him free.

The contemporary tribe of black athletes is the greatest proof of that yet.

But it doesn't have to be this way. Like the Sankofa bird of African mythology, we have to look backward to see our way forward. Studying a history of how black athletes have confronted and mastered a series of obstacles and dilemmas over the centuries gives insight into the contemporary dilemma. It's not nearly hopeless.

This book seeks to tell the story of the rise and fall of the black athlete, but also to point the way toward redemption. It will seek to tell this exciting, rich, epic story with honesty and respect for its complexities, but it will also be driven by a sense of purpose: to find in that history lessons that will help illuminate the still-darkened path to real power for the black athlete.

Morgan State's Raymond Chester makes a catch between Grambling defenders on September 28, 1968, as Morgan defeats Grambling 9–7 before a sold-out crowd at Yankee Stadium. The game showcased the inherent talent and economic potential of black institutions. *Courtesy of Morgan State University.*

The Race Begins:

The Dilemma of Illusion

LONG BEFORE THERE WAS RACE and even before there was politics, there were Saturday mornings in the playground.

Every summer, on Saturday mornings my father and I would greet
the dawn. We'd have our breakfast, put on shorts and sneakers, walk
across the street to the Martha Ruggles Elementary School playground, and practice basketball. My father was my first coach. He was
a mathematics teacher by training, and his penchant for teaching
extended to sports. He taught me how to catch a football and run a
sprint. I played Biddy Basketball at the Chatham branch of the YMCA;
my dad was the coach. An astute judge of talent, he recognized that his
oldest son needed tutoring. And that's how those joyous Saturday
morning sessions evolved. I was eight years old, my shots barely
reached the rim, but my dad constantly reminded me that there was a
lot more to the game than shooting. He said that by the time I was
able to hit the rim consistently, I'd have an idea of how to play the
game. So we worked on fundamentals: dribbling, passing, catching.
Now and then we'd play a game of one-on-one. He always won. For
a change of pace, we'd run a foot race. He won that, too. But what I
loved most about Saturday morning was the bonding. Those practice
sessions gave me an opportunity to be with my father, and be with him
on a relatively equal playing field. At every turn, I measured my physical prowess against my father's. At every picnic, on every long walk,

I'd challenge him to a race, keeping mental notes all along, noting how long he had to run hard before easing up and letting me win. He was still father, I was son, but I knew that one day, if I became strong enough, quick enough, big enough, competent enough, the dynamics of our athletic relationship would change.

Those memories, carefully tucked away in my heart, are what make sports reverberate in my soul. Not covering the big games, interviewing celebrities and superstars, but childhood recollections of a boy trying to please his parents. The deepest, most ancient pull of sports for me has always been emotional. "Race" was something you did on the sidewalk or on a dusty road on the way home from school. In the beginning, speed and quickness didn't have a color.

My father tried to shield his three children from the brutality of the racial struggles that swirled about us in the 1950s. Every now and then he'd talk about some slight or indignity he'd suffered at the hands of a white person. Mostly he insulated us from the unfolding drama of the Civil Rights movement. Jackie Robinson desegregated Major League Baseball three years before I was born, but my father wasn't much of a baseball fan, so I wasn't shellacked in Jackie's legend of black Americans in the United States.

My mother was not an avid sports fan, but she was the lion in my soul. Her brother, my uncle Eddie, was a prizefighter in his younger days (my father called him the Canvas Kid). One day, when I complained about Billy Boy, our next-door neighbor, my mother didn't advise me to turn the other cheek, or to ignore him, or to tell his mother. She essentially told me to go back and kick his ass. I remember the two of us standing in our kitchen, my mother giving me an impromptu boxing clinic. I can still hear her voice as she showed me how to throw a combination: "Bop, bop—just like that," she said, showing me how to deck Billy Boy. I never did fight Billy Boy. I faced him in the yard soon after my mother's tutorial but couldn't bring myself to throw the first punch. This was my first lesson in combat: Power without heart and strategy is meaningless.

My mother laid out the racial facts of life for me. She burst my bubble in our kitchen one afternoon when she said casually that there were more white people than black people in the United States. I was stunned. In my segregated world on Chicago's South Side, black and brown were the dominant colors. In my world, white people were there but not there. Invisible. The stores, the Laundromat, the record shops, my schools. If whites were the majority, where were they? Why didn't I ever see any?

Of course, the answers to these questions flowed into the larger ocean of segregation and racism. That, in turn, flowed back to the ritual my dad and I enacted when we watched sports.

I learned about race and racism in front of the TV set. My father and I watched football games upstairs, in our bungalow on 78th and Calumet. We sat and cheered on the red leather seat my dad had pulled out of our '56 Mercury station wagon. Televised football didn't make a lot of sense to me back then. The images were too crowded, too small, too gray. The fun of it was cheering; and cheering interests were simple in our house. We rooted for the team with the most black players. We cheered for the hometown clubs, the Bears and White Sox, but aside from that, the general rule of thumb was that we cheered for the team with the most colorful presence.

In those days, when black faces were few and far between, we cheered for the color of the skin. We had some variations to the general rule: If the team was from the South and had just one Brother, his team was our team; he was our man. Didn't matter who the athlete was underneath his uniform or his skin—his true character was less significant than his presence. Out there on the field, he became the torchbearer for the race. Content of character mattered only to the extent that we prayed these pioneers wouldn't embarrass The Race.

The ritual my dad and I engaged in was one that took place among black sports fans and non-fans throughout the United States. The ritual went further back than Jackie Robinson, Joe Louis, or Jesse Owens. It probably went all the way back to the heavyweight prizefighter Jack Johnson in 1910, when the telegram runners passed through black neighborhoods calling out round-by-round progress of Johnson's historic fight with Jim Jeffries, the first Great White Hope. When Johnson defeated Jeffries on July 4, 1910, black communities across the country exploded in celebration. Other parts of the nation exploded with violence. As news of Johnson's victory spread, mobs of angry whites beat up and, in some instances, murdered blacks. Many whites feared that the black community might be emboldened by Johnson's victory over a white man. And they were not mistaken. Those early symbolic victories were soul food.

Symbolic representation was the rule of the day, part of a timeless ritual throughout the United States' melting pot of ethnicity: Jews cheered for Jews, Irish for Irish, Italians for Italians. But the predicament of black Americans was more complex, precarious, and sometimes seemed even hopeless. African Americans were so disconnected from the American dream that sports often seemed the only venue where the battle for self-respect could be vigorously waged.

My parents and their parents sat around their radios listening to Joe Louis fights, living and dying with every punch. Louis was fighting for himself and his country, but he was also fighting for a black nation within a nation. Every time Jackie Robinson went to bat, he did so for that elusive, ever-evolving state of mind called "Black America."

In those days of suffocating, uncompromising segregation, we cheered black muscle with a vengeance. The fate of black civilization seemed to rest on every round, every at bat. "Knock his *white* ass out," or "Outrun his *white* ass," or "Block that *white boy's* shot."

Or, worst of all: "You let that *white boy* beat you?"

Each group has had its cross to bear, but although Jews and Italians and Irish and all the other mingling European races could look forward to assimilating, assimilation was practically impossible for African Americans. The indelible marking of skin color made it so.

Early in the formation of the United States, blacks became the designated drivers of the Scapegoat Express. We were the "indecent others." The nation needed a permanent workforce and a permanent pariah. African Americans, by virtue of some seventeenth-century decree, got the job. No amount of education, no amount of wealth, could remove the stigma of race. The paradox and dilemma of virulent racism is that our exclusion became the basis of our unity. The next two hundred years of our existence were defined by reacting to racism.

So our cheering assumed a deeper meaning: We were cheering for our very survival. Black athletes became our psychological armor, markers of our progress, tangible proof of our worth, evidence of our collective soul. Our athletes threw punches we couldn't throw, won races we couldn't run. Any competition or public showing involving an African American was seen as a test for us all; the job of the athlete was to represent The Race. This was a heavy burden on the one hand, but on the other it represented a noble, time-worn responsibility. You always represented.

Paul Robeson—All-American football player, activist, orator, singer, actor—never forgot his first day as a freshman football player at Rutgers when white teammates tried to kill him—and nearly succeeded. Robeson never forgot his father's angry reaction when he was informed that his son was thinking about quitting the team—and Rutgers. His father told him that quitting was not an option, regardless of how trying conditions became. "When I was out on a football field or in a classroom or just anywhere else, I was not there just on my own. I was the representative of a lot of Negro boys who wanted to play football and wanted to go to college, and as their representative, I had to show that I could take whatever was handed out."

The attitude exemplified by Robeson's father was widely embraced by African Americans—the idea that we were each connected to a national black community by a common experience, a common condition, and a common cause was commonplace.

Floyd Patterson was the first African American athlete I can personally remember who carried the burden of The Race into the ring. Patterson became heavyweight champion in 1956—the youngest ever at the time. Soft-spoken and self-effacing, Patterson was the perfect media story: a young, wayward black boy, transformed by a caring white patron—Cus D'Amato—into a champion. In June of 1959 he defended his title against Ingemar Johansson and was pummeled without mercy. Johansson knocked Patterson down seven times in three rounds, and to many of us it felt as if black folks had been knocked out. But Patterson came back and won the rematch in June 1960, becoming the first fighter ever to regain the heavyweight championship. This was one of those psychic victories for black America, all the sweeter because Patterson proved all his doubters wrong. But then things got complicated. Patterson's next opponent was Charles "Sonny" Liston, an illiterate former convict with mob connections, whom the New York State Athletic Commission described thus: "A child of circumstances, without schooling and without direction or leadership, he has become the victim of those with whom he has surrounded himself."

The scholar Maurice Berube called Liston the "stereotypical nightmare of the bad nigger, the juvenile delinquent grown up."

That was the first time I was confronted with the new complexities of race brought on by the nascent Civil Rights movement. Liston was no Floyd Patterson. That is, he was not the model Civil Rights Negro, beloved by all, especially by whites. So here were two black men fighting for the championship. Liston was regarded as a pariah; Patterson was cast as the Good Black. Even John F. Kennedy, the President of the United States, weighed in, telling Patterson that he had to "beat that guy" because a Liston victory would not be in the best interests of the Negro image. The fight definitely was not in Patterson's best interest. Liston pulverized Patterson in their first fight in September 1962, knocking him out in two minutes of the first round.

Even Malcolm X—like Liston, a threat to both whites and the Civil Rights model—weighed in on the 1963 Liston-Patterson rematch, expressing the hope that Liston would "shake Patterson up."

That he did. Liston beat Patterson even worse in their 1963 rematch. Then along came Cassius Marcellus Clay.

Clay triggered an odd transformation in the country, in my household, and within the African American community. Liston's mob connections were one thing, but Clay's connection to the Black Muslims frightened a lot of blacks and whites a whole lot more. He had been recruited into the Nation of Islam by none other than Malcolm X, the radical minister who spoke of whites as blue-eyed devils.

Suddenly, big, bad Sonny Liston was redefined. He became reassuring to an older generation of blacks who liked the old heavyweight model Liston represented and were intimidated by Clay's brashness and connection to the Nation of Islam. A conservative segment of the community was screaming, "Enough of this militant business. Enough of this talk of separation, of blue-eyed devils." They hoped that Clay would be crushed, silenced, dashed to bits by the Bear. It didn't happen. Clay, the radical, defeated Liston, the thug, to become heavyweight champion. Later he fought Patterson and humiliated him in defeat because the former champion refused to call Clay by his new name, Muhammad Ali. Those of us who were younger and beginning to develop a more militant racial consciousness were thrilled by Ali. We called any black person who refused to call Ali by his name Old Negroes, Uncle Toms, or the white man's niggers.

Ali became the first universal, seemingly omnipresent black man. He said things we only imagined saying, did things many of us had never conceived of doing. He shunned his slave name, Clay, for Ali; he refused to be inducted into the U.S. Army and risked everything, including the heavyweight championship, for principle. When Ali was stripped of his title, it was as if he were being whipped by the overseer, like those "bad nigga" slaves of old. Publicly. We were outraged at the injustice but inspired by his courage and fearlessness, which were as strong outside the ring as they were within the four corners. Ali was my Jackie Robinson, the sports figure who transcended sport to become a true role model. His example gave many of us strength—black and white, rich and poor. For me, Ali brought home the concept of principle, that there was something greater in life than wealth, though wealth has its place; something greater in life than fame, though fame has its place. And he taught me that in the right hands, wealth and fame, the fruits of athletic success, could be used as a tool in the ongoing struggle.

★   ★   ★

My junior and senior years in high school were dominated by two shocking events: Malcolm X's assassination in February 1965, and Dr. King's assassination in April 1968.

When I left for Morgan State in August of 1968, my head was filled with conflicting visions of unity and revolt: Dr. King's Dream and Malcolm's warning of blue-eyed devils. There were kernels of truth in each vision.

When my dad and I watched football games on that black-and-white TV, the black athlete, low in numbers, with so much to prove, was a symbol. The struggle was about representation on the field. Ultimately I realized that cheering for the team with the most black players begged the question. By the summer of 1968, my dilemma, our dilemma as athletes, was where we fit into the Black Power equation, what our role was to be in the liberation movement. From Jack Johnson to Joe Louis, from Jackie Robinson to Wilma Rudolph, black

athletes had been effective symbols. How could African American athletes now become the energy inside the movement?

I figured the first step was to become part of strong black institutions.

★   ★   ★

I made my college football debut in Yankee Stadium on September 28,
1968, my freshman year: Morgan State versus Grambling State in an
eagerly awaited showdown between two titans of black college football. It wasn't much of a debut; one of four freshmen to make the
squad, I was in uniform but didn't play in the game. I was just happy
to be there.

This was our first game of the season, Grambling's second. Both
teams were on a roll. Morgan hadn't lost since the fourth game of the
1964 season—a span of twenty-six games. Grambling was the defending black national champion.

The teams had played each other only once before, in 1945. Back
then, using a band and a football team, Ralph Waldo Jones, the
Grambling president, sought to turn Grambling into the Notre Dame
of black college football. Eddie Robinson, going strong as the
Grambling coach in 1968, was hired in 1941 as part of President Jones's
plan to put the tiny school in northern Louisiana on the map.
Robinson's first big move following World War II was to play Morgan,
a nationally recognized power. Morgan won that 1945 meeting, 35–0.

But Robinson kept working, Grambling kept improving, and by
September 1968, Grambling had more players on professional football
rosters than any other college except Notre Dame. This game against
Morgan would be the crowning glory for Grambling and would put
Morgan, which had built a second dynasty under its coach, Earl Banks,
in the national limelight.

The game itself, the historic setting, and the underlying theme of
black pride made this Morgan-Grambling rumble important beyond

the final score. This clash between two Historically Black Colleges in a major stadium in New York was a perfect illustration of the power of the African American college, the power of the African American consumer, and the power of the African American athlete at the historically black institution—all empowered to determine their own definitions of success.

There were a number of forces that made the game a reality. Two beer companies, Rheingold and Ballantine, were fighting for control of market share. Rheingold was first. Ballantine, running a close second, agreed to sponsor the game with the idea of increasing its take of the lucrative black consumer market.

The National Football League also supported the game. Buddy Young, one of the first African American stars in the league, had been Banks's teammate at Phillips High School in Chicago and now worked in the league commissioner's office.

The National Football League (NFL) had once ignored players from historically black colleges. The league had gotten religion in the past five years, because players from Historically Black Colleges were instrumental in helping the rival American Football League keep pace with the NFL and ultimately forced a merger two years later.

In 1967, Willie Lanier, who played at Morgan from 1963 to 1967, beat out Jim Lynch, the former Notre Dame All-American, for the starting middle linebacker position of the powerful Kansas City Chiefs. Lanier was the first African American to start and star at middle linebacker.

Lanier's accomplishment was as significant in many ways as the Morgan-Grambling game itself. In 1967, middle linebacker was regarded as a "white position" along with free safety and, to a lesser extent, strong safety, offensive guard, and quarterback, of course. These positions required smarts and good judgment, attributes that white players had and black players, according to stereotypes of the day, lacked.

Until Tank Younger of Grambling was drafted by the Rams in 1949, athletes from Historically Black Colleges were ignored by the NFL in favor of black players from predominantly white colleges. Most NFL scouts felt that black college players lacked the talent to play professional football. There was also an unstated but keenly felt opinion among NFL management that black players from predominantly white institutions knew how to play with white players; in other words, they knew their place. League officials were anxious about how black players from black colleges would adjust to playing alongside white players—and accepting subordinate positions.

Coach Robinson said, "Tank, this is a great opportunity for black college football. If you fail, it's no telling when another player will get an opportunity. They'll say, 'We took the best you had and he failed.' "

Younger enjoyed a stellar NFL career (1949–1958) and was inducted into the College Football Hall of Fame in 2000.

The Urban League, then led by Whitney Young, embraced the game as a means of reaching out to the black community following the devastating urban riots that summer. Proceeds from the game were supposed to go to the Street Academy, a Harlem-based initiative sponsored by the Urban League, designed to help teenage dropouts return to school.

Young, who had been denounced by fiery congressman Adam Clayton Powell Jr. as "Whitey" Young, saw sponsorship of the game as a way to counter a growing sentiment that moderate Civil Rights leaders were selling out to white political interests. None of us was aware of it at the time, but the subject had become so heated that a former black school principal in New York City had been arrested in New York for making threats to assassinate Young, Roy Wilkins, and other Civil Rights leaders who he thought were selling out the mass of African Americans to white interests in exchange for position, personal gain, and prestige.

This internecine violence, symbolized by Malcolm's murder, reflected a complicated new development. Where previously our anger had been turned on whites, it was now also trained on those blacks who supposedly acted as agents of white interests—so-called Uncle Toms. Integration added a layer of complexity to black unity that hitherto had not existed.

Eight months before the game, Sammy Young Jr., a freshman at Tuskegee Institute in Alabama, the black school founded by Booker T. Washington, went to a filling station about a block off the Tuskegee town square and used the white men's room. The white filling station owner was so enraged that a Negro had dared to use his toilet, a public facility, that he shot him dead. An all-white jury acquitted the owner.

Robert Kennedy was murdered in June of that year. In August, the Chicago police routed protesters at the Democratic National Convention.

The most traumatic event took place in April, when Dr. Martin Luther King Jr. was assassinated in Memphis. Dr. King's death triggered weeks of rioting across the country.

With unrest and revolution erupting around the world, and with the Civil Rights movement in full and bloody bloom, Morgan-Grambling was an intriguing subplot in the violent drama being played out in the United States.

In fact, this game was a footnote to Dr. King's death, for it was at his funeral in Atlanta that Coach Banks and Coach Robinson signed the contract to play the game. Although there was no formal dedication, the inaugural Morgan-Grambling game would be played in Dr. King's memory. This added to the powerful spirit in Yankee Stadium that afternoon.

The big question surrounding the inaugural Classic was whether there was enough interest in a game between two historically black schools—one from Maryland, one from Louisiana—to attract a crowd in New York. Could they fill Yankee Stadium?

When our Morgan State team bus rolled up beside Yankee Stadium the Friday before the game, the marquee in front shouted the answer in big, bold letters:

MORGAN VS. GRAMBLING: SOLD OUT. NO TICKETS AVAILABLE.

By four o'clock Friday afternoon, we had finished a light workout at Macombs Dam Park, next to Yankee Stadium. As the bus pulled out of the Yankee Stadium parking lot and prepared to take us back to our hotel in Midtown Manhattan, Coach Banks's gruff voice thundered down the aisles, rolled up to where the driver sat, and commanded, "Let's go back through Harlem!" Our bus rumbled over the Macombs Dam Bridge into Manhattan and then up the 155th Street viaduct. Then we made a left turn—into another space and time. A turn into Harlem, U.S.A. I'd heard about Harlem in high school—a tough area, the capital of black America. Harlem was the place of dreams. To be here, live and in color, was electric. Two years earlier, in his book *The Crisis of the Negro Intellectual,* author Harold Cruse had described Harlem as "a community that still represents the Negro's strongest bastion in America from which to launch whatever group effort he is able to mobilize for political power, economic rehabilitation and cultural re-identification." We reached 125th Street and Lenox Avenue, the heart of the neighborhood, at five o'clock.

The eagle flies on Friday, and this Friday the eagle seemed to be flying especially high. It was the end of another hard week. Spirits were soaring. Brothers and sisters of all shades of brown walked the streets, talking and laughing, flirting and flaunting. Horns honked, music blared. This was one great, busy drama of huge Afros and processed hair. Black women were dressed in earth-toned African dresses or in hot pants and hoop earrings. Red, black, and green liberation flags flew everywhere. Sensory overload.

Streetcorner revolutionaries on speakers denounced blue-eyed devils on one corner; Jehovah's Witnesses proselytized lost souls on another. Cars double-parked. Cool cats sported canary yellow suits, while Superfly brothers in shades leaned against shining Eldorados with gangster whitewalls. One brother was driving a convertible with a leopard-skin top.

Coach Banks was the resident expert on Harlem. An All–Big Ten guard at Iowa, Banks played professionally for the New York Yankees of the All-America Football Conference before a knee injury cut his career short. He'd earned his master's degree from New York University. Like most football coaches, Earl Banks was a dictator. What made him tolerable, even enjoyable, was that his life contained a rich reservoir of experience, and he'd built a rapport with everyone from hustlers and tavern owners to the white drugstore owner in Iowa who had talked him out of quitting Iowa's football team. Coach Banks had an anecdote for every situation, and he would use the gospel preacher's inflection or the piercing vernacular of the street to deliver master-pieces of storytelling. As we passed through Harlem, he pointed out the hot spots: the Hotel Theresa, the Red Rooster, and the Showman's Lounge. "You can always tell the prostitutes," he advised, "because they wear white boots."

In 1966, Stokely Carmichael, then chairman of the Student Non-violent Coordinating Committee, espoused a dramatic paradigm shift for African Americans called "Black Power." The name bespoke unity, and called for black America to consolidate its resources to achieve political and economic power.

The Harlem I glimpsed that afternoon captured the essence of that slogan. Harlem felt like the spiritual and cultural capital of black America. In my eyes, Harlem defined the essence of "the Revolution," a revolution that had escalated the day Martin Luther King was assas-sinated. Dr. King's death was a signal that the nonviolent phase of the movement was over. His assassination ended a chapter in the Civil Rights movement that symbolically began in 1955 when Rosa Parks sat down on a bus in Montgomery, Alabama, and refused to get up for the white man who had demanded her seat. Between 1955 and 1968, protest was aimed at eliminating segregation. After King's death, the impetus, at least in my mind, was no longer asking whites for access or approval, but pushing for autonomy, empowerment, and self-definition. We were entering a new phase of the struggle. I certainly was.

We were no longer appealing for understanding from white society or asking to be allowed into its castle; we would build castles of our own, build strategies and programs that gave us a voice—and power. There seemed to be a new wave of struggle, a new way of thinking about things. We were taking all of the raw components of our lives and turning them into revolutionary weapons. Even our music was revolutionary: Nina Simone's "Young, Gifted and Black," Curtis Mayfield's "We're a Winner," James Brown's "I'm Black and I'm Proud."

I was just getting into jazz; there was a whole genre of so-called protest music. Many of the masters of the music were strong, independent black men and women who used their music as a vehicle, as a powerful expression of pride, anger, frustration, and hope. In my mind, the Morgan-Grambling game sprang from a spirit of independence. In our own way, we were part of an emerging new phase of resistance. Athletics was part of the revolution.

★   ★   ★

The teams came out for the pre-game introductions and were greeted by a thunderous roar, which, together with the blaring of the bands, formed a great sheet of sound. As I ran out on the field, I looked up. As far as I could see—nothing but Grambling black and gold and Morgan orange and blue.

John "Frenchy" Fuqua, Morgan's star running back, remembered the only thing he was thinking about was not embarrassing himself when he ran out for the introductions. "I was just praying, 'Lord, please don't let me trip and fall.' "

Frank Lewis, the Grambling wingback, was mesmerized—not by the crowd or the stadium, but by the historic moment the game represented. "What stood out in my mind was that here were two black schools playing in New York; Morgan State had that 26–0 record. That was the only thing that was exciting to me. I was thinking about how big a game it was. I didn't focus on the city and the stadium, just that two black universities had sold out the stadium at a neutral site, and that that was something that wasn't happening too often. It was almost like it was some national game."

Morgan scored on the fourth play of the game, a 47-yard pass to Raymond Chester. Grambling answered just before the half with a 37-yard pass from Frank Holmes to Frank Lewis to tie the game. In the locker room at the intermission, Coach Banks gave a classic halftime performance. He slung the blackboard around and furiously scribbled X's and O's. Above one X he wrote the number 81, and circled it: Billy Newsome was Grambling's defensive end. Newsome had single-handedly scuttled our "46 power," a running play that hadn't been stopped in four years.

"We're making this lemon look like an All-American!" Banks roared.

Newsome was in fact an All-American. Seven Grambling players and three of ours would be drafted the following spring.

Coach Banks glared at the two players responsible for blocking Newsome and scrawled some new blocking schemes on the board. When one of the players tried to say something, Banks cut him off and roared, "I want you to put your head in his gut and I WANT YOU TO DRIVE HIM OUT OF THERE!"

In his fury, he drew the line all the way off the blackboard. The chalk snapped and broke into little pieces as it hit the floor.

Early in the fourth quarter, Grambling lined up deep in its own territory to punt the ball. On the sideline, Coach Banks grabbed Ray Chester, who had played a great game as tight end, and tossed him in as defensive end. During the course of the season, I would learn that Coach Banks believed in inspirational substitutions. In the heat of the moment, if someone was screwing up, he'd roar, "I need someone to rush the passer," or "I need someone who can block." He'd grab the closest player and say, "Can you do it?" The answer always had better be "yes," or you might not play for the rest of your career.

Chester stormed across the line and blocked the punt. The ball rolled out of the end zone for a safety, and Morgan led 9–7.

Now Eddie Robinson was forced to use Grambling's "secret weapon," James "Shack" Harris. In truth, Harris was anything but a secret. At six feet four, 215 pounds, with a powerful arm and a "drop-back" style, scouts predicted that Harris would become the first African American quarterback to "make it big" in the National Football League. In the fall of 1968, quarterback was the sacred position, reserved for white players only. The history of black quarterbacks in the NCAA and NFL was limited: Willie Thrower had played for the Chicago Bears in 1953; Sandy Stephens had led the University of Minnesota to the Rose Bowl but had never played professionally; Eldridge Dickey, a star ambidextrous quarterback at Tennessee State, was drafted by Oakland and actually beat out Ken Stabler for the starter's job. But Dickey, like many talented black athletes before him, was ahead of his time, part of an era when athleticism in a quarterback was a dirty word. Dickey was eventually switched to wide receiver.

But Shack had all of the "necessities."

Harris nearly passed up the opportunity to play professional football. Drafted by the Buffalo Bills in the eighth round of the 1969 draft, Harris was demoralized over not being drafted sooner. He felt slighted and devalued. If not for a pep talk from Eddie Robinson, his coach and mentor, Shack might not have reported to camp. While Harris contemplated whether to report to the Buffalo Bills training camp, Robinson took him to Grambling's football stadium one afternoon and laid out the historical facts of life.

Harris's decision, Robinson explained, had to be based on something much larger than his disappointment over not being a higher pick. "He said if I didn't go, we might not ever have a black quarter-back in the pros," Harris told me years later. "We sat on the bleachers, just me and him. He told me that there was no question that I would make it as a quarterback, but if I didn't go, I might be keeping other guys from getting a chance. If I didn't go, it would be hard for anyone else because he thought it would be a long time before another black quarterback came along with my ability."

James Harris reported to camp and in 1974 became the first African American to start a regular-season game as quarterback. Harris would play twelve seasons in the NFL. In 1999 he became one of the few African Americans in the league's front office, as director of pro personnel for the Baltimore Ravens. Baltimore won the Super Bowl in 2001. In January 2003, Shack was hired as vice president of player personnel for the Jacksonville Jaguars.

★   ★   ★

Fortunately for Morgan on this particular autumn afternoon in 1968, Shack was hurt. He'd injured his ankle playing pickup basketball before the season and had missed most of Grambling's opening game against Alcorn State. Robinson wanted to hold him out of this game, too. But here in the fourth quarter in New York, on the greatest stage of his career, Robinson had no choice. Even Robinson had miscalculated the magnitude of this game, and he may have underestimated Morgan. Now, with his back against the wall, Coach Robinson reluctantly yielded to the moment. He signaled Harris into action.

Harris made a dramatic entrance onto the field from the Grambling sideline. He made his way slowly, visibly limping. He ducked into the huddle as Grambling fans went wild. Four times the officials had to stop the clock as the frenzied crowd drowned out Harris in his attempts to call the signals.

Grambling started on its own 23-yard line with 3:36 to play.

Harris completed four passes on the drive: Zip!—to Charlie Joiner.

Zip!—to Lewis. Zip!—to Joiner. Then he hit Lewis with a 37-yard pass to the 1-yard line, with 37 seconds left. The stage was set for a finish that could not have been believably scripted: a goal-line stand in the biggest game in black college football history.

Grambling's fullback, Henry Jones, gained nothing on first down. A second-down pass fell incomplete, and Jones gained just inches on third down.

Now it was fourth-and-goal from the 1, with 16 seconds to play. Eddie Hayes, our senior safety and team captain, remembered having a sinking feeling that Grambling would kick a field goal and Morgan would lose 10–9. Instead, Robinson valiantly chose to go for it. Later he would explain that Grambling's field-goal kicker was unreliable. I will believe to the end of time, however, that Robinson wanted to make a point—six points, actually: He wanted to run the ball down Morgan's throat.

The crowd was going crazy. Shack was raising his hands, wasting precious seconds trying to quiet the crowd. He didn't call time-out; the clock was running and Grambling had to rush the play. Jones took one final plunge into the line.

There was a tremendous collision as Chester and the entire Morgan defense collided with the 245-pound Jones and the rest of the Grambling offense. The referee took what seemed like several minutes to disentangle the players and determine whether Jones had scored. Chester, unconscious, was later carried off the field to a great ovation. As the official continued to dissect the pile, the tension mounted and the stadium fell practically silent. I remember looking around and wondering how 64,000 fans who had been so raucous all afternoon could suddenly be so still.

Finally the official held the ball over his head and flipped it up in the air. The game was over. Morgan held! The winning streak was alive at 27! The stadium—host to another epic—erupted in a loud burst of cheers and shrieks.

Now black, gold, orange, and blue all mixed together. I watched Ed Hayes walk off the field crying, saw Frank Lewis on the other side crying. Players on both sides were overcome, not just from the effects of a hard-fought game, but over the recognition of a historic event. Black folks had come to New York and put on a grand spectacle. What had been invisible had become visible, from the great athletes on the field to the dollars and wallets of a black community. This was the same untapped potential that the Brooklyn Dodgers' general manager Branch Rickey had observed two decades earlier when he attended Negro League games and felt a surge of black power that he craved to capture for his Dodgers.

This place, this trip, this football game, was the harbinger of promise, of all that could be. Not "integration" on white society's terms, but self-sufficiency. We didn't need to add to anyone's empire—and all the negatives associated with it. We needed strong, enduring African American institutions in which black people could have a defining say in matters that affected their expanding community. This was the dawning of a new day: black athletes, black institutions, black folk flexing their economic and cultural muscle in a collective way.

This inaugural Morgan-Grambling afternoon was a model of possibility of how sports could be used to achieve a greater good. The athlete could be something more than an entertainment bloodhound. That afternoon at Yankee Stadium conjured up memories of Negro League baseball games of the 1940s and Harlem Rens basketball games at the Renaissance Ballroom.

This was a snapshot of our past, our present, and—I hoped—our future.

I walked off the Yankee Stadium turf bursting with pride, thankful to be part of something this big, this black, this beautiful. We had the athletes, had the fans, had the money. This day, I thought, was the beginning of something. After all that had happened in 1968—the assassinations, the riots, the protests—things would never be the same again; there was no going back. I felt that something new had awakened in us.

Twenty-five years later, I would still be waiting. The dream was a mirage.

Harlem, 2003

Spirits echo as another dawn overtakes Harlem. Soft bursts of purples, oranges, and blues fan out over the Harlem River. Amber streetlights framed by my living room window glow like fireflies, peeking through a scattering of trees. Buildings cast long shadows in all shapes and sizes. The morning's pastels illuminate ribbons of highways and rails that bring in the noise and funk from the suburbs and points north.

The wild beats of the inner city, the "jungle rhythms," the "soul," that inspire so much romance and lore, yield to this peaceful early-morning interlude, a warm-up act for the bustling, full-scale drama of daybreak.

This is my home. This is Harlem.

The area is Sugar Hill, the building is "409." For most of the 1930s, 1940s, and 1950s, 409 Edgecombe Avenue was one of the most prestigious addresses in Harlem for African Americans. The building was completed during World War I. The first black family moved into 409 in 1929. The building quickly became home for many luminaries of black society: W. E. B. DuBois, the father of black sociology; Walter White and Roy Wilkins, executive secretaries of the NAACP; Thurgood Marshall, the first black Supreme Court justice; Jacob Lawrence, artist; Elizabeth Catlett, sculptor; Lucky Roberts and Jimmie Lunceford, musicians.

Marvel Cooke, who worked as DuBois's field secretary, lived in 409 from 1932 until her death in 2001. Cooke once told me that the great Babe Ruth lived at 409 in the early 1920s and kept an apartment on the thirteenth floor. A number of New York Yankees had lived in 409, she said. I'd never heard that, but it made sense. Yankee Stadium is a fifteen-minute walk from 409. Turn left out of the building, make a quick right down the 155th Street Viaduct, walk across the Macombs Dam Bridge, over the Harlem River and the Major Deegan Expressway, down the winding ramp, past the handball courts, and you're at the stadium press gate.

What an amazing transition. When I walked off the field in 1968, I never would have guessed that the arc of time would carry me back to Harlem. In retrospect, that Morgan-Grambling game was the beginning of a bridge, a transition from the black world in which I had been raised and a white-controlled sports industry in which I would work.

As much as I enjoy the memory of that idyllic autumn day in '68, time has crystallized realities in a way that has made me realize that 1968 was a mirage. Just as I realized in 1968 that the issues we were confronting were deeper than the simple lessons on race I had absorbed on those afternoons with my father, the years since 1968 have taught me that the issues go deeper than the powerful symbolism of one game. The idea that athletes, given a forum, would all follow the example of Ali and Tommie Smith and John Carlos has been shown to be mistaken. The notion that black people—once they'd infiltrated the world of sports in sufficient numbers—would follow the example of Curt Flood and work to change the economic exploitation of the sports industry was wrong. The idea that "soul," black style and artistry, was the one thing that couldn't be appropriated and commoditized by white power has proven to be laughably false. And the black institutions that I thought would be the vanguard of the revolution have been stripped bare by the progressively rapacious forces of sports capitalism.

Even the Harlem I thought I saw in 1968 was an illusion—the streets teeming with the colors and sounds of black folks did not match the reality of white ownership. Like the sports industry they "dominate," African Americans were not in control of this community; they merely rented. On 125th Street, for example, 95 percent of the consumers are black, while 95 percent of the stores are owned by non-black people. This mirrored the world I discovered as jazz critic for the *Baltimore Sun* between 1978 and 1982, and the world of sports I'd covered for the *New York Times* beginning in 1982. Black on the outside, white-controlled on the inside.

Harlem was a plantation.

*   *   *

And to understand just how deep the dilemma of the black athlete goes, that's the metaphor we return to again and again: the plantation. Because the heart of the dilemma, I eventually came to understand, is the quest for power, power as illustrated by on-the-field representation, power as demonstrated in off-the-field control, power as symbolized by physical domination, power articulated as political revolution. The plantation is the enduring metaphor because that quest for power began with the attempt to assert control over our individual lives and freedom in the hellish years of literal bondage. For black athletes in the United States, the roots of black muscle are buried in the blood-soaked plantations of Virginia, South Carolina, Mississippi, and Georgia, where the majority of slaves were first brought to America for their physical labor. The plantation is where the black athlete's dramatic march through history began. The roots of this tribe of black athletes run deeper than the fable of Jackie Robinson, deeper than the myth of Joe Louis or the legend of Jesse Owens, deeper even than the spectacle of a defiant Jack Johnson pummeling the Great White Hope into submission at the turn of the century. To understand the plantation is to begin to understand the present dilemma. So it's to the plantation that we will return to begin to unravel the dimensions of the black athlete's centuries-long quest for power.

Tom Molineaux represents the beginning of the African American athlete's march across time. Born into slavery on a Virginia plantation, Molineaux won his freedom with his fists. He would later challenge English champion Tom Cribb in the first "Fight of the Century." *Schomburg Center for Research in Black Culture, The New York Public Library.*

TWO

The Plantation:

The Dilemma of Physical Bondage

Now Joseph and all his brothers and all that generation died,
but the Israelites were fruitful and multiplied greatly and became
exceedingly numerous, so that the land was filled with them.

—EXODUS 1:6–7

Copthorne Commons, Sussex, England, December 10, 1810
2:40

TOM MOLINEAUX CURSED UNDER his breath and shivered as he made his way toward the scales for a pre-fight weigh-in. Under normal conditions, Molineaux enjoyed these events. They gave free rein to his flair for drama. They allowed him to connect with the crowd and absorb the atmosphere of the moment. But these were hardly normal conditions. Strong, gusting winds, bitter cold, and slicing rain this December afternoon had washed away the moment. This was a day for neither beast nor man to wage a fight, especially not a fight of this magnitude: Molineaux, the impetuous black American challenger and former slave, versus Tom Cribb, the undisputed, unrivaled champion of England.

Molineaux grumbled halfheartedly to Bill Richmond, his manager, sponsor, and tactical guru, "Why not postpone the fight until a day when the weather isn't so harsh?" But Richmond knew the mere hint of a postponement could trigger a riot.

The British people were known throughout Europe for their rowdiness. Eighteenth-century Britain was a flurry of riots brought on by everything from bread prices to new machinery. Even now, there was internal agitation in England caused by the rise of a radical working class. In an odd way, Molineaux, with his background in American slavery, had become the inspirational symbol of England's working class, which was largely sympathetic to the black resistance in America.

The five thousand fans who stood ankle-deep in mud at Copthorne Commons had no idea they were witnessing the beginning of a historic timeline of the African American presence on the large stage of professional sport. To them, this was "the fight of the century," but in reality it was merely the first act of a long-running drama that would play itself out back in America for the next two centuries. Even as the United States grew in global stature, the extremely visible struggle of black athletes for a fair opportunity became a constant, often haunting reminder that the principles of liberty and fair play, on which the nation was built, were compromised. Even if they didn't know about the struggle to come, the crowd that day knew that this fight was more than just a physical struggle. There was something else at stake.

For all these reasons, plus the sheer carnal pleasure of a championship fight, there would be no cancellation. Most of the crowd had come here from London, almost twenty-five miles away, to see this bold, black phenomenon named Molineaux, this foreigner, mysterious in so many ways, who came to England from a plantation in the American South. While historians agree Molineaux existed and was an accomplished fighter, there is disagreement over Molineaux's account of his slave origins.

Molineaux had barreled into London earlier in the year, loud and raucous, proclaiming himself the boxing champion of the United States. To the amazement, disgust, and fascination of Britons, this black Yankee boasted and bragged and told London journalists what he would do to English champion Tom Cribb if ever granted the opportunity. Cribb, for his part, had defeated all challengers in London. Unchallenged, he had retired and gone into the coal business.

Then Molineaux came along. His looks, manner, and brash attitude stirred a fever that spread through London. The retired champion at first rebuffed Molineaux, at one point disparaging him as a "mahogany impostor." But after he'd heard enough from Molineaux, Cribb sent word to the challenger that before he would consider a championship fight, Molineaux would first have to fight a pair of tune-up matches against opponents hand-picked by the champion. Then and only then, Cribb said, would he decide whether Molineaux was worthy to share the same ring with a national hero.

Molineaux accepted the terms and promptly wiped out the first challenger, a fighter called "The Bristol Unknown," in thirty minutes. Next came Tom "Tough" Blake, a hard-nosed veteran. Molineaux, in an extraordinary display of unpolished power, knocked Blake senseless in eight brutal rounds. The victory over Blake was so stunning that there was now a hue and cry throughout London for a Molineaux-Cribb match, and Cribb was forced to acknowledge that the black American was his chief contender. The stage was set.

Under British boxing custom, Cribb would have to surrender his title if he refused to fight a legitimate challenger. At the same time, he was duty-bound "to prevent the championship of England from being held by a foreigner" or, worse, as one English writer called Molineaux, "a Moor." This fight had become larger than Cribb. For the first time in Cribb's career, and the first time in recent English boxing history, a boxing match carried implications for the entire country. Even while sympathetic to the claims of enslaved American blacks, the English were in no hurry to see one take their boxing crown.

Born in Virginia, Molineaux was a product of the American plantation system. His father had been a fighter and a sailor in the War for Independence. Molineaux's uncles were fighters as well. When his father died, Molineaux, still enslaved, became an apprentice cabinetmaker. He began fighting slaves from other plantations and won several bets for his plantation owner, Algernon Molineaux. According to one story, Algernon Molineaux received a challenge from Peyton Randolph, a local planter, who said his best fighter could beat Algernon's best. Tom either volunteered or was volunteered to accept the challenge. Algernon supposedly hired a British sailor named Davis to whip Molineaux into shape—literally. Algernon had Molineaux flogged when the sailor complained that Molineaux wasn't training hard enough.

It was Davis who told Molineaux of the thriving professional boxing culture in England, of the money he could make with his fists in London. When the slave fight came, Molineaux handily defeated his opponent and won a substantial amount of money for his owner, who, as a reward, set Molineaux free and gave him $500. Molineaux worked his way north, first to Baltimore, then to Philadelphia, and finally to New York, where he lived for five years. According to one account of his life during this period, Molineaux fought several bouts, and in 1809 "we find the black assuming the title of 'Champion of America.' And he would appear to be the first man to call himself such."

After a string of triumphs, Molineaux took work on a frigate bound for England. He landed in Bristol, walked to London, and was directed to Bill Richmond, a fellow African American and a top boxing trainer.

If Molineaux was the root of a black presence, Richmond was the very seed. Born in Staten Island, New York, in 1763, Richmond had come to London in 1777—more than three decades before his protégé.

Richmond was brought to England as a servant to General Earl Perry, who saw to it that Richmond was given a solid education. In fact, he became better educated than most native-born Englishmen. He attended school in Yorkshire and was apprenticed to a cabinet-maker. Somewhere along the line, Richmond was introduced to England's bustling, well-developed sporting culture. He discovered that some men made enough money from their skill with a cricket bat, in the saddle, or with their fists to live comfortably. (The United States would not develop a broad-based, commercialized sporting culture for nearly a century.) Richmond learned to play cricket and attended horse races and prizefights. One evening he saw a match between a pair of fifty-year-old fighters. What made the greatest impression on Richmond was that one fighter quit after three rounds and still earned four pounds for his effort. Richmond decided to become a fighter on the spot and soon earned a reputation as a skilled one. During his days in the ring, he himself fought Cribb when Cribb was an up-and-coming fighter with a growing reputation. Cribb battered Richmond so badly that Richmond decided to retire to the life of a fighter's trainer.

Richmond married well. He married a white Englishwoman with enough money to enable him to keep a fashionable house, dubbed the Horse and Dolphin. It was here that Richmond opened a boxing school and taught gentry and aspiring boxers the "sweet science" of boxing. It was at the Horse and Dolphin that he also met Molineaux, who had heard of Richmond's reputation and sought him out.

Thirty-two years had passed between Richmond's and Molineaux's arrivals in England. The nature of their respective emigrations, their outlooks and expectations as athletes, reflect the evolution that was taking place in the American sports scene. Richmond came to London as a servant and stumbled into boxing. To Molineaux, boxing was his ticket to independence. He came to England as neither slave nor servant. He arrived in London with the single-minded mission of becoming world champion.

Although it took place in England, the fight marked the dawn of the black presence in American sports. Fittingly, the black athlete's prototype was a man who'd won his freedom with his fists and who, not satisfied with mere physical freedom, became hungry for more. Race, as it would be for the next two centuries, was at the core of white society's resistance to Molineaux's rise. Pierce Egan, the best-known boxing writer of the era, wrote: "Some persons feel alarmed at the bare idea that a black man and a foreigner should seize the championship of England, and decorate his sable brow with the hard-earned laurels of Cribb. He must, however, have his fair chance."

England had never seen a fight of this magnitude. Hundreds sloshed through the mud and gusting winds to bear witness to a match bursting with symbolism and metaphor. Englishman versus American. White versus black. Despite the rain and wind and generally dreary conditions, the afternoon had the feel of a coronation. And for many, that was precisely what they had hoped for: a formal installation of Cribb—and by extension the English people—as King of Pugilism, protector of English virtue and conqueror of infidels. Nearly everyone gathered at Copthorne Commons had heard tales and rumors of the man the English press alternately dubbed "the American Othello" and "the Great American Moor." Rumor is one thing, seeing is something else. Here was Molineaux—broad shoulders, stout chest, muscles bulging from well-formed arms and legs. His dark brown skin struck a dramatic contrast to the sea of white faces surrounding the boxing ring that winter afternoon. The English press had framed the fight in a way that modern readers would find familiar. All the already well-formed stereotypes were in play here in this squared circle: the black man's questionable character and intellect versus the white man's claim to civilization and superiority.

An ear-splitting roar erupted as Cribb appeared and climbed on the scale for the weigh-in. He was the hearty, robust signature of England. The band blasted "Heart of Oak" in honor of Cribb and "Yankee Doodle Dandy" in the American's honor. The anticipation for the fight was unprecedented, the pre-fight tension unbearable. Now the fighters stood shoulder to shoulder on the scales, Cribb's white skin touching Molineaux's black skin. Molineaux was not intimidated. In fact, one journalist wrote that "Molineaux was in the highest state of confidence; indeed his vaunting bordered upon insolent braggadocio." Egan, covering the fight, wrote:

> The affair excited the most extraordinary sensation, not only in the pugilistic world, but also among classes that had hitherto considered boxing as beneath their notice, and who now, thinking the honor of their country was at stake, took a most lively interest in the affair. The betting was heavier than had been known in years. Odds were laid that Molineaux would be defeated in fifteen minutes, and it was considered the excess of foolhardiness in anyone who betted that he would stand more than half an hour.

Indeed, few had given Molineaux a chance against Cribb. He was supposed to have been the unsuspecting lamb being led to slaughter. The odds were 5–1 for Cribb, 10–1 that Molineaux would fall in fifteen minutes, and 100–1 that he would not last the hour.

Thirty minutes into the fight, however, the gamblers and nationalists —and most of all Tom Cribb—realized they had made a tremendous miscalculation. They had grossly underestimated Molineaux's skill, his heart, his toughness and stamina. Mostly they had overlooked his resolve. Working deftly, with a combination of quickness and power, Molineaux handed Cribb the most savage beating of his career: The left side of Cribb's face was grotesquely swollen, his nose and mouth a bloody, indistinguishable mass of flesh. In the nineteenth round, as Molineaux held Cribb in a headlock, riotous fans stormed the ring and pummeled the black fighter. Molineaux sustained a broken finger as rioters attempted to break his grip. By the twenty-seventh round, the fight crowd realized that unless something was done, and quickly, the honor of England (and hundreds of pounds) would be lost. Bad enough that the national hero would lose, but lose to a Yankee? To a black man?

What stunned these fans most was not Molineaux's power, but his finesse and strategic command of the ring. According to ancient stereotype, blacks supposedly lacked the intellectual capacity to be strategists, as well as the fortitude to be warriors. These deep-seated stereotypes, along with Cribb's national standing, made Molineaux's performance all the more stunning. "Molineaux proved himself as courageous a man as ever an adversary contended with," Egan wrote. "Molineaux astonished everyone that afternoon, not only with his extraordinary power and strength, but also by his acquaintance with the science, which was far greater than anyone had given him credit for."

In the twenty-eighth round, Molineaux inflicted so much punishment that Cribb "could not come to in time"—the champion could not get off his second knee to meet Molineaux in the center of the ring. The umpire, Sir Thomas Apreece, had allowed the half-minute between rounds to elapse, then summoned each man three times. Cribb did not rise. Molineaux was ecstatic as he awaited his award of victory in the center of the ring. Sensing he had won, he leaped in the air in celebration. In that instant the twenty-six-year-old fighter embodied one of the most compelling themes in sports, one that the black athlete would revisit in various problematic iterations over time: the use of athletics as a way out; sports as a dramatic means of improving one's station in life, of gaining economic advantage and prestige that would have been impossible to achieve without sports. Two years earlier, Molineaux had been a slave on a Virginia plantation. Now he was on the verge of pulling off perhaps the greatest upset in boxing history.

Egan described what Molineaux was still up against: "The black had to contend against a prejudicial multitude. The pugilistic honor of the country was at stake and the attempts of Molineaux were viewed with jealousy, envy and disgust—the national laurels to be borne away by a foreigner, the mere idea to an English breast was afflicting, and the reality could not be endured. It should seem the spectators were ready to exclaim, 'Forbid it heaven, forbid it man!' "

In the midst of the excited confusion and in clear violation of the rules, Cribb's handler, Joe Ward, rushed across the ring to Molineaux's trainer, Bill Richmond, and yelled, "Foul!" He accused Richmond of having placed two bullets in his fighter's hand. This charge, according to Paul Henning, covering the fight for the London *Times,* "was indignantly denied and Molineaux was requested to open his hands proving that nothing was there. The ruse, however, succeeded, and gave Cribb the opportunity to come round."

All this drama swirled as the timekeeper repeatedly yelled, "Time! Time! . . ." signaling that the bout was over. Ultimately the timekeeper, who was under considerable duress from a crowd that had already stormed the ring once, waived the rules. Cribb was allowed an additional two minutes to recover and resume the fight.

The fight continued, but a dejected Molineaux began to fade. Twelve rounds later, Molineaux found his skull crashing against the ring post, his dream crumbling into ashes. In this, the fortieth round, the black American fighter finally conceded defeat.

Despite his loss to Cribb, Molineaux became the toast of London. Aside from being a novelty, he earned the respect of the English for his audacity, gall, and pluck. After that historic fight with Cribb, Molineaux watched his fame, popularity, and notoriety grow to a level he could have barely imagined two years earlier as a slave on the plantation.

Though he was raw and often crude, Molineaux found in England a kindred spirit. Each had battle scars. England had endured a succession of invasions: the Romans, the Danes, the Vikings, the Normans. At the time of the Molineaux-Cribb fight, England was fighting France; there was the eternal war with Ireland; and friction with the United States would again lead to war in 1812.

Molineaux had his scars as well, long ones across his back that were the signature of his previous life. In London he enjoyed life and lived "the life." Molineaux sat for a number of famous artists, including Douglas Guest, a frequent exhibitor at the Royal Academy, who included his portrait of Molineaux in his gallery. He also sat for the artists Molteno, Dighton, and Sharples. He was drawn in action during his fight with Cribb by Rowlandson and by the French painter Théodore Géricault. "Everybody in England knew of Molineaux," Egan wrote. "Through advertisement and published accounts, the name of this American-born Negro was a household word."

The English press loved Molineaux because he made good copy. He had a fascinating story, after all, and was not bashful about telling it.

Three days after his first fight with Cribb, Molineaux published his challenge for a rematch in an open letter to Cribb in the London newspapers:

> *Pugilistic challenge to Mr. Tom Cribb. Sir—My Friends think that had the weather on last Tuesday on which I contended with you not been so unfavorable I should have won the battle; I therefore challenge you to a second meeting at any time within two months, to such a sum as those gentlemen who place confidence in me be pleased to arrange.*

As it is possible that this may meet the public eye, I cannot omit the opportunity of expressing a confident hope, that the circumstances of my being of a different color to that of a people amongst who I have sought protection, will not in any way operate to my prejudice. I am, sir, your most obedient humble servant, T. Molineaux.

The second Cribb–Molineaux fight took place on September 28, 1811, in Thistleton Gap, England, and created even more frenzy than the first. There was an almost hysterical air of fear and expectation at Thistleton Gap. Again the national honor was at stake. Cribb trained hard for the rematch. Molineaux, after his discouraging loss, began drinking heavily and carousing, and finally broke with Richmond. This was a significant break. Without his trainer's shrewd eye watching over him, Molineaux reportedly consumed a chicken and a quart of ale on the day of the fight. He fought six strong rounds until fatigue, lack of training, and the excesses of his social life took their toll. Finally, in round eleven, with Molineaux's jaw broken, his face a bloody mess, Cribb was declared the winner.

★   ★   ★

Except for bits and pieces taken from the English papers, barely a word was written in the United States about Molineaux's exploits in London. *The First History of Prize Fighting,* published in the United States in 1849, failed even to mention Molineaux's name. A single story about his fight with Tom "Tough" Blake leading up to the first Cribb fight appeared in the October 25, 1810, edition of the *Raleigh* (North Carolina) *Minerva.*

The fact that Molineaux's feats in England were ignored reflects, on one level, the obscurity of boxing in the United States. More than that, however, the lack of acknowledgment reflects the suffocating impact of

American slavery, an institution that refused to allow slaves—and often their masters—any news of the world that would suggest that black people had an alternative to bondage. They were certainly not going to be allowed to hear of a story that suggested that blacks could compete with whites on equal footing. American slavery was founded on the principle of benevolent authority—the notion that the white man knows what's best for the black man. The primary aim of slaveholders was to indoctrinate slaves with a deep sense of fear and inferiority; to make them accept the notion of white supremacy in all things. Heralding Molineaux's exploits in England might encourage black independence at a time when the grip of slavery and persecution had intensified. By the time Molineaux arrived in England, the distinction in the United States between free blacks and slaves was being erased by whites alarmed by the rising number of free blacks in the United States.

By 1810, free blacks in the United States were finding it increasingly difficult to stay free. A white person could simply claim that a Negro was a slave and throw him back into bondage. There were numerous instances of kidnappings, and in those cases that actually reached the law, the courts often reduced free Negroes to slavery or servitude. Making a living was also becoming more difficult. In Maryland, for example, free Negroes could not sell corn, wheat, or tobacco without a license. Several states required free Negroes to have a white guardian, and all Southern states required them to have passes. There were restrictions on travel: Molineaux's home state, Virginia, barred free Negroes from entering its borders. There were also laws against free Negroes leaving the state for any length of time.

Molineaux came of age near the end of an era in African American evolution that historian John Hope Franklin has called "the search for independence." It was a time of firsts. Phillis Wheatley, who, like Molineaux, was enslaved, published the first book of poems by a black woman in 1773. Benjamin Banneker published the first science book written by an African American in 1791. By the mid-1790s, Molineaux's future benefactor, Bill Richmond, had become the first black athlete to receive international acclaim. But now began a time when race relations and the perception of the African American permanently began to deteriorate in the United States. The Enlightenment idealism of the American Revolution, which led to widespread condemnation of the institution of slavery, was giving way to the calcification of racial categories. These categories helped define who belonged and who did not.

The Naturalization Act of 1790 was designed to consolidate an American national identity, as European immigrants were transformed (through national legislation) into free white persons. We also begin to see the effort to define the African American slave as a "living tool, property with a soul."

Richmond stumbled into professional sports; Molineaux's distinction is that he actually set out to be a professional athlete and achieved prominence in the field.

Molineaux was a pioneer in many ways, not least of which was in showing how the tools of enslavement could become the tools of liberation. The black experience in athletics is a prime example of this motif in African American life. But the irony is that sports, which would become the tool of liberation for Molineaux and so many others—as well as a tool of psychological liberation for generations of black fans—were not introduced to empower enslaved blacks in antebellum America. Sports on the plantation were used as diversions to dull the revolutionary instinct.

Many slaveholders felt that contests such as the harvest festivals, an early American form of athletic games, were an ideal way for slaves to safely take out suppressed anger, aggression, and hostility. They felt that the competition dulled the revolutionary inclination; Frederick Douglass agreed. Douglass did not like fêtes and festivals, and was generally suspicious of sports. He saw holidays as frauds created not for the joy of laborers, but for the owners of that labor. Douglass felt that such festivals were only safety valves and conductors "to carry off the explosive elements, inseparable from the human mind, when reduced to the condition of slavery. But for these, the rigors of bondage would have become too severe for endurance, and the slave would have been forced to a dangerous desperation." Douglass added:

> To make a contented slave, you must make a thoughtless one. It is necessary to darken his moral and mental vision, and, as far as possible, to annihilate his power of reason. He must be able to detect no inconsistencies in slavery. The man who takes his earnings must be able to convince him that he has a perfect right to do so. It must depend upon mere force: the slave must know no higher law than his master's will. The whole relationship must not only demonstrate to his mind its necessity, but its absolute rightfulness.

In his autobiography, Douglass mentions the holidays at Christmas as a time when "the sober, thinking, industrious ones would employ themselves in manufacturing." Douglass believed that Southern plantation owners used "those wild and low sports" to keep blacks "semi-civilized."

Because Douglass wasn't an athlete, you could assume that he didn't particularly care for athletics. This is not entirely true. Douglass recognized the power of athletics to either pacify or inspire. And Douglass did enjoy competition. Shortly after the Civil War, he watched his youngest son, Charles, play baseball for the Washington Alerts. What Douglass despised was not sport, but rather white control of sports in which blacks were involved. He opposed the manipulation of black participation in sports to enhance a system that enslaved them.

Douglass achieved his own liberation when, after months of torment, he confronted his overseer and fought him in a famously documented two-hour confrontation. Douglass called this fight the turning point in his career as a slave: "It rekindled in my breast the smouldered embers of freedom and revived within me a sense of my own manhood." What Douglass didn't see about sports was that they often allowed slaves to grasp this same sense of their own humanity and selfhood. Sports, for many of the enslaved men in particular, became a ritual of reclaiming one's manhood. For Douglass, the act of fighting, not the winning, was liberating. His liberation lay in having the courage to fight his oppressor. He translated the symbolism of confrontation in real terms. He fought a system of slavery, challenging it in a fundamental way by engaging his overseer in a life-or-death struggle. For many blacks, sports were similarly symbolic ways of physically transcending the system of bondage, a space for freedom.

This legacy of using sports to stake a symbolic claim to humanity has endured: Molineaux facing Cribb; Jack Johnson beating Jim Jeffries; Jackie Robinson facing white Major League Baseball; Muhammad Ali defying the United States government; even Latrell Sprewell, part of a black majority governed by a white minority, attacking his white coach, or, more recently, black players attacking white fans. While each of these are, like Douglass's, stories of violent confrontation, there's a crucial difference: While later athletes fought to be accepted, admired, and respected, Douglass fought to be free.

★   ★   ★

For the early African Americans, alternatives to captivity were limited: They could commit suicide, as thousands did, or render themselves useless through physical mutilation, as other thousands did. They could attempt escape, as thousands tried, or they could attempt revolt and insurrection, which many did. The consequences of escape and revolt are recorded in the grisly accounts of slaves who were caught and subsequently flogged, or those implicated in insurrections who were brutally executed.

The "smart" alternative, taken by the vast majority of slaves, was to embrace survival. In exchange for being allowed to live, slaves were forced to accept the terms and conditions of bondage, and they were assaulted by constant, often brutal reminders of their subordinate status. Plantation owners continually worked to instill in their slaves a feeling of inferiority and, conversely, a belief in the innate superiority of all whites. Africans brought into American slavery were forced to accede to the humiliation that relinquishing one's selfhood demanded. They had to adhere to a set of elaborate laws, plantation rules, and social expectations: They could not possess alcohol without their master's permission; could not trade, traffic, or barter without a permit; could not beat drums or blow horns. They were not allowed to gamble with whites, to own property, to leave the plantation without a pass. They were not taught to read or write.

Sports played a crucial role in the lives of Africans who were captured, sold, and placed aboard America-bound slave ships. Plantation games and recreation were critical to the physical and psychic survival of many slaves. Physical competition became another means of salvaging a portion of lost self-esteem. Games—play—became a way of accommodating a bizarre new reality of bondage. For slave children, so-called athletic feats were a source of great pride. The ability to perform well in physical contests usually guaranteed them the respect of their impressionable young playmates.

There was no American sports culture to speak of in the mid-seventeenth century. The high value placed on work, coupled with the scarcity of workers, made recreation virtually impossible. By the early part of the eighteenth century, however, African slaves had become an essential part of an evolving sports culture in the American South. A rising aristocracy began to use sports to increase and extend its power. In the process of accomplishing this, quarter-mile racing became prominent. This emerging elite had access to vast amounts of land as well as an increasingly prominent labor force: enslaved Africans. The presence of these African jockeys and trainers reinforced a distinctive view of labor and leisure that the elite embraced and quarter-mile racing represented.

But there was a wider range of sporting activities in which African slaves were involved. In the plantation South, slaves of rival plantations were used as oarsmen in high-stakes boat races, as their respective masters steered. Foot racing, an enormously popular sport in the United States during the 1830s, was equally popular on the plantations and provided a convenient backdrop for wagering. Plantation owners exploited the speed of the fastest slaves by entering them into races against neighboring slaves or local challengers in various town races. Some slave owners formally trained slaves and even held preliminary races to ensure that only the fastest runners would race.

One slave recalled the running of races on his plantation:

> It was a custom in those days for one plantation owner to match his Nigger against that of his neighbor. Parish trained his runners by having them race to the boundary of his plantation and back again. He would reward the winner with a jack knife or a bag of marbles. Just to be first was an honor in itself for the fastest runners from all over the country competed for top honors and the winner represented his master in the Fourth of July races, when runners from all over the area competed for top honors and the winner earned a bag of silver for his master.

Another slave, William Mallory of Virginia, recalled the number of races he ran for his owner and proudly declared that he had never been defeated. Mallory added a touch of braggadocio by saying that he was so fast that at the Civil War battle of Bull Run, he added to his legend for blistering speed when "I actually outran the bullets." Planters described the characteristics of runaway slaves in terms of their physical acumen. This ad for a runaway slave in the August 3, 1797, edition of the *Maryland Gazette* acknowledges that slaves had made owners aware of their great speed:

> To any person apprehending and delivering at this place Negro Isaac who left here yesterday morning, and is endeavoring to cross the Bay, his route will be to the Delaware State, or Philadelphia though a very timid fellow it will be difficult to apprehend him, as he runs remarkably fast . . . he is a noted rogue, runaway, and horse rider. . . .

Slave narratives make frequent reference to adult slaves wrestling and fighting each other. Slaves preferred to compete among themselves and settle scores in private. The idea of competing for the entertainment of owners was the owners' idea. In his dissertation on plantation games, David Wiggins writes:

> It was common for planters to pit individual slaves against each other in wrestling and boxing matches. They frequently took place after corn-shuckings, log rollings or other communal gatherings when slaves from all over were gathered at one particular plantation. Slaveholders like nothing better than placing a wager or two on their favorite combatant.

John Finnely, a former slave from Alabama, reinforced the idea that these black-on-black fights were the white planters' idea. "De nigger fights am more for the white folks' joyment but de slaves am allowed to see it. De masses of plantation match deir niggers 'cording to size; and bet on dem."

Sports, like dance and musical forms, became tools of survival. But even as the power behind competitions was white, the slaves seized their own meaning from them. Athletic competition became a mode of expression and transformation. "The slaves' uncommon manner of performing many of their sports and popular pastimes was in a sense a form of communication," Wiggins notes. By utilizing different styles and assuming different roles in physical activities, "slaves were able to express their deepest fears and anxieties, scorn the maladroit whites and convey their thoughts and feelings to fellow bondsmen."

In play, the slave could become master; the powerless could become powerful. Athletic competition or a mere athletic feat—lifting hogsheads, picking cotton, cutting cane—was a free space where bodies bound and scarred by chains could soar. Sporting events sometimes provided slave children with an opportunity to compete against the children of plantation owners or overseers. These innocent-appearing competitions were often more significant to Africans because the white man's games were an extension of the white man. A victory wasn't simply a victory, but often a moral triumph over Pharaoh, a step toward the Promised Land.

In one narrative, Felix Haywood of Texas told an interviewer, "We was stronger and knowed how to play and the white children didn't." Another young slave who lived on a plantation in West Virginia regarded the son of the plantation master as his friend, but didn't allow him to win at any of their games. This particular young slave believed that he had unusual strength and spirit and claimed that he was "the best of the young boys on the plantation."

Even Frederick Douglass, who frequently criticized the role sports played in dulling the angry edge of slaves, remarked with pride that black boys "could run as fast, jump as far, throw the ball as direct and true, and catch it with as much dexterity and skill as the white boys."

What slaves could not do was give a defining voice to who they were. Slavery dramatically repressed the ability of slaves to express themselves. Even to attempt such a thing would be to risk being called impudent, which could lead to severe punishment; impudence could lead to death. The range of self-expression was curtailed to an extent that is difficult to imagine. Slaves were whipped for sullen disposition or dogged countenance. "A slave must not manifest feelings of resentment." For slaves, then, sport and play, music, dance, gestures, and other forms of nonverbal communication became crucial outlets for expression and communication. Sports were transformational. Play gave slaves a measure of autonomy, which in turn provided a forum for actions and expression that, in other contexts, might be seen by authority figures as "arrogance" or "impudence."

In addition to sports, there were a number of ways that slaves with unique skills could be elevated beyond the drudgery of backbreaking fieldwork. Slaves who practiced medicine were highly valued for their ability to cure illness. Slaves with a facility for numbers were also valued, and wealthier plantation owners used slaves as blacksmiths, carpenters, stonemasons, millers, and shoemakers. But for many plantation owners, whose estates were often physically isolated and at great distances from each other, the slaves' greatest value was their capacity to provide entertainment. The plantation owners relied on slaves' singing and dancing for their entertainment and the entertainment of their guests. A slave who was an accomplished fiddler was in great demand at social gatherings, as were "callers," who used clever rhymes to provide stepping instructions for country dances. Playing at social gatherings—and later, engaging in athletic feats and contests—earned privileges slaves would not have otherwise had.

Tom Molineaux's significance is that he identified the possibility of sports as another way of achieving liberty; he presaged what would become a dominant avenue after slavery. By the middle of the nineteenth century, sports generally became a way to help young men, black and white, but disproportionately black, escape from poverty.

The plantation athlete assumed a prestigious though ambiguous status within the plantation hierarchy. There were two status systems at work on the plantation: one defined by owners and staff, and one by the slave community. Blacks who were carriage drivers, cooks, maids, and slave drivers had high status among the white community but very low status within the slave community. They were distrusted. Nat Turner specifically told fellow rebels not to tell house servants about an impending revolt—with good reason. When someone informed the servants, the plan was foiled. Within the slave community, people like the granny woman, who cared for the community of slave children, or the conjure man had high status.

"The person who couldn't be broken . . . the rebel, the one they'd whip and whip and he'd still come up fighting—that person had high status in the slave community and none at all in the white planter family," said Ann Patton Malone, a professor of history at Louisiana Tech University and the author of *Slave Family and Household Structure in Nineteenth-Century Louisiana.*

There were figures who earned special status from both the plantation owners and the slave community. An accomplished "athlete" was one such person, according to Malone. The slave athlete—the fighter, the jockey, the horse trainer—often enjoyed exalted status among fellow slaves and was regarded as a role model for slave children, to whom he passed along his various skills. The most talented enslaved athletes not only earned respect among fellow slaves, but also garnered favor among owners, who saw their prowess as an outward extension of the owner's own strength. For those in bondage, the image of the strong black body engaged in competition was a positive one, and a powerful symbol. The black athlete's strength and grace presented a powerful counter-image to the prevailing stereotypes of blacks as slump-shouldered, shuffling bondsmen with heads bowed and knees bent.

Athletic contests, and the social gatherings surrounding them, helped

slaves maintain their identity as individuals and secure their cohesion—
as much as possible—as a community. This was critical for slaves
brought to North America, where extreme measures were taken to split
tribal groups, clans, and families so that little community of belief or
practice remained. Festivals and races helped keep this community
intact, however, fostering group solidarity and community spirit. Play
taught crucial survival skills. The games of children in bondage often
reflected an astute awareness that they lived a fragile existence under circumstances that required a certain level of cooperation, cohesion, and
compassion.

While some references to boxing and wrestling appear in slave
narratives, the children generally preferred to engage in more "gentle
pursuits." In his dissertation "Sports and Popular Pastimes on the
Plantation," David Wiggins points out that physical abuse of one child
by another was considered unjustifiable and a veritable threat to the
general well-being of the group.

Like their parents, slave children viewed themselves as a distinct
body with common concerns, problems, and lifestyles. They recognized the need to remain together as a familial group, no matter the
particular circumstances.

The point is not that slave children never fought each other, "but
rather they understood it was to their mutual advantage to care for
each other and refrain as much as possible from foolish skirmishes."
Children were usually so attuned to their interdependence that they
often refrained from playing games that required the elimination of
players. Even in a game like dodgeball, which typically required that a
player who was hit sat on the side, rules were altered to allow players
to remain in the game. The reluctance to eliminate reflected an
underlying fear of having a father, mother, sister, or brother sold, or
hired out at any time. Play was an area that slave children could regu-
late, where they could ensure that their playmates would not suddenly

be removed from their midst. Child and adult slaves alike learned that survival required teamwork.

Yet, by the beginning of the twenty-first century, white sports journalism had created and fostered and perpetuated the stereotype of black athletes as selfish individual players with an incessant "one on one" mentality. In fact, the history of African American survival in the United States is the history of teamwork and a history of individual expression within the context of the larger group.

Teamwork and community represented an essential component of African American survival; this was reflected in their games and social gatherings. The most poignant example of how African Americans in bondage used "events" as a means of maintaining continuity were the harvest festivals that celebrated the earth's abundance and the techniques of producing food. These included cotton picking, hog killing, and log rolling. These activities provided a test of skills and allowed individual slaves to distinguish themselves within the group. The most significant activity was corn shucking, the process by which corn is plucked from the stalk, husked, and stored for the winter. The festival itself was modeled after traditional English celebrations and took place in autumn. Depending on the planter's resources, the festivals could be huge affairs, with slaves from other plantations joining in. Corn-shucking festivals were held throughout the United States. In the South, however, the agricultural festivals were used by plantation owners as a way of "authorizing the delegation of power attending the ownership of the land and the slaves." These festivals were not the democratic drama of the "frontier bee" in the North. In the South, work parties on the plantation involved a bringing together of workers who were not landowners but slaves.

Yet these very congregations made some plantation owners uncomfortable. Some planters viewed the coalescing of slaves into groups for team activities as potentially dangerous and actively discouraged it. In fact, in 1797 the city of Fayetteville, North Carolina, passed a law prohibiting African Americans from playing "base ball" on Sundays.

★   ★   ★

This early history of the African in America offers a first glimpse of the differences in sporting culture between African Americans and European Americans. For all the talk—and reality—of contemporary social integration and assimilation, there remains a distinct black-white aesthetic divide in United States mainstream sports. Even as more young white athletes become influenced by urban black mannerisms, there is a fundamental, if subtle, tension between their respective approaches to sport. The tension is an extension of age-old, deeply rooted differences in what sports have meant to survival.

Practically from the beginning of their coexistence in the New World, Africans and Europeans—especially the English—viewed sports through drastically different lenses. Much of this had to do with the respective sporting traditions they brought with them to the New World. In England, beginning early in the seventeenth century, there was a court-inspired assault on the recreations of laborers, servants, and tradesmen. Reformist critics across England saw that when sports contests and public displays of physical prowess competed with religion, sports won. In response, justices of the peace in places like Lancashire mandated church attendance and suggested that sporting activities be banned. The tension went back to the previous century, when officials in certain towns eliminated football matches and other events from the list of acceptable Sunday activities. Eventually, in 1617, the conflicts led to a compromise called the Declaration of Sports, which ensured the sanctity of the Sabbath morning church services and the acceptance of sports and recreation later in the day. But the declaration fell in and out of use and became a bloody bone of contention between the clergy and the sports-addicted public. For what sports actually expressed was the response to fundamental changes in England from manors, lords, and tenants toward industrialization and urbanization. Yet in spite of the power structure's ambivalence, activities like wrestling, football (soccer), horse racing, and cockfighting remained staples of English sportive life.

Sub-Saharan, non-Muslim Africans had a strong athletic tradition as well. What Westerners called "sport" was to these Africans an integral part of their ritual, spiritual, and community life. The games were as diverse as the continent itself. The men participated in a variety of games, including foot and oxen races. Women played an assortment of games, too, often using a ball and various throwing and catching techniques. For males or females, a central characteristic of all games was the use of dancing, either as a means of introducing the game or as an integral part of playing it. And great care was taken to distinguish dances that were intended for secular uses from those designed to honor the deities.

The differences between the European (English) and African view of sport carried over to the New World and widened with the advent of slavery, which created an artificial distinction in which Europeans assumed a superior position, while Africans and their progeny assumed a subordinate position based purely on race.

White planters judged an individual's worthiness by the type of work he performed. While planters saw their own recreational pursuits—horse racing, boat racing—as signatures of elite and refined society, they considered "play" as trifling, frivolous, and inconsequential to survival.

For slaves, work did not define who they were, because it reaped more benefits for the slave owner than for the worker. The realm of play—which might include work, or the way one went about work—was a free space where the slave could salvage dignity, affirm selfhood, and express flair and individuality. Sports, as well as dance and music, were vehicles through which transcendence and transformation could be achieved, in which slave could be master, the powerless could become powerful.

Indeed, in the late nineteenth century, black boxers, black baseball players, and even a smattering of black football players were flourishing. Black jockeys were legends—and money earners—in the emerging business of horse racing. This physical presence in sport was a testimony, in some minds, to African Americans' ability to survive and flourish. Their hearty physical presence prompted Theodore Roosevelt to remark: "The Negro, unlike so many of the inferior races, does not dwindle in the presence of the white man. He holds his own, indeed, under the condition of American slavery he increased faster than the whites threatening to supplant him." Three years later, in the midst of withering brutality directed at African Americans, Jack Johnson became the first black man to win what was regarded as the American white man's prize of prizes: Johnson won the heavyweight championship of boxing. This was the dawn of the American Century and of an emerging black presence in sports. In 1910, a century after Tom Molineaux was robbed of his rightful victory over Tom Cribb in London, Jack Johnson put his knuckled stamp on the forehead of American sports by defending his title against the favored Jim Jeffries, who carried with him into the ring that afternoon the prophetic label the "Great White Hope."

The hysteria over this "black rise in sports" betrayed a deep-seated fear among whites of being overtaken by African Americans. This fear triggered a mostly unconscious, knee-jerk reaction to black success by mainstream white society: changing rules and changing relationships to either eliminate or mute the black presence, whether by gentlemen's agreement, racial quotas, or globalization. As scholar and sports historian Gerald Early observed in an interview with me for the 1996 HBO documentary *Journey of the African-American Athlete,* "At this point, white society had decided it was going to use any method it could to bring him down. He was just completely a political figure at this point and it was decided that they were going to bring him down." Just as Molineaux was robbed in the ring, so black athletes across the board have been faced with ever-changing rules designed to maintain white dominance. Mostly this has meant using power to change the rules of engagement. This is the "Jockey Syndrome."

CHARLES STEWART.

MY LIFE AS A SLAVE.

THE following autobiographical narrative has been taken down almost verbatim from the lips of its hero, an old negro man, who has dictated or told the whole of it with absolutely no help but his own memory. He does not read at all, or, of course, write either, though he once knew his alphabet, and there are none of his contemporaries alive in this part of the country, all the older members of his last owner's family, with whom he still remains, being dead, and none of those among them, to whom old Charles has been a life-long servant and friend, I might almost say necessity, knowing anything about the names and dates of races and race-horses, which are given exactly as he remembers them. Nothing throughout has been altered in any way except to make the details as consecutive and

Charles Stewart became the preeminent trainer of his era. While he amassed great wealth and national notoriety, the money and fame did not change his status as a slave. *Courtesy of Cornell University Library, Making of America Digital Collection. Image from* Harper's New Monthly, *vol. 69, issue #413 (October 1884).*

THREE

The Jockey Syndrome:
The Dilemma of Exclusion

So they put slave masters over them to oppress them with forced labor, and they built Pithon and Rameses as store cities for Pharaoh. But the more they were oppressed, the more they multiplied and spread, so the Egyptians came to dread the Israelites and worked them ruthlessly.

—Exodus 1:11–12

ISAAC MURPHY WOKE UP in the saddle of exalted fame and notoriety. The date was June 26, 1890, a day after the twenty-nine-year-old jockey rode to immortality on the strong, broad shoulders of a fire-breathing colt named Salvator at New York's Coney Island Race Course. Murphy had already won what racing aficionados described as one of the greatest races of the previous decade, and he was already one of the most popular athletes in an emerging professional sports culture, which saw bicycling become a national craze and baseball the budding pastime. But with horse racing still king, this day's race victory had solidified him as "king of the hill."

Murphy made his riding debut in 1875, at age fourteen, just five days after the inaugural Kentucky Derby. Thirteen of the fifteen riders in that first Derby were black, including the winner, Oliver Lewis. That was a year of great promise for black jockeys and for African Americans in general. It was the year Congress passed the Civil Rights Act of 1875, which outlawed the exclusion of Negroes from hotels, theaters, railroads, and other public accommodations—a major, if temporary, victory.

Within the next fifteen years, Murphy, an African American, had become a celebrity. His face, with its handsome chiseled features, was known at every track in the country. More than 25,000 roaring horse-racing fans packed the Coney Island course that Saturday afternoon, not just to see a monumental showdown between two outstanding horses, Salvator and Tenny, but to watch two of the country's best jockeys fight a battle of wits and skill. For nearly a decade, there had been heated national debates over who was better (and therefore the best): the cool, unflappable Murphy or the flamboyant Snapper Garrison, his opponent in the saddle. Murphy had a gunslinger's reputation. He was known as a big-time winner in big-time races. During a career that lasted nearly twenty years, Murphy rode in every important Derby, every classic stakes race, every important race everywhere. The bigger the race, the tougher Murphy was to beat. Garrison was the young star of the industry and the best rider in a group of white jockeys challenging deep-rooted African American dominance in the sport. He was the "White Hope" before the term was coined.

The battle between Murphy and Garrison contained the combustible elements of a historic match: great horses, great riders, high stakes, and racial tension. Newspapers sent their best reporters to the race and commissioned artists to re-create the dramatic moments of a race that was seen as the next symbolic showdown between black and white. For many whites, a Garrison victory would confirm the caginess, guile, and daring that supposedly framed white supremacy. For African Americans, the race was simply one more symbolic venue to prove that African Americans could excel when the playing field was level. Competition was on a level playing field.

Symbolism aside, Murphy and Garrison were much more alike than different. Both riders had a flair for the dramatic, and both had been chided by the media for it. Garrison was so acclaimed for his dramatic races and comebacks that his home-stretch rush became known as a "Garrison finish." The *Spirit of the Times,* a popular newspaper of the day, reported on "Garrison's inordinate desire to ride a grandstand finish, in which respect he is very much like Isaac Murphy. . . . Garrison wants to win by a nose or an eyelash, if possible, as that satisfies best the vanity which is the dominating feature of this man's make-up." Likewise, the *New York Tribune* complained about Murphy's "penchant for gallery finishes." The paper noted that if Murphy was in a race he knew he could win, his strategy was to "lounge along in the rear of the field till he strikes the home stretch and comes in range of the clear vision of admirers in the grandstand." Murphy would then move up and dramatically poke his horse's nose in front of the lead horse he had overtaken. "He proceeds to hold it there in a most artistic way 'til both horses pass the judges. It is the height of Murphy's ambition to ride such a finish."

Murphy's greatest gift, aside from knowing how to handle the media, was his exquisite sense of pace and timing. Perhaps his greatest skill—a mandatory skill for African Americans at the time—was the ability to size up a situation quickly and adapt. At Coney Island that June morning, Murphy sent Salvator off like a firecracker, knowing it would take a herculean effort from Garrison and Tenny to catch him. Salvator finished the first mile in record time, then set a record for the next eighth of a mile, leaving Garrison and Tenny hopelessly behind.

Or so it appeared. Garrison's performance in the race's last hundred yards—part miracle, part work of art—was a blend of the heart and heroism that converts events into legend. Garrison frantically, mercilessly used his whip. Tenny exploded and closed what seconds earlier had seemed like an unbridgeable gap. A writer would say in the next day's paper that the manner in which Garrison drove Tenny so close on Salvator was "perfectly stupendous." Before delirious thousands, Tenny thundered down the stretch and, to the naked eye, appeared to catch Salvator at the wire. A photograph taken on the spot showed that Salvator had won by a nose. The photograph itself was worth a thousand words; for it not only showed Salvator's dramatic margin of victory, but captured the essence of two great jockeys: There was Garrison, bent over, frozen in his "monkey crouch" in the last split second of a great race, frantically flailing. There was Murphy, sitting coolly upright and proper in his English seat, oblivious of the raging storm rapidly approaching from his right rear. They called Murphy "the Machine," and this photo captured his stoic essence: cool, unflappable control.

Murphy's victory capped three years of escalating fame, notoriety, and wealth. At the start of those three years, Murphy bought seven acres of land, and he and his wife moved into a large home in a fashionable part of Lexington, Kentucky; he also bought land in Chicago. When fellow jockey Tony Hamilton was married, Murphy gave a grand reception at his house. The local paper called the reception "the social event of the year in black Lexington." One paper said that Murphy entertained more often than "any black man in the South if not in the whole country."

In 1889, Murphy bought a colt and sold him for $4,000 and began a small stable of his own. An impeccable dresser, Murphy was always accompanied by a young white valet during the racing season. Murphy bought diamonds for his wife and was often bedecked with diamonds himself. While large numbers of African Americans in the South eked out a living, Murphy lived deliciously.

At the end of those three years, Murphy was one of the highest-paid athletes in the country. His annual income ranged between $15,000 and $20,000—nearly more than the entire payroll of the Chicago White Stockings baseball team. Other top jockeys of the day made between $5,000 and $6,000. Even this was a healthy salary, considering the average worker made between $500 and $1,000 a year, a figure that would plummet in 1893 when the nation plunged into a depression. Though this was not the norm, many of the best black jockeys, like their professional basketball counterparts a century later, earned salaries and enjoyed notoriety unthinkable to fellow African Americans, particularly in the South.

★   ★   ★

What would Murphy have said if someone had told him, as he basked in the glow of his Coney Island success, that black jockeys were racing toward extinction? If the response of contemporary black athletes is any indication, he probably would have laughed in his questioner's face. During the course of conducting interviews for this book and in casual conversations, black athletes routinely said without hesitation that they thought the likelihood of such a black vanishing act was virtually impossible. The black presence in contemporary sport has become so well defined, so deeply entrenched over the past fifty years, that many fans, both black and white, as well as players feel the current situation always was and always will be. Even as the NBA actively grooms as many non-black players as it can, players from Europe or Asia, players who don't bring along with them all the street baggage of black stars, Grant Hill sees the idea as preposterous. "People are too used to seeing the game played at a certain level," Hill has said. "The league needs us."

That's what Isaac Murphy thought.

Within twenty years of Murphy's defining victory, the black jockey, a dominant presence beginning with the quarter-mile match races of the seventeenth and eighteenth centuries, would have all but disappeared. Murphy would have been hard-pressed to predict or imagine the reason for this disappearance. It wasn't because black jockeys grew too physically big, or because of any exodus from the South to the Promised Land in the North, or because blacks gravitated to more prestigious occupations. African American jockeys disappeared because of a confluence of powerful forces—owners and trainers who stopped hiring them, white jockeys who ganged up on them, and the Jockey Club that systematically denied the reenlisting of blacks. Black riders became victims of the Jockey Syndrome, or changing the rules to fit a need—the need to maintain control in the face of a perceived challenge to white supremacy.

The Jockey Syndrome is distinguished by a changing of the rules of the game when competition begins to gain ground. It usually involves a series of maneuvers to facilitate racist outcomes, including the taking away of previously granted rights and the diluting of access through coercive power and force, a phenomenon that was common outside of sports as well, of course. Black Americans would see that clearly when the Civil Rights Act they celebrated in 1875 was almost completely overturned by the *Plessy v. Ferguson* case of 1896.

The Jockey Syndrome has been the primary mechanism in American sports for tilting the ostensibly level playing field of sport away from equal opportunity and toward white supremacy.

In short, the conspicuous success of black jockeys led to their demise.

The black stronghold on the sport had deep roots. The legacy of black riders and trainers formed an unbroken chain of dramas that extended back to the Revolutionary War, when black trainers, grooms, and riders not only cared for their master's horses, but also hid them from invading British troops. Most of the grooms, riders, and trainers were slaves and former slaves who earned various levels of independence through their skill at handling horses. Like most aspects of Southern plantation life, the antebellum racing industry in America could not have survived without a black presence. Slaves and former slaves rose to prominence as jockeys and trainers.

The 1890s marked the end of interracial sports in the United States at a time when the African American presence was under attack at nearly every other level of society as well. The period between 1890 and 1915 marked the most repressive and violent period in the history of race relations in the United States. Post-Reconstruction America was brutal for African Americans, who witnessed a furious backlash of white rage against gains made by African Americans after the Civil War. By 1890, black jockeys, while not the overwhelming force they had been before the Civil War, were still a dominant force.

Prior to the outbreak of the war, black jockeys were an indispensable part of the racing tapestry in the United States, especially in the South, where the majority of African Americans lived and where horse racing was king. Beginning in the eighteenth century, when quarter-horse racing was the dominant form of racing in the United States, black jockeys were involved in the most significant matches in the sport.

Quarter racing was a unique American invention. Because the Eastern Seaboard was densely wooded, Americans would clear a pair of adjacent paths through the pine trees. These paths were anywhere from ten to twenty-four feet wide, but always a quarter-mile long. As many as twenty times a day on some properties, two horses would bolt down these two paths at full throttle, jockeys jostling each other as they sped past spectators cheering wildly. This new sport was called quarter racing, and its headquarters, on the Virginia–North Carolina border, was dubbed "the Race Horse Region." The vast black population of the region accounted for the majority of riders.

Because trainers and riders spent so much time with horses as part of their normal chores on the farm and plantation, they often developed a rapport with the animals that translated into stellar performances. The first outstanding quarter-horse jockey was a slave named Austin Carter. Carter was probably the best quarter-horse jockey, trainer, and groom in the country. With racing centered in the South, the majority of riders from the late 1600s to the Civil War were slaves.

Although popular in the North, horse racing became wildly popular in the South. As large tracks were built throughout the South, black slave riders became a sorely needed source of labor to race, train, and care for the horses. An interesting aspect of the treatment of black jockeys is that not only were they dominant, but they enjoyed a reputation for honesty and integrity—a reputation inconsistent with the virulent attacks on the black character outside the track. At a time when blacks were being demonized as beasts and rapists, black jockeys were being praised for their character. One *Spirit of the Times* writer said, "In the Colored Ranks are to be found jockeys of the most sterling honesty and integrity." Another writer, protesting the suspension of a black rider, lavished praise on him, saying he wanted to recognize the jockey's "ability combined with thorough honesty . . . without regard to race, color or previous condition of servitude."

★　　★　　★

By the late nineteenth century, the dominance of black riders had become an issue. A year before Murphy's glorious Coney Island race, this headline appeared in the *New York Herald,* the day after African American jockeys won all six races in Brooklyn: "Colored jockeys show the way." In one section the writer observed: "The sons of Ham outrode the children of Japhet with a vengeance, for not a single white boy was successful in guiding a winner past the judges. It was a field day for the dusky riders and they forced their Caucasian competitors to take positions in the background." An 1890 headline in the *Spirit of the Times* declared, "All the best jockeys of the West are colored."

So dominant had black riders become by 1890 that racing writers were looking for various "White Hopes" to break the seeming lock that black riders had on the industry. An article in *Harper's Weekly* in 1887 pointed out hopefully that a quartet of white riding stars was emerging at the new Brooklyn Jockey Club track: "The professional jockeys some years ago were Southern Negroes, and with the exception of a few cross-country riders of Irish parentage, monopolized nearly all the mounts. Today it is different. With McLaughlin, Garrison, Luke and [Andrew] McCarthy—a quartet equal to any in the world—there is but little doubt that if a horse has got it in him to win, he will have to do it with one of them on his back."

Why didn't African American jockeys initially encounter as much resistance as did successive waves of baseball players, cyclists, and heavyweight boxers?

Perhaps diminutive jockeys were not a threat to order; in fact, in many ways they affirmed the imperial order. During the early decades of the sport, condescending attitudes prevented owners from appreciating the value of trainers and jockeys to the success of their horses. For many owners, until the 1850s, jockeys were anonymous sacks of weight that horses carried.

With the emergence of a slave jockey named Abe Hawkins in the 1850s, owners realized that the trainers and jockeys who had the best rapport with horses had the best chance of winning—and bringing the highest return on their investment. Famous for his honesty and professionalism, Hawkins was lauded for his cleverness as well as his skill in the saddle. While slave jockeys, including Hawkins, were not afforded the dignity of having their first and last names used, they were allowed public praise. Hawkins was the first to be lavished with platitudes by newspapers like the *New York Herald* and the *Spirit of the Times*. After one race, the *Spirit* gushed, "To extraordinary patience and judgment, Abe adds marvelous strength and skill. With a clip of the knees and thighs that incorporate him with the horse, and arms that never tire, he always has his colt right by the head and directs unremitting observation to what others are doing. His sagacity is greatly relied on by the gentlemen who know him." Said the writer Robert Alexander: "I have seen the best jockeys in Europe, and not one of them is nearly the equal of that old darkey." Another called Hawkins "the greatest rider in the South," while a third praised his "extraordinary patience and judgment."

The rise of Hawkins represented a significant shift in the elevation of jockeys in general, and of black jockeys in particular. Hawkins, more than any jockey before him, inspired an epiphany among owners regarding the importance of the jockey and the trainer to the success of the horse—namely, that the investment in horseflesh was meaningless unless the animals were well trained and expertly ridden. Hawkins, who rode throughout the Civil War period, represents the point at which African Americans began to be portrayed as accomplished athletes with strong character, discipline, and broad knowledge of racing strategies. At a time when African Americans were widely regarded as beasts and animals, some of the accomplished black athletes were marginally being portrayed as human beings.

Hawkins's proficiency forced the racing public to see the importance of the jockey. Thanks to Hawkins's insights, as relayed by reporters, racing fans gained keen insight into the riding tactics of the top riders. Bettors began betting on the jockey, not the horse. This new attitude toward racing and jockeys elevated the diminutive riders to star status in the United States. The new breed of racetrack gamblers placed their money in the belief that a clever jockey could win even on a second-rate mount.

White riders generally did not challenge the black jockeys' preeminence because of the stigma attached to working at the same job as an African American. After emancipation, African Americans monopolized certain jobs, becoming jockeys, caterers, bathhouse keepers, tailors, butchers, coachmen, barbers, and delivery boys—jobs that required little capital and depended on white customers. These jobs were closely identified with jobs performed on antebellum plantations by slaves. According to historian David Wiggins, slaves had been exploited as jockeys by the Southern planter. "The position of a black who rode for wealthy racing stables after the Civil War was quite similar to that of a slave who rode for his master," Wiggins said. "The black jockeys were hirelings who rode primarily for someone else's business."

So long as blacks were slaves, so long as they posed no threat to the political and economic supremacy of whites, people were content to live with them on equal terms of relative intimacy. But when the slave became a citizen, when he got a ballot in his hand and learned to read, there were demands for laws and arrangements that would humiliate him and keep him in his place.

In horse racing, they needn't have bothered; many of the jockeys kept themselves in place.

Even after the Civil War, Hawkins remained loyal to his former owner, Duncan Kennar. He was grateful to Kennar for giving him an opportunity to ride horses and see the country, and Kennar was no doubt grateful to his former slave for helping to build his fortune. At one point, when Kennar's fortunes were declining, Hawkins sent word that he would lend Kennar money to tide him over. Kennar, touched by the gesture of his loyal rider, declined the offer. When Hawkins became ill, he went to Kennar's plantation to die. It was the only home he really knew.

The story of slave and trainer Charles Stewart offers a poignant example of how the Jockey Syndrome reinforces the plantation power dynamic, whereby money does not necessarily alter one's status as "slave," as long as the "owner" is the one who controls the rules that allow that money to be made.

Stewart was a slave and trainer whose extraordinary racing life underlines the freedom a black athlete could achieve even within the confines of slavery. Born in Virginia in 1808, Stewart was a rider for Colonel William R. Johnson, one of America's leading stable owners. Later he became a trainer and a manager. Though he was wealthy as the curator of Johnson's sprawling stable, Stewart was never set free. But he had so much authority and made so much money that he *felt* free. He even had an agent.

As slave revolts swirled around, Stewart bought, sold, and trained his owner's horses. In 1831, when Nat Turner led his historic slave revolt in nearby Southampton County, Virginia, Stewart was unconcerned and uninvolved; he was training horses. "I was just as free and independent as any gentleman in the land," he said in his memoirs. "I had my helpers and jockeys and grooms and stablemen under me; nobody was over me."

Clearly the irony of his condition escaped Stewart. He was "free" but could also be sold. This is precisely what had happened to Abe Hawkins, originally owned by Adam Bingaman and sold to Duncan Kennar for $2,350. Two wealthy horse owners attempted to buy Stewart from Johnson, but the owner refused their offers. Henry Clay Jr. offered $3,500. Stewart eventually worked out an arrangement with his owner in which he, Stewart, would find another owner and Johnson would agree to the sale. Stewart arranged to sell himself to Alexander Porter, a U.S. senator from California. The sale price was $3,500. Stewart was well compensated, but he was not "free." Jockeys were dependent on the land and the landed gentry. Jockeys and trainers, so thoroughly tied to the land and owners, did not capitalize on their resources in a collective way by breaking free when they had the chance and acquiring their own land and horses. It would have been difficult, but not impossible—and it would have set up a major shift in the way the business worked if they had gained control of their own highly skilled labor. Instead, they allowed whites to negotiate the terms of their freedom and were devastated when, during times of economic hardship, the spoils were taken away.

As we'll see later, this pattern of dependency and non–self-sufficiency would repeat itself centuries later when blacks were dragged back into integrated sports beginning in the late 1940s.

Before Hawkins and Stewart, there was Austin Curtis, who raced in the eighteenth century and was the first "officially recognized" great black jockey. Curtis was given his freedom after decades of loyal service to his owner, Wylie Jones of North Carolina. Jones did not set Curtis's children free, however, and one of his sons was transferred to Jones's own son, although Curtis was given use of him "until my son . . . comes of age." Curtis was also given use of a nearby home and permission to clear fifty acres for cultivation. Jones's thinking was that when Curtis's son came of age, he would take control of the land. With money he earned and saved, Curtis bought another 165 acres of land in 1803 and 145 more acres in 1808.

Even at this early date, black athletes were able to make a living, get a head start, when many of their fellow bondsmen were tied to the land with little or no prospects of improving their station in life. Thanks in large part to black jockeys, the profession was elevated and jockeys found themselves in a seller's market. But as this happened, white riders began replacing black riders in the saddle. By the 1880s, the financial rewards of horse racing had made riding a means of social and economic mobility for members of disadvantaged social groups of all races. Young men who might otherwise have found it impossible to move upward advanced economically and socially by becoming jockeys.

★   ★   ★

Just four years after the great Murphy-Garrison Coney Island race in 1890, Garrison, who rode for several horse owners, including the wealthy industrialist August Belmont, made $23,500 in a single year— at the time the highest amount ever earned by a jockey in the United States. By 1900, Todd Sloan, another successful white jockey, had become known as a lavishly spending superstar, squandering millions over a two-year period. Sloan hobnobbed with royalty, lived in the finest hotels, and traveled with thirty-eight trunks of clothing. He changed his outfits every hour, and appeared on the streets in full dress.

Only since the 1890s, when white jockeys formed "anti-colored" unions and virtually drove black riders off the tracks, had the jockey profession attained its current respectability. The acknowledgment of the jockey's importance was the beginning of the end for the reign of black riders.

By the turn of the twentieth century, black jockeys were being driven out of the industry faster than the mounts they rode. A headline in a Chicago newspaper in 1900 declared: "Race war is on between jockeys at local tracks." The story began, "Jealous because of the success of so many colored riders, the white boys have taken to desperate measures to put their rivals out of business." While Jimmie Lee, one of the last black jockeys to win a major sweepstakes race, in 1908, was considered by the "white boys" acceptable,

> some of his compatriots of color became a trifle cocky in the jockey rooms; especially in the East. The white boys retaliated by ganging up against the black riders on the rails. A black boy would be pocketed, thrust back in the race; or his mount would be bumped out of contention; or a white boy would run alongside, slip a foot under a black boy's stirrup and toss him out of the saddle. Again while ostensibly whipping their own horses those white fellows would slash out and cut the nearest Negro rider. They nearly ran the black boys off the tracks.

Isaac Murphy could not be run off the track by other jockeys. He was too revered, too respected, too good. Murphy was not so much a victim of the syndrome as its trigger. It was almost as if the powers that be determined that there would not be another Isaac Murphy.

In August 1890, Murphy was suspended from riding at Monmouth Park, New Jersey, on the accusation that he had ridden while drunk. There were long-standing suspicions that Murphy was a hard drinker, but his good relationship with the media kept his problems out of public view. The Monmouth Park episode became a scandal because Murphy had been seen as a paragon of virtue, integrity, and honor. He claimed he had been drugged, and began seeing a doctor. Despite these upheavals, Murphy won an unprecedented third Kentucky Derby in 1891, setting a record that would stand until 1930.

He was suspended again in 1894 for being drunk. From that point on, his mounts were treated suspiciously, and owners refused to put Murphy on their best horses. If he lost, he was accused of being drunk or not putting forth sufficient effort. The proud Murphy was shattered. He told one writer, "I am disgusted with the way they treated me in the East during the summer. When I won it was all right, but when I lost they would say 'There's that nigger, drunk again.' I tell you, I'm disgusted and soured on the whole business."

Isaac Murphy died at age thirty-five, on February 12, 1896. His death, on Lincoln's birthday, marked the end of an era and the beginning of the end of the reign of black jockeys.

The year Murphy died, the Jockey Club was formed and became the national administrative arm of the horse-racing industry. Among its other responsibilities, the club licensed jockeys. In many instances, black jockeys were not relisted. That practice, along with a reluctance of white horse owners to hire black riders, and a black exodus from the South in the face of escalating violence directed at blacks there, reduced the pool of jockeys. The root of the change was greed, money, and racism.

Jimmy Winkfield was the last great black rider. Winkfield rode back-to-back Kentucky Derby winners in 1901 and 1902. He left the country shortly thereafter (his daughter says he was chased out by the Klan) to race in Russia and Poland, where he became a wealthy star. Ironically, he was chased from Russia during the Revolution because he was considered part of the bourgeoisie. Winkfield subsequently led a caravan of horses, women, and children from Russia to Poland. He eventually moved to France, where he raced, bought a farm, and ran a successful stable. But the defining episode of Winkfield's life, one that framed the tenacity of racism, took place many years later in 1966, when Winkfield returned to the United States for what would be his final visit. He went to Louisville to attend the Kentucky Derby—his first since he won the event in 1902. The turf writers learned that Winkfield would attend the race and arranged to honor him the night before the race. But when he showed up at the hotel, Winkfield ran into Jim Crow. Because of his race, he was informed that he couldn't come through the front door.

Over the years there has been a debate over what actually happened to black riders. Sam Lacy, the late sports editor of the Baltimore *Afro-American* newspaper, said the disappearance of black jockeys was not a hocus-pocus mystery.

"What made the colored boy drift away from the jockey profession which he dominated at one time? It isn't difficult to answer this one. The colored boy has not faded out of the hard boot business through any choice of his own. He was forced out as he is in everything else where the white man's money and influence dictate the course of events."

Although horse racing presented the first widespread example of the Jockey Syndrome, its first victim was not a jockey but a baseball player. The exclusion of African Americans from baseball was part of a trend as far back as the 1850s, when "informal agreements among organized amateur teams barred black participants."

★   ★   ★

A year before Isaac Murphy's great race at Coney Island in 1890, Moses Fleetwood Walker, a talented catcher from Ohio, played his final game in professional baseball. On the surface, Walker's exit from baseball seemed a mere drop in the bucket of America's emerging segregationist culture. But Walker's retirement was the beginning of a tidal wave that swept African American athletes out of integrated sports by the end of the nineteenth century. In 1884, Walker became the first African American to play major-league baseball. Five years later he left baseball bitter and disillusioned, convinced that black and white Americans could not peacefully coexist in the United States. Walker became an advocate of the Back to Africa movement. He may have been the first black athlete of his stature to play an active role in the black freedom movement.

Unlike horse racing, whose roots are buried deeply in the nation's raw beginning, baseball was a phenomenon of the nineteenth century. By the mid-1800s, baseball was making the transition from a game played on farms and lots to a highly commercial enterprise with good salaries for a select few. Baseball was among the first American sports to enter the realm of the emerging entertainment industry. The first professional baseball team was formed in 1869, the first professional league in 1871, and by the late 1880s the game had become a commercialized amusement business.

Baseball players were tied to their teams for life—or until their teams no longer needed them—but they were happy to be so chained. The pay was good, and jobs were limited. The players' grateful attitude was summed up by the star player of the time, Willie Keeler, who said, "I'm thinking of these suckers, the owners paying me for playing ball. Why, I'd pay my own way if that was the only way I had to get in a ball game."

Then as now, the media took a "they should be grateful" attitude toward players' salaries. *The Sporting Life* newspaper observed: "Columbus has a deaf mute and Cleveland a one-armed pitcher, Toledo a colored catcher and Providence a deaf center fielder, and yet these men can earn about $2,000 per annum apiece." At a time when laborers made less than $600 a year, a career in baseball was an attractive way to make a living. The best Negro League players were making $500 a year. By 1898, rising salaries and ferocious competition for jobs triggered the complete purge of African Americans from white-controlled baseball.

One reason that Walker would be so broken by his exclusion from baseball was that he felt he was better than the average African American and should be treated as such. He was a mulatto. His mother, Caroline Walker, was a midwife, his father was a doctor and a minister, and his family lived in a large home. Walker attended Oberlin College and played on the school's first varsity baseball team. He transferred to the University of Michigan, where he played one season.

In 1883, William Voltz, a former sportswriter, hired Fleetwood Walker to play for Toledo in the Northwestern League. During his first season, Walker had his initial encounter with a ragged version of the Jockey Syndrome when Cap Anson, the manager of the Chicago White Stockings of the National League, threatened not to play if Walker was allowed to play. Voltz refused to concede, and even sent Walker, who was scheduled to have an off day, to right field. He told Anson that if Chicago pulled out, Toledo wouldn't pay the guarantee. Anson backed down and the game was played.

A year later, Walker became the first African American player to play in the major leagues. But his entry into the game was hardly the emotional national saga that would make Jackie Robinson and Branch Rickey immortal fifty-four years later. There was no national "search" for the right black man to break the color barrier. Walker came in through the back door when Toledo, which played in the Northwestern League, was invited to join the American Association, which itself had received major-league status in an agreement with the National League in 1883. At the time, other black players were playing with white minor-league teams; some all-black teams competed in the leagues as well.

In Walker's case, the Jockey Syndrome manifested itself in a variety of ways. The covert backroom meeting of the old boys took the basic format: In 1887, International League owners agreed in a vote not to offer future contracts to black players. Then there were the more extemporaneous manifestations, such as Cap Anson's threat to Toledo. It manifested itself on the field, too. In Toledo, Walker worked with a pitcher named Tony Mullane, who conceded that he did not like blacks, but admitted that he respected Walker's ability and said Walker was the best catcher he had ever worked with. But Mullane refused to take signals from Walker, lest he allow a black man to be in a leadership capacity. "Walker was the best catcher I ever worked with . . . but whenever I had to pitch to him I used to pitch anything I wanted without looking at his signals. One day he signaled me for a curve and I shot a fast ball at him. He caught it and walked down to me. He said, 'I'll catch you without signals, but I won't catch you if you are going to cross me when I give you signals.' And all the rest of that season he caught me and caught anything I pitched without knowing what was coming." The fact that catchers didn't wear gloves in his day made Walker's task all the more remarkable.

Unlike with Jackie Robinson, who would integrate modern Major League Baseball in 1946, Walker's presence did not lead to a deluge of black players, or the scouring of Negro teams for black players by major-league teams. Walker lasted less than one season in the majors. He broke a rib in July 1884, was released from the Toledo team a month later, and never reentered the major leagues. No more black players played in the major leagues until Robinson signed with Brooklyn, though there were numerous attempts, mostly by major-league managers, to sign black players.

The next five years saw Walker embark on an odyssey of trying to get back into major-league baseball. He played with Cleveland of the Western League briefly, then with Waterbury of the Eastern League for two years. In 1887, Walker got a position with Newark of the International League, where he worked with a black pitcher, the great George Washington Stovey. In an exhibition game against Chicago, Walker was confronted once again by Cap Anson, who again threatened to pull his team if Walker and Stovey were allowed to play. This time Walker's team backed down.

By 1887 the climate had changed. Baseball salaries began to rise in the 1880s and into the first decade of the 1900s. There was a tremendous talent surplus brought on by the collapsed Players League and the American Association, and this resulted in ferocious competition for jobs. Team rosters were limited to 14 players until 1897; only 170 players could play in a given season. In 1897 the rosters expanded to 18. Owners, with the help of sportswriters, constantly reinforced the idea that players should be happy and grateful. The naked truth is that had talented black players been allowed to compete, they would have taken jobs away from white players. So black players, victimized by racism on the one hand and economic-based exclusion on the other, were left out. White baseball owners, while perfectly willing to lowball white players, were not ready to use black players as a means of achieving their end; they still had a sport to build. When the International League re-formed as the International Association, the Jockey Syndrome was still in place. The International League, for a period, had agreed not to ban black players, but to restrict them to one per team. When the Newark team folded, Walker moved to Syracuse of the International Association. Syracuse already had a black player but was able to use a grandfather clause to get Walker onto the roster.

By this time the cumulative effect of turning the other cheek, acting in a way that made whites feel comfortable, began to eat away at Walker's renowned restraint. At a game in Syracuse, Walker took the day off and sat in the dugout in street clothes. The Toronto manager asked Walker to leave the stadium. Heated words were exchanged. According to one account, Walker was surrounded by fans and allegedly brandished a loaded revolver and threatened to put a hole in someone in the crowd. He was arrested but released, and the next day he was in Syracuse's lineup.

Walker's last season of baseball was 1889. He was the last black in the International Association. As a result of that 1887 owners' meeting, no contracts were handed out to new black players. Nine years later, blacks were banned from all levels of white-controlled baseball.

On April 1, 1891, Walker was walking home from a bar when he was confronted by a group of white men. Words were exchanged, Walker pulled a knife, and a man named Patrick Murray ended up dead. Walker was tried for second-degree murder and acquitted.

In 1898, Walker was arrested, convicted, and sentenced to a year in federal prison for mail theft in connection with his job as a clerk in the post office. He was released in 1900 and began work as the owner of the Steubenville Hotel in Ohio. He also managed an opera house in nearby Cadiz. In 1908, the year Jack Johnson won the heavyweight title, Walker and his brother Weldy edited a paper called *The Equator.* That same year, Walker wrote *Our Home Colony: A Treatise on the Past, Present and Future of the Negro Race in America,* a forty-eight-page book in which Walker advocated emigration to Africa for all blacks. In the book, Walker wrote, "Even forced emigration would be better for all than the continued present relations of the races." Walker felt that whites and blacks were too different to live peacefully in the same country. It's not hard to see why he'd think that, given his experiences in the sport he loved.

★   ★   ★

In the end, Isaac Murphy and Moses Fleetwood Walker made fatal miscalculations in negotiating a racist sports industry. Walker, greatly influenced by his father's teachings and the prevailing attitudes of the day, felt that his privileged upbringing and his light skin, along with merit, would allow him to prevail.

Murphy was simply too grateful at the beginning of his career and too blinded by opulence at the end of it to anticipate black riders being pushed out of horse racing. Walker's and Murphy's miscalculations define what would become the Achilles' heel of African American athletes to this day: the failure to anticipate, plan, and organize; the wholesale dependence on a racist white power structure for

sustenance; and surprise and consternation when the money and support are withdrawn. Just as black jockeys failed to accumulate an ownership stake in their industry, contemporary black athletes have little
ownership stake, and thus are vulnerable to the same Jockey Syndrome.

In any event, Murphy and Walker were merely the tip of the ice-
berg of an emerging African American presence in sport.

And there's no question that among some powerful white
Americans, the black presence in sports was becoming a threat. At the
turn of the twentieth century, the prevailing wisdom among racialists
was that African Americans, because of irreparable genetic deficiencies,
would not survive. So for those who wished the country's "Negro
Problem" would just "go away," the black athlete became an uneasy
symbol of the African American's deeply rooted presence in America.
This resilience was crystallized over the next century by the predom-
inance of African American athletes in white-run sports, even under
the regime of the Jockey Syndrome. No sooner had one star or group
of stars been purged than another, usually in another sport, emerged.

In 1896, the year Isaac Murphy died, a pair of eighteen-year-old
teenagers—a boxer in Galveston, Texas, and a cyclist in Indianapolis,
Indiana—embarked on respective odysseys that would propel them to
international fame. One would revive his sport, the other would define
his. Their presence would have a far more resounding impact than
Murphy's.

★   ★   ★

Jack Johnson and Major Taylor stripped away the United States' democratic veneer as the country embarked on a century of dominance and
expansion—in the name of democracy. As much as lynching and racial
violence revealed the nation's bent toward violent racism, Johnson and
Taylor exposed America's deep-rooted fear of the fair fight—a fear
that stalked and haunted the nation, even at play. As a widening international audience weighed the United States' deeds against its pro-

nouncements, African Americans—burnt, castrated, strung from trees—became a profound symbol of the nation's contradictions. But even when bloody evidence of racism diminished or was hidden, black athletes revealed its existence.

Both Johnson and Taylor were born in 1878: Johnson on March 31 in Galveston; Taylor on November 26 outside of Indianapolis. Johnson, the third of six children, embarked on the independent life early on. Between the ages of sixteen and twenty, he trained horses, painted wagons, baked bread, and unloaded ships.

Taylor grew up on the farm of a well-to-do white family for whom his father worked as a coachman. The farm owners later "adopted" Taylor when he was eight, to be the playmate and companion of their son. While Jack Johnson lived the rough-and-tumble life of a fighter in training, Taylor helped himself to large doses of the good life, alternating between the black world of the farm and family and his adopted family's world of expensive toys, upper-class values, and private tutors. When the white family left for the Midwest, they left Taylor behind but also gave him his own late-model "safety" bicycle, which had become all the rage. The expensive toy became Taylor's ticket to international fame.

Johnson began boxing locally in Galveston, and slowly gained a reputation as a nimble, skillful fighter with a mean disposition. Taylor grew up in the predominately white world of bicycle racing. He worked in bicycle shops, one of which employed him as a mascot of sorts to do tricks on his bike, and dressed him in a soldier's uniform (thus his nickname, "Major"). He moved in with Birdie Munger, a former cycling great, who inspired Taylor's career. Under Munger's direction, Taylor was introduced to professional cycling.

Despite their different upbringings and worldviews, Johnson and Taylor would be victimized similarly by the Jockey Syndrome as white society became more reliant on rules and legislation to accomplish what once had been done through violence and intimidation. The two confronted the Jockey Syndrome in drastically different ways, with varying degrees of success. Taylor, much as he did on the velodrome, slipped through cracks and darted through openings. Johnson, much as he did in the ring, pounded down the door.

In 1890, Charles Pratt, the father of competitive cycling, sent out a call for cyclists around the country to converge on Newport, Rhode Island, for a convention. Pratt's goal was to form a national association that would put all riders under one umbrella. By the end of the week, the 5,000 cyclists had gathered and formed the League of American Wheelmen.

Over the next ten years, cycling became a fad of epidemic proportions. By 1890 there were more than 100,000 cyclists in the United States. Clubs were organized in nearly every town in the nation. There were white clubs and black clubs, clubs for women and children. A women's club in Manhattan performed intricate drills on bicycles. Everyone was riding. As bicycling became a spectator sport, velodromes were built everywhere in the United States, and large crowds came to watch the "scorchers," as cyclists were called, shoot around the board tracks at breakneck speed. Bicycle riding was the new national craze, racers the daredevil heroes of the day.

At that 1890 jamboree, neither Pratt nor any of the other cyclists had any idea that a humble, well-mannered twelve-year-old African American boy on a farm in Indianapolis would emerge as one of the greatest cyclists in the sport's history.

Taylor won his first race in 1892, at age thirteen. He had gone to watch the race, but Munger, the owner of the cycling shop where he worked, insisted that he enter the ten-mile race. White riders immediately showed their resentment by barring Taylor from all city tracks in Indianapolis.

Taylor dominated cycling competition during the height of the sport's popularity. By 1899 he had won the national and international championships and was the most recognized African American athlete in the United States. Great and enduring as his legacy would be, Taylor's racing career, virtually from the beginning, was defined, framed, and circumscribed by the Jockey Syndrome.

During the 1892 League of American Wheelmen convention, a faction introduced legislation banning blacks from membership, but the body refused to consider the question. A year later a similar motion was introduced to include the word "white" in the membership rules; that, too, failed to achieve a two-thirds vote.

In 1893 the Associated Cycling Club of Chicago barred black riders from participating in the Pullman Road Race. At the 1894 League of American Wheelmen convention, a motion barring blacks from membership passed out of fear—so the argument went—that the association might lose its Southern chapters if integration prevailed. Black riders who were already members could remain in the association. The impetus for the vote was a letter favoring segregation, allegedly written by Frederick Scott, president of the Union Cycle Club of Louisville, the largest black cycling club in the South. Scott correctly surmised that continued segregation would strengthen his black association. Indeed, after the 1894 ruling, black racing clubs grew. Taylor joined the predominately black See-Saw Club in Indianapolis in 1895.

In 1896, Taylor received an invitation from the Capital City Cycling Club to race against the record of Walter Sanger, one of the sport's early champions. Taylor beat Sanger's record by 8.2 seconds and was subsequently banned from the track.

After a hard-fought race in Massachusetts in which Taylor finished second, the third-place finisher grabbed Taylor from behind and choked him into unconsciousness. The rider was fined and a group of white riders took up a collection to help him pay it. In 1897, Taylor pulled out of the national circuit races because Southern promoters refused his entry when racers refused to ride against him.

While the Jockey Syndrome tied Taylor in knots, the underlying racism of the syndrome concealed what was also at the root of his popularity. This would be the conundrum that black athletes and promoters would face for decades to come: fighting on the one hand for a level playing field, yet playing on America's obsession with race to sell tickets and promote events. Taylor, like nearly every legendary athlete from Tom Molineaux to Jackie Robinson, was propelled to national and international heights of fame largely because racial tensions and combustible feelings projected into a sporting match between black and white. One writer explained: "The crowds wanted action, drama and danger and the struggle between Taylor and his white rivals was basic and understandable and fit the black–white hysteria of the era. Taylor was a young David taking up against several Goliaths at once. Taylor's races were filled with unstated but obvious racial symbolism."

In virtually every race, he found himself competing against the field, much like black jockeys of the same era who found themselves under attack by clusters of white riders. Many of Taylor's most ingenious racing tactics were developed to overcome the often dangerous maneuvers opposing racers used against him. His best—and most obvious—tactic was to get the lead early and keep it. In this way, Taylor dominated cycling from 1898 to 1901.

By the end of 1899, Europeans, especially the French, were eager to see this mysterious black champion. Taylor was a hero in France, and found himself elevated to the status of superstar. He was recognized everywhere he went. Crowds waited in his hotel to ask if he had passed a good night. When he arose at 6:00 a.m. and went for a walk, the walk became news in the Paris papers. The staff of the sports newspaper *L'Auto-Vélo* took Taylor to see Little Chocolate, the clown, the only other famous black in Paris at the time. He spent time in the Café Esperance, the cyclists' hangout. Taylor, the *negro volant,* was so well known that mail addressed to "Major Taylor, Paris, France," reached him. Maurice Martin, owner of *L'Auto-Vélo,* took Taylor to be examined by distinguished doctors at the Academy of Sciences to test racial stereotypes of the day. The doctors found him to be absolutely perfect except for overdevelopment of the thighs due to bicycle racing. A French journalist wrote to a friend in Chicago:

> . . . not one may be compared with [Taylor] in the matter of politeness and good behavior. We were literally amazed to find him better educated than the average foreigner who comes over and possessed of far better manners than our own riders. When we think of some of the harsh treatment to which this man has been subjected on account of his color, we cannot refrain from uttering the strongest words of disapprobation of such acts, nor from thinking that some parts of your country must be in a state of savagery.

Taylor left Paris on June 28, 1901. In four months he had been in twenty-four races. He had taken eighteen firsts, four seconds, and two thirds. He lost only two match races, and came back to avenge those defeats. In Paris, Taylor was welcomed into the social life of the sport. There the racism he encountered at home was replaced by curiosity and tolerance. There was ignorance of black culture and some condescension, but no hostility. For the first time in his life, he found it an advantage to be black.

Taylor, like Isaac Murphy, made a lucrative living through racing. He bought a large home in a white neighborhood in Worcester, Massachusetts. In Taylor's mind, this was evidence of his elevated status. Like Moses Fleetwood Walker, Taylor felt that his home, his standard of living, and the respect he received from the white community separated him from the "typical Negro."

In retirement, Taylor never filled the void created by the end of his legendary career. Cycling died out as an American passion around 1902, and what also died out was the notion of Taylor as an American hero. He was just another black man, who happened to have once been an athlete. Taylor had a penchant for invention, and felt he only needed formal education to flesh out his skills. Yet, despite his accomplishments, Taylor was refused admission to Worcester Polytechnic Institute, supposedly because he did not have a high school diploma. His daughter, Sydney, and wife, Daisy, subsequently watched venture after venture fold. "He was a racer," his daughter recalled, "not a businessman." When the Major Taylor Manufacturing Company folded, Taylor lost $15,000. A motor-oil business also failed. He was a salesman in 1917, a machinist in 1918, and a partner in a firm called Taylor & Quick the following year. Between 1922 and 1924, he owned the Major Taylor Tire Shop. In 1926 he was listed as an auto repairer.

The Jockey Syndrome shaved precious years from the athlete's sports life and real life, creating as it did the stress and frustration of knowing that whatever heights one attained might have been higher but for the pressures of racial animosity and the silent spike of discrimination operating in high places. The most devastating effect of the Jockey Syndrome, regardless of the generation it strikes, is how it eats away, not simply at the victim, but at the victim's family relationships.

I met Sydney Taylor-Brown some time ago, when we sat in her Pittsburgh home and talked well into the evening about her father and the meaning of his life. She recalled the fanfare surrounding her father's races, and being made to feel special because she was Major Taylor's daughter. They were not close. He discouraged her from becoming a physical education instructor because people might think she was a lesbian. He admonished her for going out without a hat on a sunbaked day, lest she get dark. For his part, Taylor attended a black church, but was not really "of the people." Said Taylor-Brown, "I don't think he was proud to be a Negro."

Her father respected Jack Johnson's triumphs over racism, but did not like Johnson's outrageousness, his cavorting with white women and openly living the fast life at a time when blacks were expected to be seen, not heard. As with Moses Fleetwood Walker, the source of Taylor's indignation over race did not stem from his pride as a black man. He resented not being allowed to become part of the fraternity of white men as other ethnic groups had done.

As his fame evaporated piece by precious piece, Taylor sold all the material markers of his fame: diamonds, necklaces, furniture. Finally came the most crushing blow: He sold his home and moved his family into an apartment. In 1930 his wife left him, taking their daughter, and moved to New York. Taylor was crushed by the specter of failure and could not stay in Worcester. He left for Chicago, where he died in 1932 after a lingering illness. He was buried in a paupers' cemetery. Sydney did not learn of her father's death until her husband received a copy of his obituary that appeared in the *Chicago Defender.* A larger obituary appeared in Paris, the scene of his great international triumphs.

Taylor was devastated by his sharp descent. "He had been a famous athlete and treated with such respect; I'm sure that was very hard for him to handle," his daughter recalled. She reflected on what it must have been like to be an African American athlete living so large one moment and sinking to such depths in the next. Only as an adult had she realized the enormous pressure her father must have been under to be successful, to contend with racism, swallow his pride, and then watch his fame crumble before him. "Losing his money and his health and his wife and his daughter—I think it was too much," she said. "I think it was a shame that he had to end like that. I didn't realize it then, because I was always mad with him. But I sure do wish I would have called him back and said, 'Daddy, I didn't understand what it must have been like to be a black man back in those days.' I feel terrible to think that he died alone in a hospital."

★   ★   ★

Jack Johnson's timing was always superb. Just as he was mastering his craft as a boxer, the nation was hungry for a fight.

The infatuation with cycling had faded and Americans wanted something more physically direct. Boxing surfaced as the sport of the moment. Velodromes were converted into boxing arenas; boxing was a fitting sport for a nation beginning to sow its international oats. Prizefighting thrived because the sport helped to satisfy the rapidly growing urban audience for commercial spectacles. By 1900 the sport of boxing not only attracted its traditional rowdy core audience, but it was gaining support from "respectable" people who once scorned the sport.

This was an era of muscle-flexing and rugged competition in politics and business. Boxing was a human drama that reduced the values of American society to a pair of gladiators. More than any other sport, it spanned the gulf between rich and poor, upper and lower classes, because in its raw, primal violence and drive toward domination, it captured the spirit of the age. As one commentator wrote: "There is in every man a trace of original savagery and it is probably no worse to gratify this by looking at a fight than by scolding one's wife, kicking the family cat or trying to bulldoze a legislature in the interest of Tammany."

Unlike Taylor, who enjoyed a meteoric rise from 1894 to 1900, Johnson took the long road. When Arthur John "Jack" Johnson was born, the United States was mired in depression, though his hometown of Galveston was prosperous. His fighting career was inspired by his mother, who, after he lost a schoolboy fight, told him that if he was beaten again he'd get a worse whipping at home.

Johnson's first taste of organized fighting came in humiliating "battle royals." These were a form of boxing that were more racist ritual than sport. They took the form of young blacks fighting each other in a ring in front of white spectators, who threw coins to the victor. These spectacles were very much like the plantation fights in Tom

Molineaux's days, when neighboring owners would pit their black slaves against each other.

After leaving school, Johnson trained horses, painted wagons, baked bread, and unloaded ships. By the time he reached his late teens, he was "locked into a profession" as a fighter. He worked as a sparring partner and sometimes fought circus boxers.

By 1899 he was defeating the best of the local fighters. After beating Jim McCormick, he decided to try Chicago. In 1901 he got a chance to fight Joe Choynski, a great fighter past his prime but still respected. Before the event, black minstrels and a quartet sang some songs; this was followed by a battle royal between two one-legged "colored boys." The referee gave a speech about maintaining order during the interracial main event. Then Johnson's bout began, and in the third round Choynski knocked Johnson out. Immediately after the bout, the fighters were arrested.

White boxing fans were uncomfortable, particularly in the South, with interracial matches. In 1897 an interracial fight was stopped by Henry Long, who said, "The idea of niggers fighting white men—why, if that darned scoundrel would beat that white boy the niggers would never stop gloating over it, and as it is we have enough trouble with them."

But, unlike cycling and baseball, boxing was not protected by the Jockey Syndrome. Those sports were tightly organized and lent themselves to backroom manipulation to change the rules when needed. Boxing, however, depended on individual fighters to "draw the color line." John L. Sullivan, the first great nationally acclaimed fighter, vigorously defended the color line. "In this challenge I include all fighters —first come, first served—who are white. I will not fight a Negro. I never have and I never shall." He never did. Nor did his successor, Jim Corbett.

The emergence of Jack Johnson was for many whites an embodiment of the Great American Nightmare: a bold, independent African

American competing for a job on a level playing field. As one writer observed: "With money in his pockets, physical triumph over white men in his heart, he displayed all the gross and overbearing insolence which makes what we call the buck nigger insufferable."

Johnson won a shot at the championship in part because there was relatively little money in boxing at the time. Jim Jeffries retired largely because the sport was bankrupt. When Tommy Burns won the championship in 1906, Johnson stalked him literally across the face of the earth, first to London, then to Australia. There, Burns relented in the face of the biggest payday of his career. The electricity of race—black man, white man—would again guarantee a huge gate. There was more at stake than the title of pugilistic champion of the world. Australians had a long history of racism against their own brown-skinned inhabitants. When Truganini, the last Tasmanian, died in 1876, the *Hobart Mercury* editorialized, "I regret the death of the last of the Tasmanian aborigines, but I know that it is the result of the fiat that the black shall everywhere give place to the white."

The sentiment was not borne out by the fight. By 6:00 a.m., five hours before the scheduled start of the fight, there was a crowd of 5,000 waiting at the gate. When Johnson entered the ring before a full house of 20,000, there were a few cheers, but mostly catcalls and racial epithets. The fight was a mismatch. The writer Jack London described the fight as one between a "colossus [Johnson] and a toy automaton," between a "playful Ethiopian and a futile white man," between a "grown man and a naughty child."

Much like the Molineaux-Cribb fight one hundred years earlier, racial stereotypes were smashed that afternoon. Burns was counting on the "scientific" beliefs of the day: that blacks had no endurance, hard heads, and weak stomachs. Only those races from northern climes had the stamina for a long boxing match. Johnson won the fight in the fourteenth round. Burns was led away, dazed, covered with blood but still game, screaming for the police to give him another chance.

Jack Johnson had become the first black heavyweight champion of the world in Australia. Johnson's victory set off national hysteria in the United States that revived boxing, as armadas of white men responded to Jack London's call for a "White Hope." Johnson successfully defended his title against Jim Jeffries in 1910. When he entered the ring to fight Jeffries, the band began playing "All Coons Look Alike to Me," a minstrel song written four years earlier by Ernest Hogan, who was black. After the fight, riots broke out throughout the United States; eight blacks were killed by roving gangs of whites.

Yet Johnson became the ultimate victim of the Jockey Syndrome. When the color line was not enough to contain black momentum, powerful forces dug deeper. The government began its pursuit of Johnson in 1912, when the mother of an eighteen-year-old white woman pressed abduction charges against him. The Federal Bureau of Investigation enthusiastically pressed for a Mann Act conviction. That case fell through, but the government continued to dig until it found a former lover who gave damaging evidence and testimony. A grand jury voted to indict; Judge Kenesaw Mountain Landis, who as baseball commissioner years later would play a key role in keeping blacks out of baseball, quickly issued a warrant for Johnson's arrest, charging him with transporting Belle Schriber from Pittsburgh to Chicago for the purpose of prostitution and debauchery. Johnson's subsequent marriage to his young white lover inflamed public opinion against him and incited one Southern congressman to call for a constitutional amendment that would prevent white women from being "corrupted by a strain of kinky-headed blood." Johnson refused to back down, even in the face of criticism from segments of the black community and practically the entire white community. His bold demeanor on the stand reinforced his image as "Bad Nigga." Johnson was sentenced to one year and a day in prison. The Mann Act had been successful. A *New York Call* writer observed: "Johnson is black and has more money than is good for a black man. The Department of Justice must aid the 'white hopes' in taking away the superfluous cash of the stupidly brazen Negro pugilist. . . . Anglo-Saxon America is relieved of a most dangerous menace to the preservation of its color."

Johnson fled the country in 1913 and sailed to Europe, where he remained a fugitive for seven years. In 1915 he agreed to a title fight against Jess Willard in Cuba. The lingering and unproven theory surrounding the fight was that in exchange for losing, he would be granted clemency in the States. Johnson lost the title to Willard, and while no clemency was granted, the virulent anti-black violence that had begun so abruptly and intensely in 1890 subsided, as if Johnson's defeat were a reassuring sign of white dominance reasserting itself. After the 1915 fight, Johnson went to England, Spain, and Mexico before returning to the United States, where he served eight months of his term.

Johnson didn't go out meekly, but the same way he came in—loudly. He was killed in a car accident in 1946, the same year Jackie Robinson signed a major-league contract to make him the first African American to reach the big leagues since Moses Fleetwood Walker in 1884.

Like Jackie Robinson, Joe Louis, and Muhammad Ali, Johnson has enjoyed incredible longevity. Ali in his prime kept Johnson's name alive and often invoked Johnson as a model for his own audacity. But there would not be another black heavyweight champion until 1937, when Joe Louis defeated James Braddock. Even then, Louis and his managers had to make sure the public was reassured that he was no Jack Johnson, at least not in public. Johnson became the archetype of racial confrontation in sport. Hysteria over his emergence and triumphs created the notion of the Great White Hope, which still exists both as a metaphor and a reality.

★   ★   ★

In the early twentieth century's turbulence, including the rapid formation and collapsing of sports leagues and the exodus of black athletes from white sports, a young pitcher from Calvert, Texas, named Arthur Foster began to make a name for himself. Foster would be more of a visionary than Johnson, Isaac Murphy, Major Taylor, or even Moses Fleetwood Walker, who became a proponent of the Back to Africa movement.

After years of watching talented black players get rebuked, denied, pushed out, and frustrated, Foster had a new vision of a Promised Land. In Foster's view, the Promised Land was not white leagues, but self-sufficiency. Foster agreed with Walker's premise that blacks would never have a fair break so long as they were dependent on the largesse of whites. But he disagreed that the only way to rectify the situation was to return to Africa.

Foster was convinced that this rapidly growing tribe of black athletes could create a homeland of its own. Foster's focus was baseball. His Promised Land was the Negro Leagues.

Arthur "Rube" Foster was the founder of the first Negro National League and part of a Renaissance generation of African Americans in the 1920s. He sought to organize black talent in order to empower and energize the African American community. *Courtesy of National Baseball Hall of Fame.*

FOUR

The Negro Leagues:
The Dilemma of Myopia

Where there is no vision, the people perish.

—PROVERBS 29:18

IF THE JOCKEY SYNDROME EVICTED African American athletes from integrated major-league sports, Negro Leagues offered a
home. As blacks were phased out of integrated sports through legislation, intimidation, and coercion, they relied on a sports world of their
own. Ironically, the suffocating humiliation of colored-only and white-
only was the best thing that happened to the still-developing community of African Americans only a generation or two out of slavery.
Segregation forced African Americans into a spirit of cooperation and
nudged them toward a useful, if hazy, concept of "unity" predicated as
much on survival as on true kinship. Segregation forced African
Americans into a spirit of interdependence that celebrated the parti-
cle of existence that mainstream society attacked: their humanity.

Pushed to the margins of society by de facto segregation and Jim
Crow laws, scorned as "outside others" and left to their own devices,
African Americans built a range of businesses: banks, salons, hotels,

restaurants, and theaters. In 1904, Robert Motts opened the Peking Theater on Chicago's South Side. Motts's theater grew out of black frustration with having to patronize "white" theaters through the back doors.

Arthur "Rube" Foster's Negro National League established a parallel world of baseball in the black community. Foster, known as "the Father of Black Baseball," was part of a Renaissance generation of African Americans in the 1920s who sought to redefine, celebrate, and make sense of the African American presence in the United States. Black poets wrote their poems, black singers sang their songs, black artists made their art. Foster used his baseball league as a canvas to express a new physical art form, which by the end of the century African American athletes would show off for the whole world.

Foster founded his Negro National League (NNL) in 1920. This universe of black baseball was run by African Americans and was largely dependent on an African American fan base, though it appealed to a cross-section of fans who appreciated the fast-paced, daredevil, "Africanized" style of play that became the league's resonating, rousing signature. Foster knew baseball like no other man—black or white. He had been a star pitcher, an innovative manager, a stern but generally benevolent team owner, and now was the driving force behind a groundbreaking league.

Historian John B. Holway has called Foster one of the most impressive figures in baseball history. He describes him as a combination of Christy Mathewson, one of baseball's great pitchers; John McGraw, the great manager of the Yankees' first dynasty; Connie Mack, a founder of the American League; and Kenesaw Mountain Landis, Supreme Court justice and baseball's first commissioner.

Yet Rube Foster has become a mere footnote in the epic story of sports integration in which Jackie Robinson is a central character.

In some ways, however, Foster is an even more significant figure than Robinson. Foster used black resources to build a baseball league that nurtured talents like Robinson while establishing an economically viable alternative to Major League Baseball. Robinson became a symbol of the process of integration, a process that ultimately enriched white institutions while weakening and in many cases destroying black institutions. White America determined the pattern of integration; the white power structure chose blacks who made whites feel comfortable, who more or less accepted the vagaries of racism. This was the Jackie Robinson model of how an integration-worthy African-American behaved: taking abuse, turning the other cheek, tying oneself in knots, holding one's tongue, never showing anger, waiting for racist sensibilities to smolder and die out—if your spirit didn't die first. This model was hardly progress for black athletes. It was, in fact, a reversal of the paradigm for black involvement in sports that Foster and others had created out of a hard necessity.

Foster represents a significant—and rare—departure from the pioneering tradition that defined—and, to a large extent, still defines—the journey of African American athletes. The history of the black athlete is often presented as a history of "pioneering": Tom Molineaux went from slavery in Virginia to boxing celebrity in England. Moses Fleetwood Walker became the first African American to play major-league baseball. Isaac Murphy glamorized the stature of the jockey in thoroughbred horse racing. Jack Johnson became the first African American heavyweight champion. Jackie Robinson desegregated Major League Baseball. Althea Gibson became the first African American to win a major tennis tournament. Tiger Woods won the Masters golf tournament.

Foster was also a pioneer, but not in the same way. His innovation wasn't being the first black in a white-defined institution. He was a man of clear, resolute, and uncompromising vision: He wanted a professional league of black baseball that was owned, organized, managed, and played by African Americans.

Foster was not a dreamer; he was a shrewd, determined businessman with superior organizational skills. His Negro National League marked one of the last times that African Americans controlled their own major-league sports organizations. His Negro National League also offered a glimpse of what an African American community could achieve by effectively nationalizing its athletic gold. The lasting genius of Foster's legacy is that he was able to organize African Americans, to unite and move them as a group toward a collective goal.

Foster's vision extended beyond forming a league for the sake of simply playing baseball. He wanted to "unite those who seemingly could not be united." Foster was trying to prove that this could be done, but it would take a super effort to solve the perplexing question of why Negroes appear to unite with anybody and everybody but will not unite with themselves.

As early as 1906, Foster saw the need to organize black baseball. In the seminal days of the labor movement in the United States, he saw ballplayers—black and white—as a specialized labor force. He knew that integration with Major League Baseball was inevitable. When integration came, Foster wanted the Negro League he envisioned to have a monopoly on the commodity that Major League Baseball would desperately need: black ballplayers. His league, with players coming from all sections of the country, rural and urban, would have a corner on the market.

He wanted his league to be so competitive, so well run, that when the national pastime was integrated, the NNL would be in a position to dictate rather than be dictated to. His theory was that the league's strongest teams would be absorbed intact, not picked apart like a carcass by so many buzzards.

Foster realized that the black-owned monopoly on black muscle he envisioned could not be accomplished using the working model of the day for black teams—barnstorming. This method lacked focus, and was subject to the control of white booking agents. In barnstorming, teams scoured the countryside, playing hit-or-miss exhibitions against woefully inconsistent competition, from local neighborhood teams to white major leaguers looking to make some extra money on the side.

Foster grew up in this barnstorming tradition. He was born in Calvert, Texas, in 1879, a year after fellow Texan Jack Johnson, the first black heavyweight champion. Foster's father was a Methodist preacher, and like many African Americans, the elder Foster saw participation in sports as a sinful indulgence. At the time, the attitude of many earnest, hardworking African Americans toward sports was that it led to nothing constructive and that, as an enterprise played for the pleasure of white people, it was degrading to blacks. Yet, by the time he was thirteen, the younger Foster was a train-hopping baseball vagabond.

His mother died in 1899. When his father remarried and moved, baseball became a sanctuary and an obsession for Foster. Like Johnson, Foster lived the rough-and-tumble life. He became the baseball equivalent of the itinerant bluesman, a teenage troubadour who traversed the country, hopping trains, catching freights to this game or that. The essence of Foster's character is revealed in his response to an invitation from Frank Leland, the African American owner of the Leland Giants in Chicago. The owner, in his telegram, warned Foster that with the Giants he would be playing against the best (white) baseball teams in the area. Foster replied, "If you play the best clubs in the land, white clubs, as you say, it will be a case of Greek meeting Greek. I fear nobody."

★   ★   ★

Foster moved to Chicago at seventeen, stayed for a year, then moved to Michigan to play semi-pro baseball. By 1902, he found his way east, where black baseball was thriving. He pitched for the Cuban X Giants in New York City. And even though baseball was rigidly segregated, John McGraw, manager of the Giants, asked Foster to tutor Christy Mathewson, his young right-hander. In 1903, Foster went to Philadelphia and played with the Philadelphia Giants, where the first baseman was none other than Jack Johnson. In 1906, after a dispute over pay with the team and after seeing players undervalued and disrespected by booking agents, Foster left Philadelphia and vowed that he would no longer accept racial abuse or meager salaries from men who booked the games. He returned to Chicago to manage the Leland Giants, taking several Philadelphia Giant teammates with him. He became Leland's team secretary treasurer and negotiated shrewdly with mostly white booking agents, thereby drastically increasing percentages of the gate for Giants players.

Ultimately Foster came to realize that barnstorming, for all of its charm and short-term benefits, was choking the life out of black baseball. Barnstorming was a losing proposition for black teams, which were at the mercy of white booking agents. The booking agents were the liaisons between black teams and the white baseball owners of the stadiums in which they played. Agents like Nat Strong and Ed Gottlieb, and later Abe Saperstein, could make or break teams simply by determining who played where and when. Foster was determined to break this choke-hold of agents acting as conduits between the white power structure and black owners. Foster realized that if total self-sufficiency was ever to be achieved, black teams had to reduce their dependence on booking agents. The only way to purge baseball of the network of powerful white booking agents who determined where teams played and which teams received the more lucrative dates was to form a league. The only way to do that was to organize. Writing for the *Indianapolis Freeman* in 1906, Foster wrote of black baseball:

Organization is its only hope. With the proper organization, patterned after the men who have made baseball a success, we will, in three years, be rated as other leagues are rated. We have the players and it could not be a failure, as the same territory is traveled now by all clubs, with no organization or money. It would give us a rating and standing in the daily papers which would create an interest and we could then let the best clubs in our organization play for the world's championship with other clubs of their leagues.

Foster ended by saying, "It would be a crime for the Negro who has such an abundance of talent in such a progressive age to sit idly by and see his race forever doomed to America's greatest and foremost sport."

If the Negro National League was going to corner the market, blacks would have to seize control of their resource: black players. Foster recognized by 1920, and probably earlier, that the emerging battle with the booking agents—the Strongs, Gottliebs, and Sapersteins—was a battle for control of the raw resource of an emerging industry. The battle over control of black athletic muscle would be a consistent underlying theme for the duration of the century. This was a battle African Americans would be hard-pressed to win, because they didn't know such a battle was being fought. Indeed, the African American community—and this would be its imprimatur during the next several decades—willingly turned black muscle over to whites, initially in the name of integration, ultimately for want of a dollar.

As word spread about Foster's plan to organize a black baseball league, there were attempts by the white-run Eastern League of Colored Baseball to buy Foster out. Nat Strong, the white founder of the Eastern League and one of the earliest and most powerful booking agents, offered to provide Foster, then president of the Chicago

American Giants, with a team of his own and the opportunity to play in a $100,000 stadium if he cast his lot with the Eastern League of Colored Baseball. Sol White, a player, manager, and chronicler of early black baseball, wrote of Strong that "there is not a man in the country who has made as much money from colored ball playing as Nat Strong, and yet he is the least interested in its welfare."

Foster turned down Strong's offer. He fought Strong to a draw; his mastery at booking, achieved during years of booking games in Philadelphia and in Chicago as Leland's secretary, prevented Strong from controlling all of big-time African American baseball. Foster's fight was one of principle. Dave Malarcher, one of Foster's baseball confidants and the man who succeeded Foster as manager of the Giants, recalled that Foster turned down numerous opportunities to play in white semi-pro leagues because he felt he was needed in black baseball:

> Foster had had an opportunity to leave Negro baseball, and go into white semi-pro baseball because he was the leading drawing card outside of the major leagues back in those days when he was pitching. But Rube told me he refused to go because he knew that all we had to do was to keep on developing Negro baseball, keep it up to a high standard, and the time would come when the white leagues would have to admit us. The thing for us to do, he said, was to keep on developing, so that when that time did come, we would be able to measure up.

Foster realized that the strength of the black league wasn't just that it was packed with quality players who were otherwise denied a shot, but that it had also developed a distinct, though hard to define, Africanized style of playing baseball. This style was characterized by exciting, daring base running, spikes-first slides into second base, and bunting for base hits. Foster's league became a showcase of this black style of ball, distinguished by nonstop rhythm.

Foster launched his league in December of 1920. He invited eight owners of the strongest black teams to Kansas City for an inaugural meeting that would result in the formation of Foster's Negro National League. Although he did not want white ownership, one white owner, J. L. Wilkinson, who owned the Kansas City Monarchs, was part of the founding group. Wilkinson had strong Midwestern connections that were crucial if the new league was to move forward. This meeting in Kansas City showed Foster at his organizational best. To the amazement of the owners gathered, Foster had already secured a charter of incorporation for the league. The group of owners agreed that each team would have its own stadium to nullify dependence on the whims of major-league owners and booking agents who served their interests. This, however, turned out to be an overly ambitious plan that never materialized. They also agreed on high-minded bylaws that outlawed "raiding" of players on one team by owners of another.

In an odd way, considering the racist times, black players before the formation of the NNL were much freer to move around and jump teams than their counterparts in the majors, who were bound and kept in their place by a Reserve Clause. And it was that very clause, which bound players to a team for life, that Foster adopted from Major League Baseball. Foster realized that this was one case where unchecked "freedom" did not serve the best interest of his burgeoning baseball league—it's questionable whether this tactic was necessary to the league or just an owner's reflexive instinct for control. Ironically, whether done for the league's survival or to amass power, this was the same form of "slavery" or "bondage" Curt Flood would oppose fifty years later when he challenged the Reserve Clause.

Whether because of the racial river they followed or Foster's personal habits (he did not smoke, drink, or carouse), the owners added a morals clause in the charter that levied fines for ungentlemanly conduct on or off the field. Later, Foster would kick one of his star players off the team for breaking curfew.

The new black league showcased the unique style of black baseball in the context of an organized league. Each city had a team to cheer, stars to identify with, and a pennant race to follow. And now profits were made by black entrepreneurs, and no longer solely by white hands.

★   ★   ★

Foster wasn't the first black entrepreneur to try to organize black baseball. Attempts to organize black teams into leagues began at least as early as 1887, the year blacks were banned from baseball by way of so many "gentlemen's agreements." The League of Colored Baseball Players was born and quickly died. In 1906 the International League of Independent Baseball Clubs was formed and included two white teams. In 1910, Major R. Jackson, a former manager of the Chicago Unions, and Beauregard F. Mosely, a black lawyer, businessman, and executive with the Leland Giants, called a meeting of black baseball officials to form a National Negro Baseball League of America. They were reacting to the ongoing backlash against African Americans and a desire for self-help and racial pride. The league never materialized.

Why did Foster's league take root and blossom when the others failed? Much of Foster's success had to do with the turbulence of the times, his relentless drive, and an emerging African American consciousness. America had witnessed steadily mounting violent white backlash against aggressive black demands for first-class citizenship. The demand for Civil Rights was escalated by the talk of democracy that led up to World War I. By the end of 1919, the Ku Klux Klan had become a virulent force in the United States and set the tone for a climate of violence and intimidation against blacks, Japanese, Roman Catholics, Jews, and all foreign-born persons. Blacks in particular were under attack as never before—physically and psychologically—by whites who blamed African Americans for an increasing range of post–World War I woes ranging from high unemployment to encroachment on economic and social space.

In a manifestation of fear and jealousy that undergirds the Jockey Syndrome, increasing numbers of whites felt resentment at what they perceived as blacks' advances in gaining social ground. The mere existence and proximity of African Americans infuriated many whites. The attitude is reflected by the comments of a theater manager in Chicago who was asked to explain why African Americans were prevented from buying theater tickets on the main floor of one of Chicago's premier playhouses. The manager said that it was not the "conduct of the Negroes [that] was objectionable, but their mere presence."

This attitude explained the subtle discrimination behind the new black ghettos in the North as well as the ironclad segregation of the South.

A succession of riots beginning in the first decade of the 1900s saw outbreaks of white mob violence and terrorism as a means of keeping blacks in their place and out of economic and social competition with whites. As we've seen, when Foster's friend Jack Johnson defended his heavyweight boxing title against Jim Jeffries in 1910, roving crowds of white vigilantes rioted, killing and beating African Americans.

By 1919 the violence directed at African Americans had reached genocidal proportions. Indeed, it was the bloodiest year of racial violence the United States had seen since emancipation. The harmony, sacrifice, and national unity that marked the previous war years dissolved into bitter disillusionment amid tight competition between blacks and whites for resources in the North—and into the resumption of Jim Crow's violent reign in the South. Black soldiers coming back from the war with higher expectations of better treatment were met instead by redoubled efforts to relegate blacks to pre-war status on the bottom rung of society's ladder.

Lynch mobs murdered seventy-eight African Americans in 1919; black soldiers returning from duty were not exempt. In fact, the soldiers in uniforms with rifles incited fear among whites that this black subservient underclass was now armed and dangerous. Of the seventy-eight lynchings in 1919, ten victims were war veterans, some of whom were lynched in their uniforms.

On July 27, 1919, tension in Chicago exploded into a bloody ten-day race riot after a black teenager drowned while swimming, apparently under attack from a white mob. What distinguished this bloody race war from previous black-white clashes was the aggressive nature of black resistance to white violence: Blacks fought back. Rube Foster embodied this aggressive new attitude. He was the model of the emerging "New Negro," a phrase coined in 1919 by young black radicals as a way of distinguishing themselves from the traditional, accommodating black leadership.

The New Negro fought back. Now the shedding of black blood meant the shedding of white blood. White mobs descending on black neighborhoods in Chicago were met with force. The new black attitude was encapsulated by the Claude McKay poem "If We Must Die," which contained the couplet,

> *Like men we'll face the murderous cowardly pack,*
> *Pressed to the wall, dying but fighting back!*

Foster's Negro National League created a universe in which the black presence was accepted, nurtured, and celebrated. The league became a base of power for African Americans in the rapidly growing industry of baseball. The six-team league, in addition to creating excitement, created employment and gave black newspapers teams to cover. The black press played a pivotal role in the formation of the league: Two reporters helped draw up the founding constitution.

The black press supported the league by giving teams coverage, writing up accounts of home games, and profiling the league's star players.

★   ★   ★

If Rube Foster was the Negro National League's greatest strength, he was also its weakness. Foster attended to every single detail of the league he created. As manager, he ordered team uniforms and he bought equipment. In the dugout for his team, the Chicago American Giants, Foster called nearly every pitch and orchestrated every key play. As commissioner, he settled disputes—including those involving his own Chicago Giants, often in favor of the other team. Foster sent his own players to weaker teams in order to maintain competitive balance in the league. He earned a substantial amount of money—he took a percentage of the gross of each gate—but he poured much of his own money into shaky franchises and guaranteed hotel bills for teams stranded on the road. Foster was the benevolent dictator of his league. Though he was criticized for his domineering, heavy-handed management style, even his harshest critics conceded that without his unique ways, black baseball would have remained in the wild, risky, barnstorming wilderness. When he threatened to leave in the face of mounting criticism in 1926, Foster was given an overwhelming vote of confidence by owners.

His unyielding dream, though, was to see the elimination of racial barriers that blocked the entry of blacks into major-league baseball. Foster's vision was to see entire black franchises admitted, as well as individual players.

In 1926, Foster met with Ban Johnson, the American League president, and John McGraw, the legendary manager of the New York Yankees, to discuss plans for his American Giants to play big-league teams that visited Chicago on their off days. Commissioner Kenesaw

Landis apparently killed the idea and dealt "a crushing blow to Foster's already fragile psychological condition."

Years later, Foster's son speculated that the emotional straw that really broke his father's spirit was not so much the pressure of keeping teams of African Americans together and fending off attacks from booking agents. What broke his spirit was that meeting with McGraw and Johnson. His son suspected that during the meeting Foster had proposed some form of merger between his Negro League and Major League Baseball, and that McGraw apparently told Foster that the time was not right for an African American presence in Major League Baseball. The realization that his league would remain indefinitely estranged may have broken Foster's will. The world of black baseball would never become joined with the larger world of white baseball. Foster feared that white ball would take what it needed, then crush black ball to pieces and watch it die.

By December of 1926, the pressure of holding together the fragile world of black baseball had cracked Rube Foster's battle-hardened armor. Six stress-filled years of being the heart, soul, and uncompromising guiding light of Negro League baseball had become too much for Foster to bear. He conceded as much in an article for the *Chicago Defender* when he wrote: "Oft times I have felt that the task was hopeless. I felt ready to give up. The strain placed upon me has proved great, almost beyond endurance."

There were signs of instability as early as 1924, when friends told Foster to take a break. He took a vacation, but there was no relief. There was no distinction for Foster between baseball and his life; the two were intertwined.

Then, thirteen days before Christmas, 1926, Foster broke down. George Sweatt, the Giants' veteran outfielder, heard a loud commotion coming from Foster's downstairs apartment. He heard Sarah Foster, Rube's wife, shout, "Oh no, don't do that!" Sweatt ran downstairs and knocked on the door. Sarah, flustered and panic-stricken, said, "There's something wrong with Rube, he's just going crazy down there. I'm going to have to call the law."

Sarah called the Chicago police to the Fosters' apartment building on Michigan Avenue. Several officers were needed to subdue the six-foot-two, 240-pound Foster. After a violent struggle, the legendary pitcher, manager, and founder was put in a police wagon and taken away. After a weeklong diagnosis, Foster was declared mentally incompetent and committed to the state asylum at Kankakee, Illinois. His friends came to visit him, but when there came an opportunity for his release, his wife refused to sign him out. He remained committed until his death on December 12, 1930, at the age of fifty-one.

Historians trace the demise of Negro League baseball to the desegregation of modern Major League Baseball, beginning with the arrival of Jackie Robinson in 1947. But the demise of black baseball began that December afternoon in Chicago, twenty-one years earlier, when Rube Foster suffered a nervous breakdown. Without Foster to push every button, plug every hole, whip and intimidate, the Negro National League floundered and finally died in 1932. The remaining owners lacked Foster's vision, drive, and commitment to black baseball, as well as his business instincts, his tenacity, and his presence.

Foster's death created a vacuum in vision and leadership within black baseball that would never be filled as fully and as completely as he had filled it.

Other people in other sports have tried. Bob Douglas formed the Harlem Rens, the first full-salaried professional African American basketball team, in 1923. Douglas's Rens were a model of organization. The Rens competed against white professional teams, and even won the first World Professional Basketball championship in 1939. The Rens became the first black-owned team to join the National Basketball League in 1948, but they were not asked to join the

National Basketball Association. Without a strong league in which to sustain itself—a black base of power—the Rens could not contend with an ocean of prejudice, and dissolved in 1949.

Fritz Pollard, the great Brown University All-American, and the first African American head coach in the National Football League, reacted to pro football's exclusion of black athletes by forming two all-black barnstorming teams. Without the sustaining force of an African American league, however, Pollard's two teams, and other semi-pro teams, died.

A new Negro Baseball League was formed in 1933 by Gus Greenlee, who was the opposite of Foster. Foster was a baseball man. He knew the game and loved it. Mostly, though, he knew the business of the game from top to bottom. Greenlee, however, was hardly washed in baseball tradition; he was the numbers king of Pittsburgh, a gambler. The Negro Baseball League that Greenlee founded in 1932 is the league most people have in mind when they speak of "Negro Leagues." Unlike Foster, the new wave of owners lacked vision. More than that, they lacked the dawn-to-dusk commitment required to make black baseball truly succeed.

There were good ideas here and there, but none that was connected to a collective vision or philosophy of self-sufficiency. Greenlee, for example, built his own stadium, as did Alex Pompez, the flamboyant owner of the New York Black Yankees, to avoid paying exorbitant rental fees to Major League Baseball owners. But these owners were the exception. Most black owners rented from major-league teams as part of an exchange that paid rich dividends for the major-league team owners.

Although there were African American banks, Negro League teams did not have the same access to capital as the white major leagues. The black-owned banks that did exist lent money to institutions only for life-and-death survival. Baseball, and sports in general, was considered incidental to the larger aspects of African American survival and so did not qualify.

Without clear goals and strong-willed leaders, black baseball couldn't purge outside influences. In fact, most of the owners depended on revenue from barnstorming and accepted the existence of booking agents as a fact of life. The presence of white booking agents who monopolized black baseball in Rube Foster's era continued. Cumberland Posey, owner of the Homestead Grays, referred to Abe Saperstein, the Chicago-based sports agent, as "a symbol of those who are attempting to edge into professional Negro athletics and to eventually control them." Greenlee, owner of the Pittsburgh Crawfords, had a series of clashes with Nat Strong over who should control black baseball. Greenlee said he understood why Strong opposed a black baseball league, but noted that "he fought the idea with every weapon at his command."

There were high points, such as Greenlee's creation of an East-West All-Star game. This annual game, held in Chicago's Comiskey Park, became the centerpiece of the new Negro League. The East-West Game became the black social event of the summer.

But the all-star game could not protect Negro League baseball from the coming invasion, not that black owners even saw an invasion coming. Integration, inside and outside of sports, was seen—or at least sold by so-called Black Leaders—as the panacea. Even an avowed activist like Audley "Queen Mother" Moore, a Civil Rights worker and black nationalist, was taken in. Moore was a hero to many residents of Harlem, where she worked with Marcus Garvey, the Jamaican-born black nationalist leader, and his Back to Africa movement. She was also an advocate of reparations for slavery, tenants' rights, and education for the poor. Her outrage over the suffering of blacks in America led to years of political action. "They not only called us Negroes, they made us Negroes," she once said, "things that don't know where they came from and don't even care that they don't know. Negro is a state of mind, and they massacred our minds."

Moore fought to get black players into the majors. She organized a committee that launched a campaign to integrate baseball. By the end of the 1940s, Moore realized the blunder that had been made in blindly pushing for integration. "But when I look back on that struggle now, that was because I was fighting, I was a communist, but I didn't have my right mind. Now remember—I was a Negro," she recalled in an interview.

> I've been a Negro and I know the condition of the Negro mind. A Negro follows, he's incapable of scrutiny, he's incapable of analyzing and he's incapable of perception. A Negro is functioning with a European mind, a European mentality. So he's not himself, so he doesn't know what's good for him and what's harmful for him and he'll do most anything. If people are going, he'll go, and this is the way the Negro is.
>
> Had I not been a Negro, I would have fought to get our teams in the big leagues. But what I did was kill the teams. We had teams. I found that out later. When our teams played in the communities throughout the country our communities were ablaze with activity—our hotels, we had hotels and all, we used to have taxis, shoeshine boys, old women selling candies and peanuts and everything. There was activities; our youngsters [had] something to aspire to. There was activities right? Well, honey, now you have a Negro or ten Negroes or twenty Negroes there, but the white man gets all the gate; he gets all the receipts from the ball[game], the profits. I would have fought to put our teams in. That's a qualitative difference.

Between 1943 and 1946, black baseball was more popular than ever. Owners, content to be kings of their own tiny hills, were blinded by short-term gain. Without a tenacious, dictatorial, Fosterian presence to manage resources, the two black leagues—the Negro National League and the Negro American League—never found a way to operate in a manner that ensured that black baseball would have a viable future. The owners did not see the integration armies lining up on the horizon and had no coherent plan of action for how to face the onslaught that was about to take place.

An onslaught led by Branch Rickey.

★   ★   ★

By the late 1940s, Major League Baseball was hungry for new blood, fresh blood. Black blood. Negro League owners had failed to grasp the implications of Major League Baseball's manpower shortage, its slumping attendance, and its desperate need for new talent, which the black leagues held in abundance.

In the lore and legend of baseball integration, Rickey, like Robinson, has become a legend of mythic proportions. There are all manner of stories about Rickey, schools of thought about who he was, and debate about whether his motives were social or economic.

The reality is that Rickey was a baseball man; he was also a shark. The Brooklyn Dodgers' board of directors quietly authorized Rickey to go after the most lucrative pool of untapped talent: the Negro Leagues. Rickey knew that players—black, white, and brown—were the lifeblood of any league, of any team. As the United States braced for World War II, and major-league owners fretted over how they would keep players, Rickey began recruiting players from Cuba. Rickey was fair and Rickey was a barracuda—but he was a barracuda first.

Rickey exploited a psychological soft spot within the African American community—the desire to "measure up"—that made the invasion go infinitely smoother. In his years of scouting Negro League teams, he became intimately familiar with the athletic ability of black players—and with something far more essential. He became familiar with the sense of longing, the burden of proof, that haunted many of them. Rickey understood how desperately black players wanted to play in the major leagues and, more significantly, how desperately the national black community, with a hunger for access to the mainstream, wanted black players to play and succeed in the white man's game. Indeed, this element of black life—this hunger to succeed—was the commodity Rickey was after when he campaigned to integrate Major League Baseball at the behest of the Dodgers' directors.

Major League Baseball, with Rickey as its point man, masterfully used the black community's Civil Rights fervor to keep owners from aggressively standing in the way of "integration." Rickey exploited the integrationist leanings of the black community to crush opposition. When J. L. Wilkinson, the white owner of the Kansas City Monarchs, resisted, Rickey effectively shouted him down. Rickey said Wilkinson was not Frederick Douglass. Rickey and Wilkinson exchanged charges and countercharges of carpetbagging. A tug-of-war ensued over using black muscle for white gain.

Black baseball owners could not agree on a strategy. The owners were torn between wanting integration and wanting to remain a viable business. These latter-day owners of Negro League baseball mistakenly felt that they would be involved—in a profitable way—with the "integration" process. Some felt that their teams might be purchased and incorporated into the Major League Baseball minor-league system.

That was not part of the plan, however. The treatment of the Negro Leagues was brutal and disrespectful.

The Negro Leagues were invaded for talent much as Africa was invaded for human labor. In each case, invading forces received inside help to facilitate the trade. Negro League baseball became the first supplier of black players to Major League Baseball, as Rube Foster had anticipated. How baseball went about acquiring black players was not what Foster had in mind.

Some owners eagerly sold players; others watched helplessly as players were signed and snatched away, their biggest stars snapped up and absorbed into white baseball with no compensation for the team. Worse, there was no respect for the leagues that had produced Jackie Robinson, Satchel Paige, and other great players. Rickey brazenly snatched Robinson from the Kansas City Monarchs, saying, "There is no Negro League as such as far as I'm concerned." Rickey said that black baseball was under the control of "rackets," referring to the several Eastern owners with gambling associations. Rickey insisted that Negro Leagues "are not leagues and have no right to expect organized baseball to respect them."

This was a corruption of Foster's dream. From everything we know of Foster, he would not have allowed Rickey and the others simply to barrel in and snap up whomever they pleased without compensation or respect. Foster wouldn't have hesitated to use any means at his disposal to keep his league viable, even if he had to ruthlessly exploit the opposition of the major-league owners who were against integration.

Baseball was unofficially integrated in 1945 when Robinson signed a contract with Montreal. (Interestingly, three of the greatest landmarks of African American sports history took place outside the United States, a testament to this country's racist response to the emergence of black sports figures: Tom Molineaux fought for the boxing championship in England; Jack Johnson won the championship in Australia; and Jackie Robinson integrated baseball in Canada.) In 1947, Robinson's contract was purchased by the Dodgers. Just one year later, in 1948, the black leagues were in shambles. Many of the Negro League owners, so engrossed in the period of prosperity, never saw what hit them until it was too late. Effa Manley, the co-owner of the Newark Eagles, said, "Our troubles started after Jackie Robinson joined the Dodgers." Manley, who was white but often passed for a fair-skinned African American, said, "[Black fans] are stupid and gullible in believing that Rickey has any interest in Negro players other than the clicking of his turnstiles."

But Manley was the naïve one in another sense. This normally shrewd woman thought that integration would help black leagues. In 1946 she said, "If our men made good in the majors, fans all over the country would want to see the teams that they came from. Just as Joe Louis made other Negro fighters popular, so would Negro big-league stars increase interest in other Negro players." Manley also felt that if the Negro Leagues disappeared, the flow of black players into the major leagues would disappear. She did not conceive of Major League Baseball teams developing black players in their own minor-league system, because so many of the minor-league teams were located in the South.

Manley was wrong. She had put too much emphasis on merely having players in the major leagues and not enough weight on negotiating an appropriate role for the Negro Leagues in the integration process. Black participation in ownership was demolished for decades to come.

Unlike Rube Foster, who had worked tirelessly—until his death, in fact, despite being institutionalized—to keep black baseball efficient and organized, the new owners lacked the combination of vision and dedication required to fight, much less win, a war for black resources—human gold.

In a scathing critique of Negro League baseball, the late Sam Lacy, writing in Baltimore's *Afro-American* newspaper, said that since Robinson signed with white baseball, "Colored baseball has been acting after the fashion of a mongrel puppy licking at the heels of a prospective master. The years that were spent by friends of the sport [the writers] in an effort to straighten out colored baseball went for naught until Branch Rickey reached into the ranks and took out one of its young stars. When that happened, but not until then, colored baseball operators began to see the implications."

Wendell Smith, writing in the *Pittsburgh Courier,* said,

> Organized baseball has practiced a vicious policy of discrim-
> ination against Negro players, and in so doing made it pos-
> sible for the segregated Negro leagues to flourish and
> prosper. While wallowing in the mire of segregation and dis-
> crimination, the owners of Negro League baseball were the
> beneficiaries of that vicious system and they benefited
> greatly. So much so, that the gold blinded them and they are
> now firmly caught in their own trap.

Still, before the major leagues fully took the measure of black baseball and became energized by the influx of new players and the exciting new dimension that black players brought to their clubs, the Negro
Leagues functioned as Rube Foster envisioned—as a minor-league
system for Major League Baseball, albeit without official designation.
It was a situation that was not sustainable in the long run without some
kind of negotiated formal arrangement.

The final blow for the Negro Leagues came in 1951 when the
Southern-based network of minor-league baseball teams was desegregated. Now the major leagues had no use for the Negro Leagues, and
they slowly died. Major League Baseball had no use for any competing leagues, and was not interested in allowing African Americans to
sit collectively at the ownership table. By the 1960s, black baseball was
effectively dead; Major League Baseball had prevailed.

Historians and journalists would spend the next thirty years sifting
through the ruins of Negro League baseball, finding survivors, recon-
structing records, and establishing a segregated wing of the Baseball
Hall of Fame. Foster was elected to the Hall of Fame in 1981. But the
deed—and the damage—was done, and a pattern was set: A black
institution was dead, while a white institution grew richer and
stronger. This was the end result of integration.

For all of its apparent benefits to white society, segregation had severe drawbacks for whites. The first was that it unified African Americans and helped consolidate their power.

Henry A. Scomp said that segregation was leading to a "decline in white influence over blacks, which could only result in a growth of racial friction—unless of course segregation was carried to its logical extreme of geographical separation."

Segregation helped maintain a social order, but created a fear that, removed from the gaze of whites, African Americans would become free of the spell of white supremacy. In an 1891 pamphlet, William Cabell Bruce, a Baltimore lawyer, wrote that most Southern Negroes still remained "under the spell of the conscious mastery" of the whites. He warned, however, that the process of segregation was creating a situation where the Negro, increasingly isolated from "the direct influence of the whites," would become "more and more aggressive." In white minds, the danger in allowing blacks to be off on their own, unto themselves, was that it allowed them to withdraw completely "into separate communities, beyond the reach of effective white surveillance."

In an 1899 article, Phillip Alexander Bruce wrote that disenfranchisement meant that Negroes were "no longer a menace to organized government, but they continue not the less to be a menace to the moral well-being of the communities in which they live." He said the "whites no longer exercised a beneficial influence over the blacks now that they were concentrated in separate enclaves."

Many of those who shared the belief in African American biological doom, "wanted some modification of racial separation to guarantee a greater degree of white control."

Integration of the major leagues effected just this result. It pulled black athletes back into the mainstream, but in a way that kept them on the periphery of real power, safely within sight.

⋆　　⋆　　⋆

The life and death of black baseball is symbolized by the lives of Rube Foster and Jackie Robinson. Foster built black baseball and Robinson, inadvertently, helped tear it down. Like Foster, Robinson was a pioneer. Although a generation and different approaches separated them, the two men represented the same general ideals: integration and empowerment. But Robinson did not realize the complex effects of segregation on black and white communities, and failed to balance the goals of integration and empowerment. In the end, he achieved one without the other.

Rube Foster came out of a political ideology of building strong black-controlled economic, political, and social institutions that could empower the black community from within. His ultimate goal was not to keep black and white baseball segregated, but to integrate an entire black-owned team into Major League Baseball in order to preserve community and continuity. Robinson represented a tradition that emphasized the necessity of achieving full integration "and the eradication of all barriers to equality within the United States." Each man essentially gave his life for the cause of initiating an African American presence in Major League Baseball. Foster died at age fifty-one in 1930; Robinson died at fifty-three in 1972.

Robinson was criticized by many African Americans for seeming to represent the white interests that helped kill Negro League baseball. The impression was reinforced in 1949 when he testified against Paul Robeson, a man who in 1949 told a gathering at the Paris Peace Conference that "it is unthinkable that American Negroes would go to war on behalf of those who have oppressed us for generations . . . against a country which in one generation has raised our people to full human dignity of mankind."

The House Un-American Activities Committee subsequently asked a number of prominent African Americans to refute Robeson's statement. Robinson, the Symbol of Integration, was the prized speaker. Robinson told the committee that Robeson did not speak for the American Negro. He said that Robeson's claim that Negroes would not fight against Russia "sounded silly."

Near the end of his life, however, Robinson admitted that he had been naïve in 1949. In his 1972 autobiography, he wrote:

> In those days I had much more faith in the ultimate justice of the American white man than I have today. I would reject such an invitation if offered now. I have grown wiser and closer to the painful truths about America's destructiveness and I do have increased respect for Paul Robeson who, over a span of twenty years, sacrificed himself, his career and the wealth and comfort he once enjoyed because, I believe, he was sincerely trying to help his people.

★   ★   ★

Fifty-nine years from Jackie Robinson's debut and seventy-six years after Rube Foster's death, black athletes today represent a majority in professional football and basketball and a smaller but significant number in Major League Baseball. Yet, decades after the demise of Negro Leagues, African Americans are largely excluded from the managerial hierarchy of baseball in particular and professional sports in general.

By the beginning of the 2006 Major League Baseball season, four of thirty big league managers were African American. There were no African American owners. The most alarming statistic is that the percentage of black baseball players in the majors had dropped to 9 percent. They are largely excluded from ownership, which creates a domino effect. As sports became a multibillion-dollar global enterprise, African Americans were largely shut out—shut out of front-office positions, presidencies, vice presidencies, and a wide variety of positions that flow into sports. "America's destructiveness," in Robinson's phrase, had worked its magic on what was once a thriving, black-owned industry, stealing its talent base and laying waste to its power. Foster would be appalled at how completely his dream had crumbled.

On September 12, 1970, fullback Sam Cunningham led his integrated University of Southern California team onto Legion Field in Birmingham, Alabama, against Bear Bryant's all-white Alabama Crimson Tide. In the wake of USC's 42–21 victory, Alabama fans realized the Crimson Tide—and Deep South schools in general— could not compete on a national level without extending their recruiting reach to include African American players. Alabama's epiphany spelled the weakening of black college football. *Courtesy of National Baseball Hall of Fame.*

Integration:

The Dilemma of Inclusion Without Power

"Today, there are two Negro organized leagues, just at the threshold of emergence as real financial factors. Organized Negro baseball is a million-dollar business. To kill it would be criminal and that's just what the entry of their players into the American and National Leagues would do."

—WENDELL SMITH, 1943

MY JUNIOR SEASON AT Morgan State College began in Pittsburgh on September 12, 1970. For the third year in a row we opened our season with Grambling. Yankee Stadium was being renovated, so the third annual Whitney Young Classic was played at Three Rivers Stadium, home of the Pittsburgh Steelers. Black college football was gearing up for another outstanding season. One of the many barometers of a program's success, or of a league's success, was the number of players drafted by professional teams. By this measure, the National Football League's spring draft marked yet another stellar showing for the nation's Historically Black Colleges and Universities, or HBCUs: 135 athletes from 31 schools were drafted.

Two players, Kenny Burroughs from Texas Southern and Ray Chester from Morgan, were first-round picks.

A number of schools had multiple draftees. Grambling had eight players drafted, bringing to seventeen the number of Grambling players drafted over two years. Tennessee State had five draftees, twelve in two years. Johnson C. Smith University in North Carolina had four, followed by three Morgan players—Ray Chester by Oakland, Mark Washington by Dallas, and George Nock by the Jets.

There had been a strong HBCU presence in the recently played Super Bowl III as well, where the New York Jets pulled off a stunning upset of the Baltimore Colts in 1969. The Jets roster included Johnny Sample and Emerson Boozer from Maryland State, Winston Hill from Texas Southern, and Verlon Biggs from Jackson State. The Colts had Willie Richardson from Jackson State.

The HBCU influence on pro football came into full focus when the National Football League announced its Seventy-fifth Anniversary Team. Of the forty-eight players selected, seven—roughly 13 percent—were from HBCUs. Two of them, Roosevelt Brown and Willie Lanier, were from Morgan.

★　　★　　★

We didn't realize it that September afternoon in 1970, but the world of black college football was about to undergo a dramatic—and traumatic—transformation. While we were playing our game against Grambling, a drama was unfolding that same afternoon in Birmingham, Alabama, where the University of Southern California (USC) was playing the University of Alabama.

On September 12, 1970, USC traveled to Birmingham to take on Bear Bryant's Crimson Tide at Legion Field. For many of the white—and black—fans at Legion Field that day, USC must have seemed like a team from the distant future.

Although USC had a lot of Brothers on the team, the Trojans were not merely desegregated; the team was fully integrated—numerically, but more important, stylistically. Jimmy Jones, a black man with a towering Afro, was USC's quarterback at a time when African Americans at predominantly white universities rarely played quarterback.

But the star of the afternoon was Sam Cunningham, a six-foot-three-inch, 245-pound sophomore fullback who spent the afternoon running up and down the chests of Bryant's defense. Cunningham rushed his way into immortality that afternoon; he became the Paul Bunyan of the game's lore.

Playing in his first varsity game for USC, Cunningham carried the ball eleven times, gained 135 yards, and scored two touchdowns. USC crushed Alabama 42–21.

Cunningham would be called the catalyst for integration in the South, and the game drove home the point that George Wallace's June 1963 proclamation—"Segregation now, segregation tomorrow, segregation forever"—would have to be modified to accommodate the great black athlete.

★   ★   ★

The irony of Cunningham's stardom and notoriety is that of all USC's black players, Cunningham was probably the least wrapped up in the social significance of the game. Unlike many of his teammates who were from the South, Cunningham did not understand the social significance of USC's playing Alabama *in Alabama* with a team packed with black players. He was raised in Santa Barbara, California, in an integrated community full of blacks, whites, browns, and yellows.

Cunningham and I were the same age—he was born in August 1950, and I was born in September. On September 12, 1970, we were twenty years old and our experiences in sports illuminated the rapidly changing and complex racial terrain for African Americans. But, unlike Cunningham, I was born in segregated South Side Chicago and attended a Historically Black College in Maryland on a football scholarship. Despite my emerging social and political consciousness, the implications of USC's playing Alabama in Birmingham escaped me. Cunningham also didn't immediately grasp the significance of the game.

He certainly didn't expect to be come a cultural lightning rod.

When we finally met, thirty-two years later, at Cunningham's home in Inglewood, California, he said the weight of that game unfolded like a flower, petal by petal. "It was just one game. At the time it was just a football game," he said.

The black-white angle that had so many reporters and his USC teammates in an uproar was lost on Cunningham. "Playing with white ballplayers was what we always did as kids," Cunningham said. "Neighbors and friends, that's what it was."

Cunningham said that when he landed in Birmingham, he was so consumed by the prospect of playing in his first game that everything else was a blur. He remembered hearing the coaches tell the players not to leave the hotel, for fear of what might happen given the racial tension of the moment.

"I'm a sophomore. I'm not a star on this team, not a leader on this team. I'm not anything," he said. "I had no animosity in my heart toward these people, there was no premeditation of going out here and changing the world, nothing. It was just a football game, my very first varsity football game. I was hyped behind that. First road trip. I didn't have a clue what was going to happen. I didn't even know I was going to play, other than on special teams."

During the walk-through practice the Friday before the game, Cunningham began to understand the significance of the game. There were 5,000 people watching the Trojans practice. In the stands, fans were talking trash: "Bear's going to get him some meat."

While Cunningham battered the Crimson Tide, the speedy Clarence Davis peppered USC with an assortment of darting runs and pass receptions that underlined the Crimson Tide's lack of speed. Alabama may not have needed to get blacker, but it needed to get faster. And if the two were synonymous, so be it.

The USC-Alabama game spawned a number of myths. This would be Bryant's last all-white football team, though the game did not cause him to immediately reverse his all-white recruiting philosophy and go out and begin signing every highly touted black athlete in Alabama.

In fact, Bryant had already signed Wilbur Jackson in December 1969 out of Carroll High School in Ozark, Alabama. Because of a National Collegiate Athletic Association rule prohibiting freshmen from competing, Jackson did not play his first game until 1971. Still, the loss to USC did not give Bear Bryant "religion" in terms of recruiting black players.

One of the myths that arose from the game was that after it was over, Bryant took Cunningham from the USC locker room, brought him to the Alabama locker room, and had him stand on a bench. Then he supposedly said, "Now *that's* a football player."

"That's a myth," Cunningham said. "Although it is hard to say it's a myth because it's been told so many times. I think one of the coaches made that story up, I'm not sure which one. I do know that Coach McKay would never have let that happen. He's not going to let one of his players parade over there. That would be rubbing it in their faces. That's just part of the lore, all the fallout."

A number of Cunningham's white teammates, years later, would make the game larger than life. John Papadakis, a senior on that 1970 USC team, wanted to make a movie of the USC-Alabama game. Papadakis and a few others interested in doing the documentary asked Cunningham to look at the script.

"They were all hyped about it," Cunningham said. "Finally I told them, 'John, I kind of like to remember it as it was, not as you guys may want to make it.' Every time I sit down and talk about it, which is not a lot, I try to remember it as close to how it was happening that day because that's how it happened. If I sit up and let the thirty years creep into my brain about what has happened since then, I lose perspective."

Another school of thought about the game is that Bryant knew USC was a much stronger team, but felt that the only way he could make a case for integrating his program was to have his team humiliated by a Trojan team that was heavily laden with black players.

Cunningham doesn't completely dismiss this idea.

"The powers that be who set the game up must have known that something was going to happen. Fortunately it happened to help the Bear get where he needed to get."

In fact, what stung Alabamans more than Cunningham—and what escalated the tide of change—was the performance of Clarence Davis, the Trojans' senior tailback, who was born in Alabama. He was born in Bessemer, right outside of Birmingham. His family moved to New York in 1958, then moved to California two years later.

Davis was fourteen years old in 1963 when a bomb ripped through the Sixteenth Street Baptist Church in Birmingham, killing four girls and stunning the nation. Davis's mother knew the mother of one of the children.

The public's fascination with his return to Birmingham seven years later, playing for USC, reflected their ambivalence toward black people, which became more troublesome as black athletes became more prominent—and more vital to the sport. The peculiar fascination with Davis reflected the way sports-crazed Southerners were struggling with race: On the one hand, they were steeped in the white South's revulsion at the presence of blacks, but on the other, they couldn't suppress their admiration of—and need for—the black physical presence. It was writ large in the South in 1966, but it's a paradigm that continues to define the dilemma of race and racism in sports in the United States: Behind the cheering often lurks angry resentment.

The person who may have derived the most enjoyment out of the afternoon was Davis's mother, Maria Davis. She flew from California to watch, to bask in the excitement of a game that many blacks in Alabama thought would never happen. It was her first trip back to the state she'd left in 1958. "I was excited, I was happy," she recalled. Mrs. Davis understood what she was watching, what it meant. Why this game was important.

She wanted to savor every second. "It was a very important game for me," she said. "When we lived there, you couldn't play a white team," she recalled. "You played black schools. To look to see how the changes had come, that was something."

Maria Davis was born in Livingston, Alabama, on October 8, 1929. She was five years old when her family moved to Birmingham. Mrs. Davis had tried to shield her son as much as possible from the mental scourge of segregation. That meant avoiding public transportation as much as possible. "We always had a car," Mrs. Davis said. "When we went places, we were in the car. And they were too small to know how the people were there. How the blacks had certain places to sit. They never experienced that. They were too small to wonder why the whites didn't go to the same school they went to."

Her schools were all black. She had to sit in the back of the bus. When Clarence was born, "he never rode the bus but one time in his life, back there in the South. He didn't know about this because we moved to New York."

She was a housewife in Birmingham. Her husband didn't allow her to work. "He was a good provider," Mrs. Davis said. "We had our difficulties [which] I didn't want my children to be involved in."

The USC-Alabama game was the second time Clarence Davis had returned to Alabama since he was seven. He'd come back for his father's funeral at age sixteen.

"The people wanted to see him, because this was his home and he was playing with 'SC." The team stayed out in the suburbs. "They couldn't come out of the rooms; the food was served in [their] rooms," Mrs. Davis recalled.

The USC team stayed at a Holiday Inn outside of Birmingham. Mrs. Davis remembers getting involved in some trash-talking with one of the employees, the window washer. "He said, 'I don't know why y'all here.' 'We're going to beat your butts.' " She told him if USC lost, she would come back and wash windows.

"The white people were booing them and booing them." When they got on the bus on the way to the game, they had to have security guards. "When the game was going on, it was terrible," she recalled.

"Some people were hollering things like 'Nigger, go back to California,' 'Nigger, go back.' Just dirty names."

"The black people were happy because of Junior," Mrs. Davis continued. "They were excited about the black players 'SC had, and knowing someone on the team. It made the blacks feel good," she said. "His father was well known, I was well known, and so, by us being raised there, being as our child plays against the white man, people were very happy."

Mrs. Davis made the usual case in favor of integration: She celebrated the access that integration had brought, and the chance it offered for athletes like her son to play on the largest possible field, to test themselves against white competition in a fair fight. But in spite of all the clear benefits of integration, the losses sustained by the African American community as a whole went beyond a ballplayer or two out of this community or that. The community's soul was compromised as well.

The USC-Alabama game began a chain reaction that escalated the African American presence in white Southern sports. After the game, one reporter quoted Bryant, referring to Davis, saying that he would never again let a great black talent leave the state of Alabama. While the Civil Rights movement challenged the nation to live up to its founding ideals of liberty and justice, The physical ability of both Cunningham and Davis provided pragmatic evidence that African Americans were needed if Alabama and other Southern schools hoped to compete on the national stage. Jerry Claiborne, an assistant coach at Alabama, reportedly said after the USC game that Sam Cunningham had done more for integration in two hours than Martin Luther King Jr. had accomplished in more than a decade. The mentality behind that statement, giving a football player more credit for integration than Dr. King, demonstrated that the basis for integration—in the minds of many white people—was not to embrace quality, but to seize an opportunity for exploitation.

Integration in sports—as opposed to integration at the ballot box or in public conveyances—was a winning proposition for the whites who controlled the sports-industrial complex. They could move to exploit black muscle and talent, thus sucking the life out of black institutions, while at the same time giving themselves credit for being humanitarians. Integration also exposed white fans to a manner of athleticism and style of play that many had not previously seen. It also introduced a type of showmanship that made the college game appealing to audiences for television's expanding sports programming.

★   ★   ★

The Morgan-Grambling game in which I played and the USC-Alabama game in which Cunningham played on that same afternoon were snapshots of two realities that were about to undergo transformation.

The Civil Rights movement was a powerful force that clashed with the United States' dominant pressure center and began to pry open previously closed portions of society. The subsequent collision had a shattering effect on the social climate in America.

But the force of that collision also shattered the African American community and scattered African Americans in hundreds of different directions. We have been trying to pick up the pieces ever since; the

contemporary black athlete expresses the still-unresolved consequences of that fracture.

There were many positive aspects of integration for African American
athletes. There was the opportunity to be educated at prestigious
"white" colleges and universities, with all the attendant advantages that
those schools bring: larger stadiums, fatter budgets, outstanding training
facilities. There was the opportunity to face a wider spectrum of competition on larger stages with access to greater resources.

But those opportunities came with a stiff price.

In the decades prior to 1970, the oppressive constraints of de facto
discrimination imposed a level of solidarity within the black community. Whatever an individual's educational attainments, economic status, or excellence on the athletic field, for example, he or she could
never entirely escape the oppressive reality of segregation.

But with oppression weighing so heavily, any sliver of daylight
seemed like relief, even if it ultimately compromised our survival by
opening a crack in our solidarity. Integration would give blacks access
to that big stage they craved, but it also gave whites access to the black
market to black wallets and sensibilities, and to black talent.

Integration also stopped a growing momentum toward independence and self-definition within the African American community.
Integration in the 1970s stifled a movement within the black community toward empowerment and community-building that began
as a result of African Americans—including athletes—being forced
out of integrated sports society in the 1880s and 1890s.

In the process of integration, there was also a psychic loss, in that many
African American athletes became estranged from the communities that
produced them. In time, many had virtually no understanding of the struggles that carried African American athletes through sports history. A generation of young athletes born after 1970 assumed that the dominant black
presence had not evolved, but rather that it had always existed.

Prior to integration, many Southern-born African American athletes were forced to attend HBCUs that were close to their homes.
This created a family-like atmosphere surrounding black schools—
they were as much a part of the community as were the families
themselves.

There was an enormous amount of civic pride associated with the
football teams at black colleges. In addition to providing a platform for
black athletes, sporting contests at HBCUs "reflected special black cultural patterns that attested to both the strength and vibrancy of the
black community."

This was especially apparent when rival teams would play one
another. More than mere games, the contests were an opportunity for
the entire community to band together and support their team and
celebrate themselves. The Morgan-Grambling showdowns were prime
examples of this element at work.

In addition, having the black athletes close to home allowed them
to serve as role models for their own families, as well as for the entire
community. Networks of relatives remained strong because the family members were always close by. After integration, however, black
athletes began moving across the country in pursuit of their individual athletic destinies. They often left both their families and extended
families behind, and as a result became alienated from their communities. Many black athletes no longer felt as if the place where they
grew up was home. As the profitability of the sports industry—starting at the college level—increased, the disconnection imposed by
white institutions on black athletes became more deliberate and
pronounced.

★   ★   ★

From the 1880s, when the first African Americans played at predominately white schools, to the early 1960s, the majority of black athletes

who aspired to play at the top level of college football had few options. Although they could play at mainstream schools in the West, Midwest, or East, they faced unwritten quotas that limited the number of black players on a school's roster. In the South, integration came late to the mainstream schools, giving Southern HBCUs the pick of the recruiting litter. Well into the 1960s, Jake Gaither, the legendary coach of Florida A&M, had the first crack at black athletes in the entire state of Florida. Eddie Robinson, the Grambling coach, had the same access in Louisiana; Marino Casem of Alcorn State and W. C. Gordon of Jackson State shared Mississippi.

The general feeling of black officials may have been that white racist attitudes in the South were so deeply entrenched that black colleges would have indefinite access to a rich pool of African American athletes for decades to come.

This unchecked access to black talent fostered a lack of foresight and vision and led to complacency. Why upgrade athletic facilities? Why beef up the athletics department budgets? Why expand? Why instrumentalize athletic programs in ways that so-called mainstream colleges had done for decades—using sports to add revenue and boost the reputation of the school—and then invest in upgrading not just the athletic facilities, but the national reputations of entire universities? Presidents, coaches, and athletic directors at the HBCUs would pay a steep price for taking their resources for granted and not maximizing their facilities and competitiveness when they had the chance. The problem was that black coaches, on some level, liked the segregation arrangement.

The Achilles' heel of those Africans who became entrenched in the slave trade, since their initial confrontation with the West, was often the failure to plan and predict. Similarly, the failure of black institutions to anticipate and plan came back to haunt them. Apparently none of the head coaches, athletic directors, or presidents at HBCUs considered what might happen when predominantly white schools in the South "got religion" and began recruiting black athletes en masse.

★   ★   ★

Over time, inevitably, a growing number of white coaches, like Bryant, and athletic directors began to realize that their segregated teams could no longer compete successfully against integrated schools. The rest of the nation was using African American athletes from the South to beat the Southern teams. For example, the Loyola University Ramblers had won the 1963 national basketball championship with a team of mostly black starters. In 1966, Texas Western (now the University of Texas–El Paso), with an all-black starting lineup, upset Adolph Rupp's University of Kentucky Wildcats to win the national title. Sandy Stephens, an African American, was the quarterback of the 1960 Big Ten champion Minnesota Golden Gophers, he led the team to the Rose Bowl. Michigan State won the national championship with a defense anchored by Texans Bubba Smith and George Webster. And now, in 1970, Alabama was being embarrassed at home by a heavily integrated USC team.

The realization that integration was necessary to maintain competitiveness was complemented by the fact that integration bore few practical costs for white teams. The key to the ultimate appeal of integration for white coaches was that it would not mean a corresponding loss of power; in essence, whites could have their cake and eat it, too. Integration on the sports field would not mean the transfer of power from whites to blacks any more than the black workforce in the cotton fields threatened white control of antebellum plantations. Blacks had not shared in the fruits of their industry then, and would not share in it now.

But for black coaches and others, exactly the opposite phenomenon occurred. Under the integration arrangement, many black institutions were either dismantled or downsized; those educators who had been heads of departments frequently became assistants or were made heads of smaller divisions. Black head coaches became assistant coaches. The old high school became the middle school, and the principal from the white high school remained while the principal of the black school became the principal of the middle school. And in sports, the white coaches got the upper-level positions while blacks got the junior varsity jobs.

In what would become a model of the new post-integration sports, blacks at the college level were pushed into prominence for their stellar athletic ability, but were not pulled into the executive and coaching pipeline with equal vigor. This pattern became firmly entrenched as the years went by. The disparity between black presence on the field and representation in the administration was illustrated in a survey by the National Collegiate Athletic Association. The four-year study by the NCAA's Minority Opportunity and Interests Committee, released in 2001, showed a negligible increase in minority-group athletic administrators over the years.

For example, of 5,889 vacant administrative positions between 1991 and 1994, only 10 percent were filled by blacks. Such positions typically include administrative assistants, equipment managers, graduate assistants, strength coaches, trainers, coaches, academic advisers, auxiliary services personnel, faculty representatives, compliance coordinators, eligibility officers, ticket managers, sports information directors, promotions/marketing directors, business managers, and athletic directors.

The number of associate and assistant athletic directors—key career paths to upper administration—actually declined between 1991 and 1994.

Of 122 new athletic directors hired by predominantly white colleges between 1990 and 1994, 15 were black, according to NCAA figures. Currently, 32 of 897 athletic directors in the NCAA's three divisions are black. Of the 107 Division I-A schools—the big-time football schools—a mere 4 have black athletic directors.

And for all their overwhelming numbers on the field, blacks represent 3.9 percent of the total number of head coaches in all three divisions. Segregation at the administrative level was a "protective tariff for whites."

★   ★   ★

The repercussions of integration went beyond the Negro Leagues and Historically Black Colleges. Prior to the integration of the NFL, there were a number of all-black professional teams that were relatively successful. The first all-black professional team, organized by Fritz Pollard in 1928, was the Chicago Black Hawks. The Black Hawks became well known for playing—and beating—white professional and semiprofessional squads. Another of the more successful all-black football teams was the Brown Bombers of Harlem. Organized by Herschel "Rip" Day, the Bombers are best known for beating the white Newark Bears in 1936 by a score of 41–0. Although the Black Hawks and Bombers were the two best-known enterprises, a number of other all-black teams were also operating successfully.

This success, however, came prior to the integration of the NFL. After the NFL began allowing blacks in, all of the most talented black players left their original teams to join the league. Wharton School of Business professor Kenneth L. Shropshire wrote, "Once integration occurred, black sports-team ownership completely disappeared. . . . Integration, a godsend for black athletes, was a disaster for black owners, who were defenseless even to protest." Similar to the destruction of baseball's Negro Leagues, black professional football organizations stood no chance against the larger and more powerful NFL.

With the dissolution of Negro League baseball and the collapse of the fragile football league, blacks would never again have as great a

stake in the sports industry, and would spend the next five decades trying to regain lost ground. The employment and promotion of African
Americans in the sports industry would be an issue in sports for the
next fifty years.

★   ★   ★

Almost no one could have predicted the numerous negative ramifications of integration. In fact, some of the most vocal supporters of integration were the same ones who were perilously impacted once it
occurred.

Even so, and in spite of the evidence pointing toward the overall
harm that integration caused in the African American community, there
are still many critics who argue that none of these results can be attrib-
uted to integration. Furthermore, some maintain that the benefits that
individual African Americans have received outweigh the harm that
may have occurred to the black community. Although many of these
arguments are compelling, they do not fully reckon with the problems
that may have been unleashed within the black community because of
integration. The next section of this book will begin addressing those
problems in detail, but make no mistake: Though integration was a
major pivot in the history of the black athlete, it was not for the
positive reasons we so often hear about. Integration fixed in place
myriad problems: a destructive power dynamic between black talent
and white ownership; a chronic psychological burden for black athletes, who constantly had to prove their worth; disconnection of
the athlete from his or her community; and the emergence of the
apolitical black athlete, who had to be careful what he or she said or
stood for, so as not to offend white paymasters. At the same time, it
destroyed an autonomous zone of black industry, practically eliminating every black person involved in sports—coaches, owners, trainers,
accountants, lawyers, secretaries, and so on—except the precious on-
the-field talent.

★   ★   ★

Integration created a multitude of unforeseen problems for the white power structure as well. For one thing, black success in mainstream sports forced the media to recast the long-held stereotypes that rationalized the exclusion of black athletes—that they were physically and mentally inferior to whites. There now had to be a rationale for black dominance.

After the 1966 Texas Western game, black success in basketball began to be explained away by a new rationale: "Okay, maybe blacks are tough enough and smart enough to beat whites, but that's only because their bodies are so well suited to the game. They can run faster, jump higher. What do you expect?"

Reintegration of sports also created an insatiable demand for black athletes and the style many of them carried with them to college and pro leagues. This style would be the source of great entertainment and much hand-wringing for white coaches and commentators.

But what is "African American style"? Where does it come from? What function, beyond entertainment, does it serve? The gestures that make up black style—the chest bumps, high fives, shakes and shimmies—are more profound than simple mannerisms. Style is a specialized form of black expression, a consequence of being "outside of," or "other." From Harlem to Bedford-Stuyvesant to Watts to isolated segregated areas, style grows up fresh and uncut. African American style is a reaction to racism. Those segregated regions of black life evolve in different ways, resulting in distinctive music, speech, manner, and ways of doing things. The various Negro League teams played by the same rules as their white counterparts—but any spectator could tell they played a different game.

Black Style is a state of mind; something felt, something seen and immediately identified as one's own. Ralph Ellison wrote that he and his young friends back in Oklahoma "recognized and were proud of our group's own style wherever we discerned it—in jazzmen and prizefighters; ball players and tap dancers; in gestures, inflection into-nation, timbre and phrasing. . . ."

What exactly is "black style"?

The answer goes beyond surface gestures and pantomime, deeper than the basket catch, the alley-oop pass, and even the Ali Shuffle. The essence of style is connected to something infinitely more powerful than trying to colorfully celebrate a touchdown or slam-dunk a bas-ketball. Much deeper. Painfully and profoundly so.

Ralph Ellison examined the question from another perspective: What would the United States be without "the Negro"?

He wrote: "Without the presence of Negro American style, our jokes, tall tales, even our sports would be lacking in the sudden turns, shocks, the swift changes of pace (all jazz shaped) that serve to remind us that the world is ever unexplored, and that while a complete mas-tery of life is mere illusion, the real secret of the game is to make life swing."

The arrival of Muhammad Ali marked the dramatic confluence of Black Power and Black Style. *Santi Visalli Inc./Hulton Archive/Getty Images.*

In the late 1950s, San Francisco receiver R. C. Owens introduced verticality to professional football. Owens's ability to out-jump hapless defenders led to the creation of the "alley-oop" pass. The phrase would become popularized as a basketball term. *Courtesy of the San Francisco 49ers.*

Style:

The Dilemma of Appropriation

IN THE SUMMER OF 1963 I stood in front of a black-and-white television, watching a baseball game between the San Francisco Giants and the hapless Chicago Cubs. I don't remember the inning or the score—just that Ron Santo, the Cubs' third baseman, hit a deep fly ball in the gap between right and center.

The fans screamed. The batter took off. Most centerfielders—even the great ones—would have to scramble to get to the ball and would shamelessly display the effort of getting there.

Willie Mays drifted across the outfield like Charles Coles, the great tapdancer whose footwork was so sweet and smooth that they called him "Honi." He arrived at his spot under the baseball with no apparent sweat, even though he'd had to run for what seemed like miles to get there.

Then, instead of raising his glove to catch the ball, the way every other outfielder was taught since Little League to catch the ball, Mays placed his glove at his belt buckle, like a basket, and made the catch.

Plop!

Santo kicked the ground in disgust; Cubs fans groaned and sat back down. Mays had turned a potentially dramatic moment into a routine out. The most memorable part of the play is what took place after Mays made the catch. He nonchalantly picked the ball out of his glove, tossed it back to the infield, coolly walked back to center field, flicked his sunglasses back up, and waited for the next play. His body language suggested annoyance that the batter hadn't presented a greater challenge. This was the highest, subtlest form of putdown, an unspoken challenge to the other team—and to the sports establishment that still frowned on any hint of flash and couldn't make sense of Mays's "signifying" around this thing called "black style"—a way of acting and talking in a coded way, communicating through gestures and body language.

When I think back on that catch and how it struck me, I realize I felt that Mays was talking to me: the way he ran, the way he made the hip catch, the way he coolly walked back to center field. The catch itself—the act of making a put-out—was secondary to the style of the catch.

★   ★   ★

Mays made deep inroads into my psyche that afternoon. Until I saw Willie Mays play, the idea of playing sports with soul had never entered my mind. Willie Mays introduced me to a dimension of style I thought only existed in jazz. I always knew music had the power to transport. A few years earlier I'd stood in the basement of my grandmother's house in Phoenix, Illinois, poring through piles of 78s she'd collected over the years: The record that stuck most in my mind was a tune called "Liza (All the Clouds'll Roll Away)," by Chick Webb's band, featuring a punchy, three-chorus trumpet solo. What attracted me was the cleverness with which the trumpet player had taken the basic theme of the piece, played around with it, turned it inside out, and interpreted it to his liking.

Until I saw Willie Mays make that basket catch, the idea of playing sports with that same sort of interpretive style had never entered my mind. I didn't realize that each of the elements that made blues-based music swing—its soul—had a counterpart in sports: the phrasing, the lyricism, the improvisation. The difference was that in sports the "instrument" was the body of the artist.

From then on, I watched Willie Mays whenever I could: watched the way he ran, the way he hit. I went outside and tried the basket catch. I tossed the ball up or had someone hit it to me. The ball landed on my head, hit my chest, fell to my right or my left. Catching a fly ball was hard enough. Making it look easy was impossible. I never learned to make the basket catch, but I was determined that whatever I did—mow the lawn; rake the leaves; play a sport—I would do it with the graceful ease and cool of Willie Mays.

There was something magnetic about Mays, not just the basket catch or the speed, but the familiar nuances I recognized in his body language. I felt so much in that catch—jazz and blues and all the R&B I loved. I felt the signifying, the dozens. All that in this one simple play.

Over the next five decades, Willie Mays's cool became my standard: Plain greatness wasn't enough; you had to play with style and soul.

What I didn't realize at age twelve was that you didn't just "get soul," you had to earn it, to pay for it, and the price of this ticket was steep.

★   ★   ★

Before Willie Mays came along, Jackie Robinson had introduced a restrained version of the same soul to mainstream American sports by virtue of his pioneering role in Major League Baseball. The late Curt Flood said:

> When Jackie Robinson first started playing, everyone was surprised at his antics. He stole second base. He stole third. Jackie Robinson stole home! It was something unheard of. Jackie Robinson dancing off the base, worrying the pitcher, and wanting him to throw to first base, and saying things. That style of baseball came from the old Negro leagues, that

is the way they played. Now you add to it the hit and run, the sacrifice, the stolen base, the hit behind the runner, the jockeying in and off base, that's the style that Jackie Robinson brought. Jackie Robinson and Larry Doby and George Crowe and Monte Irvin and these guys raised the level of competition.

And they did it with style.

Robinson was a star, but in a larger sense he was a celebrity, a monument to the black pioneer in sports: "The Black Man Who Integrated Major League Baseball."

Robinson came from the Negro Leagues but was not necessarily *of* the Negro Leagues. He did not revel in Negro League lore. Robinson endured the experience because he had to. Robinson had been conditioned to the "white life" at UCLA and in junior college. He had heard the white crowds roar and may have rather longed for the right to live that life. Indeed, it was his association with white institutions that made him attractive to Branch Rickey as the Negro pioneer to integrate white baseball. He picked up his style from the Negro Leagues, but he also knew how to tailor it to the majors.

Willie Mays was the first young African American sports superstar. Jackie Robinson was twenty-eight when he reached the majors, while Mays joined the Giants at age twenty. He was the symbol of a young, black vitality that mainstream America had never seen because African Americans had thus far been excluded from mainstream sport.

Mays became as significant to the late 1950s as Jackie Robinson had been in the late 1940s. Robinson integrated sports racially, but Mays completed the job, integrating sports stylistically. Where Robinson's great significance had been in being "the first," Mays's significance was his great talent and distinctive style. Where Robinson's presence in major-league sports announced that black players were good enough to compete, Mays's generation announced that black athletes could do more than compete: They could redefine the very game.

*   *   *

Mays was the cornerstone of a second wave of African American superstars who introduced a new dimension of soul into sports. In his three-volume treatise on baseball, David Quentin Voight said that American sports by the 1950s, particularly Major League Baseball, had begun to level off in popularity and had become boring. "Indeed," Voight said, "these were mostly clean-shaven crew-cut white boys. There was no denying their colorlessness." The American-born white athlete was bound by a certain order and custom. The black presence, beginning with Robinson, added flavor, color, and, finally, drama. This presence also superimposed the conflicts and complexities of race on the national pastime. Mays's style broke barriers that had not formally been erected yet. His style defied the "American," white way of playing—in all its sterility.

By the time Mays came to New York in 1951, black athletes were still a new commodity in mainstream athletics, but they no longer had to bear the entire weight of a nation's race consciousness. The National Basketball Association color barrier was broken in 1951 by Nathaniel "Sweetwater" Clifton with the Knicks, Earl Lloyd with the Detroit Pistons, and Chuck "Tarzan" Cooper with the Boston Celtics. The National Football League was integrated in 1947 by Woody Strode and Kenny Washington. Sports, like jazz, became a "free" space in which black athletes were free to make powerful statements using gestural modes of expression to celebrate, honor, and even chide.

Jackie Robinson had to watch every *p* and *q*, had to dot every *i* and cross every *t*, because he was the first and couldn't afford to be perceived as flashy or arrogant or "some kind of hot dog." Because Robinson had gone through all that, Mays had the luxury of being lavishly creative. He could stretch the margins. Like the boxer Muhammad Ali a decade later and the musician Charlie Parker a decade earlier, Mays was so far above the rest of the field that it seemed as if he were playing a new game.

In many ways he was. He changed the rules, from his seemingly leisurely method of catching a ball to his propensity for going from first to third on an infield out. As a defensive player with explosive speed, he raised the standard for an extra-base hit "in the gaps" between the outfielders. Mays's speed and daring fielding style effectively closed those gaps.

Miles Davis introduced mainstream America to "cool" and "hipness" in jazz in the late 1950s. Willie Mays introduced a flair and cool style in sports. He introduced the Black Thing to a mainstream public that devoured it—and has been devouring it ever since. The popularity of sports that blacks dominate today coincided with the beginning of this stylistic transformation of the game, the opening up of the game to this new way of playing. Willie Mays presaged this stylistic contour in sports. This form of integration, in the long run, would be far more traumatic for white authority figures than the mere physical presence of black players; it was this stylistic integration that led white sons and daughters to embrace the Black Thing in every part of their lives— from style of play to clothes to language.

In virtually every decade since the 1950s, black athletes have been at the core of some stylistic or structural innovation in sports. From the alley-oop pass and the spin move in basketball to the spike and the ritual of the end-zone shimmy in football. From slapping palms to donning baggy pants and executing wildly creative dunks and elaborate end-zone celebrations, the African American presence in sports has redefined and reordered the traditional way of doing things. Whether it was Jackie Robinson's daring on the base paths, Muhammad Ali's mocking brilliance and fire in the ring, Wilma Rudolph's willowy grace and speed, or Michael Jordan's aerial exploits, black athletes have brought to the field a tantalizing mix of ingenuity and grace, sensuality and strength, beauty and violence, rage and vulnerability.

In the process they have invented a new American art. Mays introduced the notion that black athletes played with a "style" that catapulted them to another level and separated them from the pack. He established that there was a level of artistry in athletics that could be attained through "black style." A level that could not, at that point, be reached by white players, who were too often shackled by limitations and expectations imposed by the very conventions Mays challenged.

Ultimately this new black style, symbolized by Mays, would become the cornerstone of America's multibillion-dollar sports industry. This elusive phenomenon has kept millions of Americans lining up for tickets, and ultimately pouring over $34 billion a year into the ever-expanding sports industry.

The dilemma for the black community is that in the post-integration world, the community has no right, no claim, indeed no way, to profit from this soul. The dilemma for the sports industry was that as the appetite for black style increased, so did the black presence on the fields of mainstream sports. As black players and style took center stage, so did a rising tension over style.

The dilemma for stewards of the game was that this "flashy" style was terribly effective and wildly exciting. Fans were coming out to watch in droves. The industry's sudden dependence on a style that many executives and media bigmouths were uncomfortable with only increased the tension.

In other words, not everyone was enthralled by Mays.

For all those who loved Mays, there were fans who became agitated by his style of play—the cap that always seemed to fly off when he ran, the basket catch, the dramatic way he ran the bases. Critics called him a "showboat," a "hot dog."

Once the novelty of Robinson and Mays wore off and the march of black athletes into the mainstream began, the knee-jerk American racism toward African American accomplishment—indeed, toward the mere presence of African Americans—surfaced. This was the same reflex that eliminated blacks from baseball in the nineteenth century, squeezed cyclists out of bicycle racing, forced black jockeys out of horse racing, and kept black football players out of the NFL.

A revealing insight into the resentment integration generated can be found in the anonymous remarks of a sportswriter in 1951. Willie Mays had helped the Giants to a World Series showdown with the New York Yankees. In the final game, the Giants started three African Americans in the outfield—Mays, Monte Irvin, and Hank Thompson—the first time such a thing had ever happened. The anonymous sportswriter wrote:

> *Willie Mays is in a daze*
> *And Thompson's lost his vigor*
> *But Irvin whacks for all the Blacks*
> *Ain't it good to be a nigger.*

A backlash had started to set in. Had Mays come along three decades later, he would have had a tremendous, integrated fan base. But in his era, white fans never fully identified with him. Mays arrived at the Polo Grounds for the 1951 season four years after Jackie Robinson had integrated baseball, and the people who ran sport and business were not certain that the middle-class Americans who were their customers were ready for African Americans to be promoted as stars, like Mickey Mantle or Joe DiMaggio or Ted Williams. At the same time Mays was beginning his career at the Polo Grounds, the Yankees brought up Mickey Mantle, a powerful, Oklahoma-born home-run hitter, blue-eyed and blond, nursed in the heartland of America. Mantle and Mays became cultural icons in America in different manners. Mantle was the embodiment of dairy farms, rolling acres of corn, apple pie, and the flag. Mays was simply a great player. He had his fans—and his money; Willie Mays was well compensated. But the element of perceived intimacy and familiarity that made Mickey Mantle a folk hero, and pulled even cold characters like Joe DiMaggio and Ted Williams into the nation's bosom, remained just beyond Mays's grasp.

Just as a black sportswriter could never be Red Smith, and Hank Aaron could never be Babe Ruth, Mays would never eclipse Mantle as a cultural icon, no matter what he did. As heroes go, Mays had hit a glass ceiling. Implied in his easy manner, his blasé attitude after a great play, and the nonchalance was an implied "fuck you"—he made it clear that his style was him, and for those who couldn't appreciate it for the genius it was, there would be no grinning and jiving to win them over; he'd given up on that. A style of play that had found an easy home and wide appreciation in the Negro Leagues was still too "black" to sit comfortably with mainstream America, even as many white Americans were thrilled and fascinated by it.

The isolation and invisibility, the bitter awareness of being accepted but not embraced, and the anger at this cultural glass ceiling—feelings that athletes like Mays shared with the majority of the black population of the country—also played out in Mays's soulful style of play. That was part of what attracted me to Mays that afternoon in Wrigley Field when he made the basket catch.

He wasn't being cool for the sake of being cool. He was cool out of a genuine urge to make a performance of the most basic athletic acts, to fully exercise his skill and creativity and his desire for jubilant expression. But Mays was also literally cool, in his air of detachment and resignation. This graceful ease and "cool" has come to be broadly associated with African American athletes—it's part of what makes them so fascinating and appealing. But this distinctive style is also a reflection of powerlessness on the part of African American athletes. For Mays, that famous style and "soul" came at the price of staying in segregated hotels, eating in segregated restaurants, and dealing with the daily bombardment of racism. For black athletes as a whole, that style in some ways underlines their inability to define themselves in more substantive ways and find acceptance. So, rather than try to fight it, to argue or plead for the acceptance that they'd never find, many black athletes let that damaged soul bleed out of them in their style on the field. But even that style, so hard-earned, is a precarious possession, one that can be—and has been—criticized, legislated out of existence, appropriated instantly and without compensation.

By the time I saw Mays in Wrigley Field that summer afternoon in 1963, the blush of innocence had long since faded. Mays was no longer the bubbly nineteen-year-old "Say, hey!" kid who'd come up from Alabama to New York City. He was a seasoned, slightly bitter, thirty-one-year-old veteran. Mays had weathered eleven major-league seasons. The basket catch and his unrestrained, flashy style of play, which had startled the stodgy baseball establishment when he broke into the league, had become old hat. His style had been copied, emulated, and improved upon, and—of course—appropriated by the system. His glory days with the New York Giants, gleefully playing stickball in the streets of Harlem on his days off, were past. Indeed, his team had moved 3,000 miles to San Francisco, physically uprooting Mays from the inner city.

At Mantle's funeral in 1995, sportscaster Bob Costas, reflecting on his own youth, recalled that Mantle was a player "we" emulated and identified with. His "blond hair, his blue eyes. The way he rounded the bases after a home run, eyes down in a sort of humble, workmanlike humility."

I don't know which "we" Bob was referring to. But the "we" I knew was out in the street, trying to emulate Mays's basket catch.

★   ★   ★

"People discovered that 'Hey, there's another level of this game that can be played—that can be played higher through the jumping mechanism; not just being able to run and catch. You can leave your feet and make a catch above everybody else.' That was an area that had been untapped," R. C. Owens said.

Owens is largely unknown to contemporary fans, and his greatest contribution to football is associated with basketball: the alley-oop.

Six years after Mays broke in with the baseball Giants, R. C. Owens, a six-foot-five-inch offensive end, was drafted by the San Francisco 49ers of the National Football League.

Owens was part of the third wave of post–integration African American athletes, those who followed Jackie Robinson and Willie Mays into the mainstream of United States pro sports. This third wave included Bill Russell, who revolutionized defensive play for centers in the National Basketball Association and was a rookie with the Boston Celtics in 1956; Jim Brown, a running back who combined speed, power, and grace, and was a rookie running back with Cleveland in 1957; Curt Flood, who shook the sports foundation by challenging baseball's Reserve Clause, and had become the St. Louis Cardinals' regular centerfielder in 1958; and Elgin Baylor, a rookie with the Minneapolis Lakers in 1958, who introduced "hang time" and "walking on air" to pro basketball. The difference between this wave of black athletes and Mays's generation was volume. There were more of them.

"More of us came on the scene at the same time athletically as potential superstars," Owens said. "We were all coming out at the same time. We were playing well. People were seeing a lot of different things; they were seeing a different style."

Each wave of black athletes has had to negotiate the changing face of racism. Jackie Robinson and Larry Doby battled exclusion, fought against the idea that blacks lacked skills. Willie Mays proved that African Americans could play and often had to play at a higher level than their white counterparts. The wave of contemporary black athletes of which Owens was a part faced a more discreet form of racism, the beginning of the more abstract racism that would confront successive waves of black athletes as the white-dominated power structure maneuvered to maintain the black-labor/white-profit paradigm in the one area in which blacks were becoming dominant: sports.

R. C. Owens played for San Francisco beginning in 1957, after a stellar basketball and football career at the College of Idaho. Owens was originally drafted in 1956, but put off his pro football career for a year and toured the nation with an all-star basketball team.

Owens introduced verticality to the sport in a way it had never been used. His basketball skills, specifically his jumping ability, laid the foundation for an aerial innovation that is known primarily as a basketball term but originated in pro football: the alley-oop.

Throughout the history of football, offensive ends and halfbacks had to outjump opposing defensive backs for the ball. Owens's alley-oop innovation, however, marked the first time a player's superior jumping ability was formally inducted into a team's playbook. The concept behind the pass was simple: The quarterback dropped back and lofted a high, arching pass in Owens's direction. As an accomplished basketball player, Owens understood the rhythm and timing of jumping, and the importance of securing position and using leverage. "It was that basketball instinct that enabled me to make those catches," he said. Owens ran to the point of reception and leaped to take it away from the defender.

For Owens, "style" became a tool for survival. He realized that if he planned to make the team, he had to do something different; fortunately for the twenty-four-year-old rookie, he could jump at a time when jumping was not considered to be an integral part of the game.

For Owens, the value of style was not simply that it came easy, that it was cultural or instinctive. No, for Owens, developing style was a matter of survival. Style actually *improved* his game; at the very least, it ensured that no one would miss what he was doing on the field. "Whatever you were doing, you had to do it in an exceptional way. Everybody could judge you, could see that you performed, you excelled: You can run, you can catch, you can block, you can tackle. Because whatever you're doing, you're doing it with great style and fashion."

Owens's approach to coping with racism was simple—and consistent with the prevailing mentality of many African Americans faced with carrying a burden of proof: "Perform."

"You would always say, beneath your breath, 'Play me and I'll show you.' And if you got the chance to catch the ball—[make sure you] score. Or, if you know you're not going to get a long pass and you get a short one, you'd better turn it into a touchdown. You'd better be inventive and come up with the performance."

That's precisely how the alley-oop came into existence in 1957, Owens's rookie season. The 49ers had lost their opening game of the season, 20–10, to the Chicago Cardinals, and faced the Los Angeles Rams the following week. "The coaches were looking for a way to not be 0–2," Owens recalled. In practice the week before the game, the offense was running the Rams' plays and Frankie Albert, the 49ers coach, exhorted Y. A. Tittle, the quarterback, to throw long passes in order to give the defense an idea of what the Rams would do on Sunday. So Tittle lofted several high passes downfield, which Owens went up and grabbed, easily outjumping the 49ers' defensive backs. After watching Owens make a couple of these catches, an excited Albert said, "He's just outjumping them for the ball. We've got to put that play in." On Sunday, Owens made two leaping touchdown catches in the end zone to lead the 49ers to a come-from-behind 23–20 victory. He scored on a 46-yard pass when he made an impossible catch over the outstretched arms of a defender. Trailing 20–16 in the fourth quarter, Tittle rolled out and hit Owens.

The 49ers kept the play in the books and started winning. On November 4, Owens caught a 41-yard pass over Jim David and Jack Christiansen from Tittle, to beat Detroit 35–31 with eleven seconds left. This boosted their record to 5–1.

Owens's jumping ability allowed him to become a "big play" receiver as a rookie. In his rookie season, Owens caught twenty-seven passes—half as many as his teammate Billy Wilson, who led the NFL with fifty-two catches. But Owens averaged 14.6 yards (the same as Wilson) and scored only one touchdown fewer, with five. In all but one of his eight pro seasons, Owens, who is now the director of the 49ers alumni association, averaged double-digit yards per reception— including a high of 20.4 yards per catch in 1959. For his career, Owens averaged 15.9 yards per catch on 206 receptions.

Style became a tool to circumvent racism and bias against black play-ers by their own coaches—it forced those coaches to pay attention. Owens said that, for him, the value of style was that it allowed black players to keep "coming up with something different so the players would say, 'Coach, we've got to use that,' or the coach would say, 'We're going to put that in,' or 'We're going to give him the ball more.' If it continued to happen more and more and more, you'd reach the point where they couldn't keep [black players] out of the starting lineup." For Owens, devising a unique style was meant to ensure that he was one of those two or four African American athletes who made the team. "You had to come up with a style so that the world would say, 'Wow, this guy is jumping out the stadium,' " Owens said. "Or if it was Willie Galimore, they'd say, 'Man, this guy's so fast, he's like a cloud of dust.' "

Willie "The Wisp" Galimore was the prototype of the new-wave running back in the National Football League. Galimore, who died in a car accident in 1963, was an electrifying runner who still ranks sixth on the Bears' all-time rushing list. Smooth, fast, quick with flashy moves, "Galimore ran at a level that other players who ran the ball just couldn't reach," Owens said. "He was one of a kind [at the time]. Of course, pretty soon you got [more] players who were black, and soon everyone was a cloud of dust. It became like a domino effect: first the running backs, then the receivers, then the defensive backs to cover them and the big, fast defensive linemen, and linebackers to keep up with them and big mobile offensive linemen to block bigger, faster defensive players."

Faced with an expanding influx of black athletes, owners—in conjunction with general managers, coaches, and managers—set artificial limits on the number of black athletes who would make their teams. "There were quotas," Owens recalled. "Usually there were two black guys on the team, maybe four. Rarely you saw an odd number; usually it was two or four." In time, quotas would be augmented by a system of steering black players to certain positions—positions that required instinct, not thought. In football, the stereotype, enforced by men with power, was that African Americans were not smart enough to be quarterbacks or centers and guards; on defense they would not play free safety or middle linebackers. In baseball, blacks would be put in the outfield, not at shortstop or second base. Being a head coach or manager in any sport was out of the question. Owens's generation had to push against those stereotypes, but first they had to get out on the field in any way they could. Their weapons were style and talent. That combination became a formula for winning in the box office and on the field. The Black Thing, as unnerving as it may have been to some, was profitable and entertaining—and therefore irresistible.

★　　★　　★

Why did it take black players to introduce "style" into sports in a more conspicuous way? Before Jackie Robinson and Willie Mays reached the big stage, style was regarded as impractical in American sports. In fact, style was all about the absence of style. Sports were supposed to showcase "the moment of truth," strength against strength, preparation against preparation. The most beloved athletes embodied an aw-shucks humility that remains at the heart of the American self-image of so-called innocence. This model of sports heroism, however, was in a constant clash with the express-yourself, do-your-thing imprimatur of "black style." The struggle between the two styles continues down to this day, but it's pretty clear who's winning the battle these days.

Owens has watched this evolution. "If you don't have that kind of [flashy] game today to help you down the floor in a full-court press, you might not be playing first team or be on the team at all—you might be on the sideline looking. You've got to have an attitude. You have to have that pizzazz."

That's today. But when Owens broke into the NFL in 1957, "having an attitude" was the kiss of death for African American athletes. "Attitude" was one of the racial buzzwords to describe black athletes in the negative. Having an "attitude problem" once was the sole province of black athletes. Attitude meant a chip on the shoulder, a surly demeanor.

Four decades later, Madison Avenue has converted "attitude" into a positive. Attitude is good. Attitude is hip and bold. Even inanimate objects have the desirable "attitude": a car with an attitude, a piano with an attitude and so on.

Owens was traded to Baltimore in 1962. The coach was Weeb Ewbank. One day in practice, Owens blocked a field goal by standing on the goal line and jumping up and swatting the ball away if it was kicked low enough. He approached Ewbank with the idea of trying it in a real game. Ewbank liked the idea. In the waning moments of a game, Washington's Bob Khayat lined up for a 40-yard try. Owens stood in front of the uprights, which were then on the goal line. The kick was on line and appeared to have the distance, but Owens leaped and knocked the ball away. Owens's block was the first—and only—field-goal attempt ever to be rejected at the goal posts in an NFL game. "They changed the rule. . . . You can't be in the goal post area anymore," Owens said. This is the Jockey Syndrome—changing the rules to stifle black excellence—applied to style. There have been other rule changes over the years of this sort.

Because of Wilt Chamberlain, the nimble seven-foot-one center who played for the University of Kansas, the National Collegiate Athletic Association widened the lane from eight feet to twelve feet, instituted offensive goal tending, and forbade the foul shooter from crossing the free-throw line until the ball hit the basket (Chamberlain would dunk his missed free throws).

With the entry of Bill Russell in 1956 and Chamberlain in 1959, the era of the tall, lumbering goon was on its way out. Russell was tall at six feet nine, but as fast as many of the point guards in the NBA. Historian David Halberstam said of Russell's innovation:

> In the past, the dominating big players had been white, usually strong but slow. When they blocked a shot it was generally because the offensive players had taken a poor shot. Russell was something completely new, the forerunner of a different player in a different game, the big man who got down court faster than the other team's small men. He blocked shots that had never been blocked before. Players on other teams not only had to correct the arc of their shots but change the very nature of their offense when they played against him.

In 1966 the National Collegiate Athletic Association adopted legislation outlawing the dunk. The legislation was aimed at neutralizing the presence of Lew Alcindor, an agile, seven-foot-two-inch center who dominated competition in high school, college, and the pros from 1963 to 1989. In 1990 the NCAA banned celebration; this included prohibiting players from taking off their helmets and from praying in the end zone. It also banned taunting. Of course, some of the recent rule changes have been less about style than simply about race, in the great tradition of the Jockey Syndrome: One promoter even attempted to place quotas on how many Kenyans could compete in a marathon.

R. C. Owens said: "It's like, they made the free-throw lane wider because you had too many guys like Russell and Chamberlain. So, well, you know, guys adjusted: Guys started flying. You could make it as wide as you want to, it won't stop you from flying."

The rules have proven futile, however, and have simply led to greater innovations. Instead of encouraging white suburban guards, for example, the three-point shot simply produced more outstanding African American outside shooters; the no-dunk rule heightened the innovation and creativity of players driving to the basket.

★   ★   ★

The introduction of African American athletes to the mainstream marked the beginning of a tremendous influx of black football and basketball players to previously segregated Southern schools. It also marked the beginning of an intense struggle to control the extent to which African American "style" was expressed through sports. For me, one of the most dramatic signals that this battle had been lost was the Cotton Bowl game on New Year's Day, 1991, when the University of Miami met the University of Texas.

At the time, Miami was nationally known and popular for a raucous style of play that included taunting, exuberant celebrations, and a steady flow of "commentary" that drove opponents to distraction. The Hurricanes' games were a combination of performance and pro wrestling match: The players danced, postured, and gestured after big plays. Earlier in the season, the school's president, Edward Foote, had warned the football team to tone its act down after a particularly ugly brawl at Brigham Young University. Accordingly, in the week leading up to this particular Cotton Bowl game, the Miami players were on their best behavior. I remember one interview session in which a couple of Miami players actually helped officials set up chairs. Meanwhile, the Texas players, enjoying a resurgent season after several down years, were talking trash. They talked and talked without admonishment. Stan Thomas, an offensive lineman for the Longhorns, referred to Miami players as "hooligans" and "thugs," and talked about how he was going to stomp the Hurricanes into the ground.

On game day, Miami whipped the Longhorns' collective asses without mercy and with great pleasure. But what was intriguing was the manner—the "What's My Name" style—in which Miami won. The Hurricanes began taunting Texas players before the game even started. The Longhorns could hear the Miami players shouting through the locker-room doors before the players came out for pregame introductions. When Texas ran onto the field, they were stunned to find Miami players greeting them, as if they were a Welcome Wagon, with obscene gestures and taunts. On the opening kickoff, Chris Samuels, the Texas kick returner, was knocked cold and the tone was set. The Miami offense, on its first possession, received three consecutive penalties—all for variations of unsportsmanlike conduct—and faced 40 yards to go for a first down. They made up the yardage on three passes. The Miami defense held Texas to minus-4 yards of total offense in the first quarter. Miami won 46–3.

Randall "Thrill" Hill caught a touchdown pass and ran out of the end zone all the way up the ramp, shouting with glee, "It's too easy, it's too easy!" Another player strode up and down the Miami sideline, like a drum major in an exaggerated high kick, as the rout continued. I felt a little guilty for enjoying the spectacle so much. This wasn't so much a lopsided defeat as vengeance. It was also great theater; indeed, the way Miami won was what reverberated all the way up to the press box. As the game went on, I alternated my view from the field, where the Hurricanes were taunting and dancing and manhandling Texas as though they were rag dolls, to the press box, where the game was being observed with tightened jaws, stern, puffy red faces, and gritted teeth.

After the game, there were renewed calls from the media to "do something" about the boisterous, intimidating, increasingly vocal and demonstrative style of play that was becoming so prevalent at virtually every level of competition. Will McDonough, the late columnist for the *Boston Globe,* wrote a scathing piece that more or less echoed the usual "loose ball" mentality. You could feel the venom. He started off by observing that "this has been in the making for close to two decades."

Two decades. That just about takes us back to the beginning of integration in the South, when large, predominately white, football universities began in earnest to get black athletes to come to their universities to play revenue-producing sports. McDonough continued, "Sooner or later, the street would take over, and it did in the Cotton Bowl in Dallas on Tuesday when the University of Miami players delivered college football's version of wilding." He said that the Miami players "exposed themselves as thugs for hire with their conduct, which included 16 penalties for 202 yards, four unsportsmanship-conduct calls, five personal fouls and a stench that will stay with Miami for a long time."

The Hurricanes, McDonough said, had gone "beyond the limits of decency" for taunting the poor, defenseless Texas players, "intimidating them in pregame warm-ups, then dancing like fools every time they scored a touchdown, and generally being obnoxious throughout the game." McDonough warned that the football powers at Boston College, then considering allowing Miami entry into the Big East conference, "should be asking: Do we really want to be in the same conference with these people and expose our players to this garbage year after year? Is this college football? Is this what we want to bring into our stadium?"

Of course, the answer to that question is simple: Yes. Yes! Hell, yes! The Big East begged Miami to join the league to bring in the very luster and hotdogging that so disgusted McDonough.

I loved the Miami performance. Loved it probably for all the wrong reasons. Loved it in large part because of the contradictions it represented: White universities embraced this Faustian pact two decades earlier when they began bringing black athletes to their campuses by the truckloads. They wanted black muscle but not the attendant zeal and style. They somehow thought these athletes would all arrive at their campuses as sanitized as Jackie Robinson. They pretended these athletes weren't going to arrive with their own baggage, baggage that a history of living in a white supremacist country had helped to pack. Style, as we've seen, developed over a long period: It developed on plantations and then on segregated fields of play; it developed in response to quotas and denials of black humanity. This historically essential element of black sportsmen was not going to vanish into the ether simply because they were now playing in leagues controlled by whites.

Dennis Erickson, the Miami coach, told his players before the Cotton Bowl game to do what they had to do to win. Which is what the Hurricanes did. Fifth-year senior Darren Handy said the players ignored Erickson's supposedly repeated demands for good behavior because "emotions just took over."

"It might be embarrassing to the university and the coaches, but it's not to the players," Handy said. "We enjoy it."

Later, Hill explained that the game was a signature performance for Miami. "This senior class is the last of the renegade classes, and we went out the way we wanted to, dancing and having fun." Dancing. Having fun! How this troubled the press and other precincts of power in college football.

At any rate, I left the press box that evening with a sense of satisfaction: The chickens, as Malcolm X had said, had once again come home to roost.

★   ★   ★

For all the emotional satisfaction that aggressive displays of black style offer to black athletes and fans, the question, however, remains: Given all of the benefits that black style—a style forged in the flames of discrimination, segregation, quotas, and dehumanization—brought to white team owners, universities, and leagues, did it do anything to enhance black power in the industry? Or was it just assimilated, albeit with some difficulty, into the existing power dynamic of white control/black talent? As black style became more popular, who really benefited? Did this black style—carved out of black suffering and creativity—ever become black power?

Quite the contrary—designers like Ralph Lauren, Donna Karan, and Tommy Hilfiger quickly became cornerstones of the hip-hop industry. Motown founder Berry Gordy sold his 15,000 Motown songs to EMI Publishing. Bob Johnson created the first African American cable TV network then sold his company to Viacom for $3 billion. Five years later, *Essence* magazine was sold to Time Warner. Call it "Soul on the Auction Block."

The fact is that black style was quickly commoditized by white power, which became addicted to this other new form of black gold. The integration of intercollegiate sports in the mid-1970s created an insatiable appetite for black athletes, which in turn triggered a strip-mining of black communities across the United States. Talented young black athletes and their families were wooed and pursued with the promise of scholarships and, often, material gifts. Black athletes had become a vital commodity in the sports industry, which necessitated a full-service delivery system to identify, prepare, and carry black muscle to "market." That system is the Conveyor Belt.

Great young talents like LeBron James epitomize the Conveyor Belt, a process by which athletic gold is mined and distributed largely to the benefit of white institutions and individuals in the billion-dollar sports industry. The "Belt" creates young African American millionaires but reinforces a "white is right" mentality that prevents athletes from galvanizing their power. *Photo courtesy of Brian Spurlock.*

The Conveyor Belt:
The Dilemma of Alienation

When you control a man's thinking, you do not have to worry about his actions. You do not have to tell him to stand here or go yonder. He will find his "proper place" and will stay in it. You do not need to send him to the back door. He will go without being told. In fact, if there is no back door, he will cut one for his special benefit. His education makes it necessary.

—G. CARTER WOODSON,
The Miseducation of the Negro

MY FIRST MAJOR SPORTS STORY for the *New York Times* appeared in April 1983. The subject was the annual McDonald's All-America Basketball Game, featuring the best high school basketball players in the country.

I arrived in Atlanta two days before the game and decided to attend one of the practice sessions. I walked over to the arena with Bob Minnix, at the time an NCAA investigator whose job was to make sure that no improper contact took place between coaches and players.

171

There was almost a revival atmosphere inside the Omni that afternoon. A congregation of sixty-five coaches, scattered throughout the arena, legs crossed, arms folded, watched as player after player executed this maneuver or that. This was part beauty pageant, part meat market, and the players were willing participants.

I'd never seen the recruiting meat market up close, and had certainly never seen anything like this. I wasn't highly recruited as a high school football player, and none of my teammates were, either. It was a different time, with a different level of pressure. The only scandal I'd been aware of back in those days involved Bernard Stephens, an all-city, all-state fullback from Chicago Vocational School. Stephens had been very highly recruited and finally chose the University of Illinois. Soon after he made his choice, news reports uncovered a so-called "slush fund" at the university used to pay athletes—including Stephens. I remember how the imagery conjured up by the word "slush" sullied Stephens's reputation. I wondered why a big white school like Illinois felt it had to "buy" a young black athlete—precisely the sort of teenager the university would otherwise ignore.

By the time I arrived at Atlanta for that McDonald's all-star game in 1983, I understood why. Money. A top recruit could mean the difference between a winning season and a losing season, a big bowl game or a short season, and all the revenue and priceless prestige that came from a successful program.

Each athlete had his own flock of coaches surrounding him. Tom Sheehey, a six-foot-eight-inch center from McQuaid Jesuit High School in Rochester, had Larry Farmer of UCLA, Gary Williams of Boston College, and Terry Holland of Virginia. Holland was also following Kenny Smith, the six-foot-one-inch guard from Archbishop Molloy in Queens, New York.

But most of the interest was reserved for Reggie Williams, the smooth six-foot-seven forward from Dunbar High School in Baltimore, and one of the most highly recruited seniors of the 1983 class of All-Americans.

Farmer, John Thompson of Georgetown, and Bobby Cremmins of Georgia Tech were the finalists for Williams's talents.

"My, my, my," Thompson said admiringly as he watched Williams maneuver on court and smoothly knock down a medium-range jumper. I asked Thompson what he thought about the All-American games. "To be honest," he said, "I don't see a lot of good in these games. By now, you've seen all the players. But you're almost compelled to attend these games if you're interested in a kid. Most coaches I know would prefer not to have these games, but if five or six coaches are interested in the same kid you're interested in, you have to come or risk having the kid think you're not interested."

"Isn't that something," I thought. Accomplished, mature, mostly white adults representing the most prestigious education institutions in the country don't want young, mostly black men with basketball skills to think they're not interested. So they show up and sit and woo and coo.

This was a snapshot of how the American dilemma of race finds its way into the realm of contemporary sports.

And John Thompson, as the rare black man with real power in this world, was not immune to its flaws. Thompson grew up in segregated Washington and was fond of telling his players how, as a teenager growing up in D.C., he couldn't even hope to attend Georgetown because he was black. Thompson attended Providence College, then played for the Boston Celtics before beginning his coaching career.

The McDonald's game in 1983 was the first of many encounters I would have with Thompson over the next twenty years. Thompson is an engaging and insightful commentator on race, but sprinkled with fascinating contradictions. He embraced his blackness (to the point that some accused him of using race as an anvil) and had nationalistic instincts. Thompson once allowed me to attend a practice session, then invited me on the court and introduced me to the team. He told me he wanted them to see a black role model, but years later I joked that he wanted them to remember that I might be a Brother, but I was also a reporter. At the same time, Thompson was an avowed capitalist whose agent, David Falk, was a white man to whom he steered most of his players.

His team had played for the national championship in 1982—losing to North Carolina 63–62 on a game-winning shot by Michael Jordan. The Hoyas had been eliminated from the NCAA tournament in the second round of the recently completed 1983 tournament. Critics felt that the successful recruitment of Reggie Williams would put Georgetown in the national championship hunt. They were right; with Reggie Williams in the lineup, Georgetown won the national championship in April 1984. With that victory, Georgetown made for itself a national reputation that would endure the ups and downs of the decades that followed, and Thompson ensured himself lucrative employment for the rest of his career. The energy and investment put into that one recruit paid off in spades. One black teenager from Baltimore who could stick a jump shot made a multimillion-dollar difference for one of the most prestigious universities in the nation and its coach. That's the logic that fuels the race for athletic talent.

★   ★   ★

The sports industry is not just a signature aspect of the American way of life, but has also become a major component of the American economy. What distinguishes sports from other industries is the nature of its raw material: For the past fifty years, the prime raw resource in the sports industry has been black muscle. The work of the industry is to extract those bodies from where they primarily reside—in the black neighborhoods of rural and urban America—and put them to work. Now a sophisticated recruiting apparatus has been created for just that purpose. The apparatus is called the Conveyor Belt.

With integration and the television-fueled growth of the sports industry, the value placed on black muscle dramatically escalated and the stakes in the recruiting game began to rise. Predominantly white colleges and universities, which once either banned or ignored black athletes, were now twisting themselves like pretzels to recruit them. Schools that had long disdained African American athletes were now going out of their way to bring them on campus by any means necessary. The arms race was on. Bitter recruiting wars would be fought over young athletes, with all kinds of perks thrown in, from financial inducements to favors for family members and friends.

The challenge for the black community over the past decades has been to figure out how to control this mad scramble for black athletic resources and harness its potential to achieve the community's social, economic, and political goals. But to do so would entail combating the delivery system I first witnessed at the All-America game in 1983 and would see in repeated variations during the next twenty years. It would require understanding and redirecting the Conveyor Belt.

★   ★   ★

The recruiting process creates a fascinating reversal of fortune: The poor become rich, and those with the least access to higher education receive scholarships to some of the best institutions in America. Since 1936, when the Southeastern Conference became the first of the major collegiate conferences to award athletic grants-in-aid, the athletic scholarship has become the centerpiece of the college sports industry. But from the large pool of potential athletes, only a handful make it to the finish line of an athletic scholarship or a big professional sports contract; the National Collegiate Athletic Association estimates that only 3 percent of high school seniors who played basketball in 2005 will continue to play in college, and that only half of those 3 percent will receive some sort of athletic scholarship.

But before the system winnows out the winners from the losers, there are literally hundreds of thousands of young athletes who will ride the Conveyor Belt at some point in their lives, even if most of us are not good enough to ride it to the end. The National Sporting Goods Association estimated that 866,000 children twelve years old and younger regularly play some form of organized baseball, 347,000 play football, 250,000 play basketball, and 36,000 play hockey. They play Little League Baseball, Pop Warner Football, Biddy Basketball, and Squirt Hockey. Traditionally, entry-level training in basketball, baseball, and football, usually starting around age eight, has been provided by national organizations like the YMCA and the YWCA, the Catholic Youth Organization, the Boys Club of America, and the Police Athletic League, and by municipal park and recreation departments.

At that level the teams are recreational outlets for the hundreds of thousands of youngsters who participate primarily for exercise, to learn physical confidence and discipline, and simply for the thrill of competition and the fun of emulating their professional heroes.

For the more talented players, however, these programs function as tributaries that carry them to progressively more refined pools of talent. The Conveyor Belt runs through a sprawling network of feeder systems: youth leagues, camps, clubs, clinics, and scholastic leagues. The feeder systems separate large pools of participants, first by age, then by ability, helping to move young people from one level of competition to the next. The Conveyor Belt transports young athletes from innocent fun and games to clubs and specialized leagues—where they find increasingly rigorous competition and better training and coaching— and finally to colleges and pro leagues. The well-trained athletes paying fans watch every weekend represent the finished product.

Most of the prestigious summer football and basketball camps are operated by white men who invite top high school players to work with and display their talent to invited coaches. At its best, the contemporary Conveyor Belt is a streamlined mechanism for developing players and offering training and showcases where talented players can display their talents for college scouts.

At its worst, the Conveyor Belt introduces young people to the worst ills of the contemporary sports-industrial complex while they're still young and impressionable. It's at the camps where many first learn about the gifted athlete's limitless entitlement. The better athletes learn that no wrong is too great to overlook, if not erase—that no jam is too severe to get out of. The Conveyor process makes a future star feel he is above the fray from an early age. Isolated on the Belt, young athletes become accustomed to hearing "yes" all the time and having adults fawn over them and give them second and third chances because of the promise of their talents. The end result is often as evident on the crime blotter as in the sports section. No matter how focused and disciplined they are on the court, young athletes are not given any restraints off the court.

Life on the Belt also often fosters dependency. Star athletes who are so inclined become accustomed to being shepherded through the system without ever having to look out for themselves, from simple perks like not having to stand in line to more serious crutches like being guided through school by tutors and structured study halls.

Warren Brown, the former executive director of the National Federation of State High School Associations, objected to the showcase games for these very reasons. Not only were the games "heavy duty" promotional jobs for the sponsoring companies, using the unpaid talents of high school students, but "We also think the games contribute to making sports bigger than life and making kids think that they're bigger than life because they are involved."

For African American athletes, the threat of the Conveyor Belt process goes beyond the ways in which it undermines character. The Belt is also designed to dull any racial consciousness and eliminate communal instincts. Instead, the Belt cultivates a culture of racial know-nothingism. Indeed, the act of "processing" athletes along the Conveyor Belt involves a significant and often subtle element of "deprogramming" potential troublemakers—black athletes who might be tempted to think of themselves, or their situations, in racial terms and who might want to use their prominence in the service of some-thing other than enriching the institution. In a university, such trouble-makers might include athletes who want to use their visibility to call attention to the need for more black head coaches or faculty on cam-pus, or athletes interested in initiating or joining in causes that might embarrass the institution. On the Conveyor Belt, young athletes quickly learn that easy passage through a white-controlled system is contingent upon not "rocking the boat," not being a "troublemaker," and making those in positions of power feel comfortable with the ath-letes' blackness.

★   ★   ★

The trick for the masters of the Belt—coaches, athletic departments, owners at the professional level, promoters and managers in sports like boxing—is to get control of young athletes early, take them away from any competitive interests—especially their own communities—and reward them with flashy goodies in order to keep them quiescent. Rudy Washington, the former head of the Black Coaches Association, once described the process:

"How tough is it to buy an inner-city kid? Buy him some shoes, take him to dinner, get him some nice clothes, maybe a car. You become his best friend, and he gets hooked, like a junkie," Washington said. "Then you control the product. The secret is controlling the prod-uct early. It's just like slavery. Modern-day slavery is what it is. And you know the saddest part? The kids benefit from the system—at least a few lucky ones—with education and money, but what they often lose is any identification with the black community."

Over time, the school-aged athlete's dislocation from the black community is manifest in the adult athlete's sense of alienation from his or her origins. In fact, among many athletes who've reached the professional level, their greatest fear is having to return to the commu-nity, to the point that some become afraid of the neighborhoods they grew up in. As Dennis Rodman has said, "I go through the projects. That's not me anymore. No longer part of my life."

Young athletes on the Belt also get a twisted education in values, ethics, and character. As the competition for players intensifies, journalists have started to uncover the lengths to which big and small programs alike go to lure blue-chip black talent to their campuses. The first big exposé I remember reading was when I was still a student athlete myself in college. It was a *Sports Illustrated* series by Jack Olsen that documented the exploitation of black athletes, especially at the college level. The articles chronicled the crippling social isolation the athletes endured, and various ways in which they were used and abandoned by the machinery of big-time sports. Because I attended a historically black school where the kinds of abuses described by Olsen were rare, I read the stories like dispatches from a foreign country. Black schools were far from perfect, but the wanton disregard for an individual's humanity was not something that took place at HBCUs.

One egregious example of the dishonesty that pervades the recruiting process is the story of Tates Locke, a former basketball coach at Clemson. Locke was so desperate to recruit black athletes to the school's South Carolina campus that he invented a phony black fraternity so black recruits would think there was actually a black student presence on campus. What were these students supposed to do once they'd signed on to Clemson? Who cared about their isolation then?

The Conveyor Belt isn't always a story about race. Every sport has one, even those sports without significant black participation: tennis, hockey, gymnastics. In sports like hockey, where a teenager can enter the minor leagues as early as junior year in high school, athletes begin rigorous competition as early as the fourth grade. By the eighth grade, many are seasoned veterans of travel. But race—and the poverty that often goes hand-in-hand with black skin in this country—adds a complicating factor to the Belt. And of all the major team sports, basketball offers the most poignant insights into the mechanics of the feeder system. Because of the growth of basketball during the past fifteen years, it has been a vehicle for both hustlers and positive forces to exert their influence.

The major difference with black athletes is the cultural dislocation and isolation the Belt encourages, and the infantilizing effect this has on the athletes themselves and the wasted opportunity it represents for the communities they come from. In the black athlete's quest for power, the Conveyor Belt represents an especially serious impediment.

Here are two stories that underline different dimensions of the Conveyor Belt. Chris Webber and Kellen Winslow represent two different lessons. Webber illustrates how one young man tried to control the Belt but in some ways failed; Winslow illustrates how parents can maintain control of the raw material that travels on the Belt.

In the fall of 1991, Chris Webber, Juwan Howard, Jalen Rose, Jimmy King, and Ray Jackson momentarily turned the Conveyor process on its ear. The five high school seniors decided they would go as a package to one university rather than blindly being transported down the Belt and distributed without having any say in the matter. Five of the top players in the United States decided together that they would play for one college team, in an effort to prove that talent, more than the coach, made the college game. These five freshman would triple the fortunes of whichever university they chose: They could either put an unknown school on the map or take a known school to the Final Four.

The significance of the so-called Fab Five was that five outstanding players understood their power. Five talented high school All-Americans gave players a glimpse of how they could empower themselves, make their own decisions, and find points of leverage that would shift the power balance from the masters of the Belt to the athletes on it.

Their story also illustrates the distinction between the rebel and the revolutionary.

In their search, the Fab Five could've gone beyond the usual suspects and made an even more explosive statement. For instance, they could have chosen a Historically Black College and then taken it to the NCAA Final Four as surely as they did Michigan, which would have shone a national spotlight on those schools, driven money and new blood into them, and provided an impressive model of black self-help. That would have been revolutionary.

Instead, they staged a rebellion and chose Michigan, a decision that in the grand scheme of things still empowered the very system of power that has traditionally smothered black aspirations. They tried to control the Belt, but in the end they showed signs that the Belt had already controlled them, limiting their thinking and ambition, and ensuring that they continued to serve the system.

While the post-integration Conveyor Belt has handily fed white-run institutions, it has starved black ones. In 1992, the year Webber came out of high school, the best black college programs, based on NCAA tournament selection, were Southern and Alcorn. Davey Whitney was the head coach at Alcorn. Did they try to recruit Webber? Why weren't the HBCUs even in a position to try to land Webber? It goes back to the dilemma of integration—black institutions were, by 1992, unable to compete.

Webber criticized black colleges for not having built a better infrastructure, not having put themselves in a position of leverage during the time when they had a monopoly on black athletes, to acquire the things that would make them more attractive to blue-chip black athletes: better facilities, larger arenas, more up-to-date training facilities—and, yes, television contracts.

"A lot of people put that pressure [on me to go to an HBCU], like, 'Come on, Chris, you can change it around, you can change it around.' But I think that process has to start within the black college association.

"Playing on BET is not good enough for me," he said. "Just like me playing on MTV is not good enough. I want the world to see. In a way I feel guilty because we could have changed that rhyme. But in a way we had to do what was best for us at that time. But we talked a lot about going to black colleges."

In any event, Webber went to Michigan, and the Fab Five created serious wealth for that Big Ten school's athletic department. Michigan, with all five freshmen in the starting lineup, went to the Final Four their first year. The next year, as sophomores, the players made a second straight trip to the Final Four. (They would lose both years in the championship game.)

The Fab Five were such a commercial hit for the university that years after those five players had moved on, the school was still selling Fab Five merchandise. Meanwhile, HBCUs continued their decline in competitiveness. A rich, predominantly white institution simply got richer from black labor, while black institutions were left struggling.

★   ★   ★

So, despite their inclination toward independence, Webber and his teammates' inability to truly oppose the power of the Belt undermined their gesture of rebellion. Webber left school after his second year and was drafted by the Golden State Warriors of the NBA. But the mental training of the Belt carried forward into his pro career.

As noted, one of the negative effects of the Conveyor Belt is that it takes the athletes farther and farther away from their home communities, particularly if they were born in the segregated, pre-gentrified inner city. The more successful the athlete becomes, the farther the Conveyor Belt carries him from that first truth of his life. For someone like Webber, who was not a "street kid" to begin with, the guilt of escape can be overwhelming.

And although the NBA is filled with black players of similar backgrounds, they've been unable to come together to form a supportive community within the league to replace the communities they've lost outside of the league. Such a community would have tremendous potential, bringing together young black men with money, visibility, and, whether they realize it or not, power. But this has never coalesced. This is because the Conveyor Belt, with its breeding of a deep competitive spirit, does not engender camaraderie and kinship. For example, Webber said that fellow NBA star Kevin Garnett is one of his favorite players, "but we don't get too close, 'cause we still got to [battle]. So it's almost better to keep a distant relationship until [our careers are] over, or until a special moment like the Olympics or all-star break."

And a lifetime of being manipulated by powerful and predominantly white coaches, boosters, administrators, team owners, and even the media leaves players fighting their own paranoia, which is another way in which potential unity is undermined: "Guys don't respect each other. I might believe the stereotypes: Your wife is making all the decisions about the money anyway; your agent is paying your bills; you ain't a man on your own anyway. You can't make the decision with me." Or, "You got five cars, I don't want somebody with five cars in the business with me. What you need five cars for?"

"There's so much of that mentality—'I'm worried about mine,' or 'We've all made it now, so what are we worried about.' "

And the Belt breeds complacency, not militancy. With their eyes on the prize of individual success and pleasing the white hands that feed them, players feel they can't risk a strategy of confrontation. Webber is aware of how this fear of the white power structure—and the goodies it provides—emasculates black athletes.

"People will be so worried about how they will be seen by history or how their commercials are going to be taken away. Now the thing is, 'Don't step out of line.' Now the cool thing is, 'I don't want to be looked at. Don't separate me; don't pick on me.' I've even felt that way a couple times, too—and that's not good. We have so much influence; I don't think we know how much we have."

"This is what the Belt teaches you," Webber added. "That one thing: As black men we can't say what's on our mind. You can never do that. I think you learn that on that Conveyor Belt, you learn you got to shut up, you learn you got to be politically correct. You learn you got to say these clichés. It's [the message] on that Conveyor Belt since the eighth grade: Keep the trouble away from me."

★   ★   ★

Ultimately, a child's movement into the world of sports shouldn't be about the athlete alone, but about athletes and their parents and guardians. Ideally, the conscientious parent walks along the Belt every step of the way, looking over the shoulder of all the operators who do the teaching, training, and coaching, making sure neither child nor handler loses focus. Sadly, in many cases, the parent or guardian is the one who loses focus. Janet Hill, whose son Grant was a star at Duke and in the NBA, estimates that only a handful of parents remain parents and not employees—just as subject to manipulation and control as the children they're supposed to be shepherding. Kellen Winslow, however, belongs to the first group. Kellen Winslow is a parent.

Kellen Winslow was an all-time-great NFL player, eventually inducted into the Hall of Fame. After leaving the NFL, he acquired a law degree. Winslow has a son, Kellen Junior, now a tight end for the Cleveland Browns. Winslow became a student of the Belt in order to help his son navigate it successfully.

"The Conveyor Belt can take you a lot of places, do a lot of good things for you, but you have to be aware that you're on one, that people want something from you. You have something that they want; you better take advantage of that.

"What's damaging about the process is the lack of awareness by the person on the Conveyor Belt," he said. "The lack of understanding that there is a system here, and that from the time that you show any type of athletic prowess—I don't care if you were four years old, fourteen years old, whatever—the moment you did something that made you different from the other kids, catch a ball, shoot a basket, the kid who's twelve years old and dunks the basketball, he's on the Conveyor Belt. And the lack of understanding by the student athlete on the Conveyor Belt or by the parent that this is taking place puts you at a disadvantage."

At the beginning of the 2000 season, Kellen Winslow Jr. announced on national television that he would attend the University of Miami.

The Hurricanes were a compromise choice. Kellen Junior had originally wanted to attend the University of Washington. His father had said no. Hell no.

Winslow used his experience, his knowledge of the business, his understanding of how these things work, to help his son make an informed decision.

"And when he came back with the wrong decision, I told him no. That's what I'm supposed to do."

"At times it was not pretty," the elder Winslow admitted. "Here he is, he's a man, everybody loves him, everybody wants him, everybody wants a piece of him, everything's good."

He had to give his son a recruiting pitch of his own. "Remember, Kell," the father said, "these people have known you for forty-five days, I've known you all your life. When they're finished with you, I'm still going to be here. I don't want you to fail, I want you to succeed. So why in the world do you think I'm keeping you from doing something that you want to do, and you're not understanding that I know this is the wrong thing?"

Winslow told his son he was prepared to go to the mat. "I told him, 'I'm going to fight you on this one.' "

"The night before we went on [a sports talk] show at Fox, I told him, 'If you get on that TV and you tell them you're going to Washington, I'm going to tell you no on national television. You don't believe me, try me.' He said, 'I believe you.' I said, 'You damn right.' "

Winslow did not like the way Washington had recruited his son.

Winslow and Rick Neuheisel,* the Washington head coach, had been teammates at San Diego. But when Washington recruited his son, they went through the coaches at school; rarely did they contact Winslow.

"When an appointment was made to make a home visit, it was made with Kellen and not with me. The meeting was supposed to be on Tuesday, Rick was coming into town. On Monday I just got back in from a trip, and Tuesday Kellen tells me that Washington is coming in. I said, 'Says who?'

"He said, 'Coach Neuheisel is going to be here.'

"I said, 'But nobody called me.' So we canceled that visit. [Neuheisel can] pick up the phone and call me. Michigan State did it; Ohio State did it."

This was both a fit of pique and a reasonable response. One of the common tactics of the Conveyor Belt is to drive a wedge between the athlete and any adult who can't be bought off, even the parent. College recruiting coaches know how to manipulate kids, cajole high school coaches, and seduce some parents. When they have to deal with a competing authority figure who won't be co-opted, they get frustrated and redouble their efforts to get a direct line to the kid. Winslow saw what was going on.

"When I know you and you can't call me, that's a problem. This is my child, this is my greatest resource right here. This is his future, and if I get a feeling that things are not going to be right in the recruiting process, how are they going to be when he gets to campus? These are details, and I preach to him details. You don't make an appointment to go to the parents' house without talking to the parents. My name is on that mortgage.

"Schools sent out scholarship papers. USC, Ohio State, Michigan State, they all called before they sent the papers. Washington did not.

---

* Neuheisel was fired in June 2003 for participating in neighborhood gambling pools on the previous two NCAA men's basketball tournaments. He sued the university and the NCAA and settled out of court in 2005.

These are legally binding documents. Suppose Kellen wants to go to Washington so bad he's going to deny his father and he forges my name. Then we have a mess.

"We sent the papers back, overnight mail.

"[Then] instead of calling me, they called Kellen at school. Red flag number three or four. There was a baseball coach or swimming coach at Kellen's high school who was a Washington alum who Rick knew— they're talking to them.

"I said no, no, no. He has a father. You might go into a lot of homes where there's not a father, but this child has a father. You might not like it, but you got to deal with it."

Winslow also wanted his son to at least consider a black coach or school. He called Bobby Williams,★ the former Michigan State head coach, because he wanted his son to meet a black Division I head football coach and a black athletic director.

"It's not about football," Winslow said. "Football is just a means to an end. If he tells me he wants to go to Grambling or Howard [Historically Black Colleges], I'm driving him, because if he has the ability to play on the next level, they're going to find him."

In the end, Kellen Junior went to Miami; the Hurricanes won the national championship in his freshman year. In the Rose Bowl game, he recovered a fumble.

★ ★ ★

Kellen Winslow Sr. was born in East St. Louis, Illinois, on November 5, 1957. His experience on the Belt was different from his son's because he didn't climb on until his senior year in high school. This variation in experience is what gave him insight into dealing with the predominantly white sports-industrial complex.

In the eighth grade, he told his mother he was going to go to col-

---

★ Williams was dismissed in 2002.

lege on an athletic scholarship. She said fine, but that it would help if he played a sport.

Instead of playing sports, Winslow had held down a job from the time he was a sophomore in high school, at UPS, where he lied about his age to get the job. But in his senior year, Winslow took a leave of absence from UPS to go out for the football team.

He went on to play at the University of Missouri, and was a first-round draft choice of the San Diego Chargers, playing for them from 1979 to 1987. He was inducted into the Hall of Fame in 1995.

His son played many sports growing up: baseball, flag football, soccer. But his father held off on letting him play tackle football until he turned fourteen. "When he turned fourteen, I wish I would have said fifteen," Winslow said.

"[When he was] a kid, you could tell he had a great deal of promise and that people were going to be after him. You could tell when he was six years old that was going to happen. But I was holding him back so he wouldn't get exposed to negative influences and bad coaching."

Unlike his dad, Kellen Junior went to all the football camps during his summers in high school: Tennessee, Georgia, Stanford.

"So the whole collegiate world knew about him before he became a senior in high school," Winslow said.

Although Winslow's own parents had met all the coaches, no one in his family was familiar with the Conveyor Belt, much less how it operated. His father had never been an athlete growing up because his mother would not let him play sports. Instead, he was in the band.

Neither parent had gone to college. "So this was a totally new experience for my immediate family. I had two cousins who had grown up with me who had gone off to college, and they were both girls. So at the time, who was going to give you insights?" His coaches were good, but "you really rely on your parents at that time for insight, and there was very little," Winslow said.

"They didn't know about this industry and they told me that," he said. "At the time you take everything a recruiter says as the gospel. But when Kellen came along and recruiters started to show up, I already knew the gospel. I had lived it, preached it."

Kellen Senior's parents were like so many parents, black and white, but especially black: just grateful that their son was going to college. "And I was the first one."

They certainly did not see him as the raw material of an industry.

"Some of the questions that I asked when recruiters came in [asking about Kellen Junior] never crossed my mind [when I was being recruited], and I'm sure they didn't cross my parents' minds because they had no point of reference, no basis to ask those kinds of questions.

"When they came in to recruit my son, I treated him just like that: You want something from him; he can do something for you. That's the only reason you're coming through this door.

"We have to get parents to understand that: You earn a scholarship, you're not given a scholarship. You have to change the language that people use; once you change their language you change their perspective.

"Once an athlete begins to see him- or herself as a raw material of an industry, the attitude begins to change. You begin to understand that nothing is made without you. It's a matter of trying to get those natural resources, all with different interests, different positions, to get them under one roof and to get them to understand. Getting the masses to understand that they do have strength, they do have ability."

★   ★   ★

This is a crucial problem with black athletes: the notion that they should be grateful for the things that they've rightfully earned, that they should come hat-in-hand in gratitude for the money and power that they themselves generate. It's this sense of gratitude and subservience—even under the bravado of many athletes' boastfulness

and preening—that in the end undermines any effort to take control
of the Conveyor Belt and the raw resources it transports. And it's the
Belt that reinforces this idea. Kellen Winslow Sr., who rode on a less
well-developed Belt than the one that kids today face, was able to see
through this deception.

Even so, he didn't stop being grateful until the end of his sophomore year at Missouri. The only reason his eyes were opened was that
his mentors, African American educators at the university, took
Winslow under their wing. He knows how rare this is today: "How
many players at football and basketball factories have African
American role models? How many have role models who will help
them open their eyes?"

Dr. Walter Daniel, the vice-chancellor of the University of Missouri
system when Winslow was a student, was also an English professor at the
school. He adopted Winslow as his "son" during Winslow's college
career. Winslow haunted Daniel's home and office, soaking up guidance.

"He asked me a lot of questions, he made me think about things,
about me being there [at Missouri], what it meant to be there. What
would I be doing if I wasn't there? He helped me understand the
advantage of being [in college] and that there was something going on
around me I wasn't aware of, there was a whole system involved, and
I was just sort of going through the motions and not aware."

Having a mentor outside the system prevented the Belt from doing
its normal work of numbing the senses and anesthetizing Winslow to
the possibilities that exist outside the athletic world.

In Winslow's case, this meant staying academically eligible. He'd
nearly flunked out the first semester of his sophomore year. "I was very
immature, I had a coach who was screamer and a yeller and I wasn't
used to that, I took that very personal. I was set to leave, go home. Once
my eyes opened up, I said, 'Okay, okay, okay!' I need to do this, I can do
that, this is a possibility. But I got to be here to be a part of it."

*   *   *

In 1956, Prentice Gautt* became the first African American to receive
a football scholarship to the University of Oklahoma. Gautt was an
invaluable mentor to Winslow because he had lived through the segregated sports history, had broken a barrier. At a time when the Big
Eight conference had increasing numbers of black players, Gautt was
a living witness to testify that life wasn't always this grand for black
athletes.

He told Winslow stories about how, as a boy growing up in Norman,
Oklahoma, he and his friends used to sneak into the University of
Oklahoma stadium and run for imaginary touchdowns, thinking this
was the closest they'd ever get to playing for the Sooners.

Then, the summer after his senior year at Douglass High School,
Gautt received a last-minute invitation to participate in the Oklahoma
State North-South high school all-star game—previously open only
to whites.

North had suffered some key injuries to its running backs, and the
coach then extended the invitation. Gautt accepted, and wound up
being named the game's most valuable player. After the game, a scout
from Oklahoma came by and said that Bud Wilkinson, the legendary
Oklahoma coach, wanted Gautt to come to Oklahoma. There was no
scholarship offer; Gautt would be a walk-on. He told Winslow how a
group of black doctors and pharmacists, who knew his family and
wanted Gautt to integrate the Oklahoma athletic program, raised
$4,000—four years' tuition—and presented it to his family.

At midseason of Gautt's first year, Wilkinson quietly put Gautt on full
athletic scholarship and returned the $4,000. In his sophomore year,
Gautt became the first black to play in a varsity game for Oklahoma.

---

* Dr. Gautt passed away in 2005.

Gautt enjoyed a brilliant career at Oklahoma, and played eight seasons in the National Football League, seven with the St. Louis Cardinals. He became an assistant coach at Missouri and earned his Ph.D. in educational psychology from Missouri in 1975. In 1994, Gautt became the senior associate commissioner of the Big Eight (now the Big Twelve) Conference.

Winslow was deeply influenced by Gautt.

"He understood the system and he took advantage of it, to be the first player of color at the University of Oklahoma, to get his master's degree, to get his Ph.D., to go out and work at the Big Eight office."

There were other black men who exercised that same sort of influence over Kellen. "The only reason I played high school football is that my high school coach, an African American man, saw something in me that I did not see in myself."

Of course, there were non-blacks who were also influential to Winslow, "but Prentice and Dr. Daniel were special because they looked like me, they had been down that road. The only reason I went to law school was because of Dr. Daniel. He planted that thought in my mind so many years ago."

But even during those earlier, seemingly more innocent days, the effects of the Belt's mental control were starting to manifest themselves. Winslow calls his generation of African American athletes, those who entered college in 1975, the generation that stopped talking about race. "I am probably the second generation after integration. We stopped talking about it, race. As a collective, our generation stopped talking about it and that put us behind. You had to do certain things, you played a certain role to be a part of the system and to survive. The athletes and the black coaches had to talk one way around each other, one way around fellow coaches and players or the white alums and white big donors."

Having witnessed both the negative possibilities of the Belt and a way to manage it, Winslow was ready by the time his son's time came. Like other athletes who become parents to athletes, he was wiser and had a deep reservoir of experience to draw from, like the parents of Mike Bibby, Kobe Bryant, or Grant Hill.

"I was just doing what was best for him, I was just being his father. And people can say I had a social agenda because I did those things; that's their opinion. If I don't bring up these subjects, knowing what I know, then I don't deserve to be his father."

He also had to look at Kellen the way recruiters were looking at him: as a coveted resource. "I tried to get him to understand that he had a position of strength now, because once he gets on campus it changes."

★   ★   ★

Winslow is unfortunately the exception to the rule. The Belt usually carries young black athletes out of black America and introduces them to a world with very few African Americans, a world of white agents, real estate brokers, bank presidents, trustees, and lawyers. The fact that so many of the athlete's closest advisers are not African American means that they're never around black models of leadership, a situation that undermines their own ability to become leaders, rather than pampered, passive followers.

When his son was a high school senior, Winslow already had his process set up. His son would attend a school where there was either a black head football coach or a significant African American presence on the team.

Winslow was attacked for his position. Even his son resisted.

"At first he didn't get it," Winslow said of his son. "But as time went on, after he had signed with Miami, he got a chance to step back and take a look at it, and got a chance to go down and spend time at the University of Miami and understand what it meant to be there, and then later on from some of his experiences, he began to understand what I was trying to get across to him."

For Winslow, the key to overthrowing the Belt is to get back to history. "The difficulty is getting players to understand where they come from. It wasn't that long ago that Shaq couldn't have played at LSU [because of segregation], it really wasn't that long ago," he said. "You want to talk about time and understanding. But when I came out of high school and I began to read and I began to get exposed to things, I got angry.

"They grow up and then one day they're fifteen, eighteen, they're twenty-one, they realize they're black. They wake up and realize that they are black men in America, and then they begin to understand what that means, because they're no longer an athlete. I'll be the first to tell you that people treat African American athletes differently than they treat African American men.

"They have to understand where they came from. Most of them don't."

★   ★   ★

The ultimate effect of the Conveyor Belt is not so much to deliver young black athletes to the pros, but to deliver them with the correct mentality: They learn not to rock the boat, to get along, they learn by inference about the benevolent superiority of the white man and enter into a tacit agreement to let the system operate without comment. By the time they reach the NBA, the NFL, or Major League Baseball, black athletes have put themselves on an intellectual self-check: You don't even have to guard them, they'll miss the shot.

The black athlete learns early on that the best way to continue the trip on the Conveyor Belt is to accept the power structure as it is. The young, talented athlete learns about the value of cultivating the far-reaching range of affiliations, connections, and alliances that can make the athlete's Conveyor Belt journey smooth; he also learns about the kinds of associations and ideas that can make it quite miserable or even terminate it altogether. Thus, even the athlete who believes in "Black Power" is given pause when confronted by a white-controlled power structure—owners, CEOs of merchandising corporations, media executives, and so on—that can make Big Things happen in the player's career.

One positive sign is that a new generation of younger black athletes are not brain-locked into the black-labor/white-wealth arrangement that has been so prevalent for so long. Many have started to use an expanded network of black professionals to negotiate contracts and represent them in a variety of business ventures. Black agents are emerging, slowly but surely, many of them young and possessed of the aggression of the hip-hop generation. This is progress of a sort, but it is not the Promised Land. In some cases, it's merely black exploitation replacing white exploitation. To really honor the struggles of the past, however, the ultimate goal must be to create a new and better model, not to replace an old form of oppression with a new one.

Michael Jordan is one of the most intriguing athletes of the twentieth century, a sports icon like Babe Ruth but not a paragon of principal like Muhammad Ali. Jordan was a marketing maven who never capitalized on his potential to mobilize African American athletes. Had he said, "Jump," they would have jumped. Instead, he chose to remain publicly neutral in all matters political and racial. The essence of Jordan's legacy is what he accomplished; the tragedy is what he could have done.

The River Jordan:

The Dilemma of Neutrality

And Moses said unto God, "Who am I, that I should go unto Pharaoh, and that I should bring forth the children of Israel out of Egypt?"

—E X O D U S   3 : 1 1

ON AUGUST 28, 1963, Martin Luther King Jr. stood at the foot of Lincoln Memorial in Washington, D.C., and addressed 250,000 people who converged on the nation's capital. The March on Washington, at the time, was the largest demonstration in the nation's history.

That summer was one of great national crisis, as well as deep personal anguish. On August 4, a month shy of my thirteenth birthday, I lost my mother to breast cancer. We had been living in Phoenix, Illinois, a tiny hamlet outside of Chicago and hometown of basketball star Quinn Buckner. The United States was being ravaged by the cancer of racism. The world sat and watched as the self-appointed bastion of democracy confronted its demons: police brutality and vigilante violence aimed at African Americans demonstrating for equality. In a span of three months there were an estimated 1,412 Civil Rights demonstrations. Many of the protesters faced tear gas, police dogs, and high-powered water hoses as they fought for their right to vote, their right to equal access to public facilities. Sociologist Manning Marable said that some decades are worth only a year, but some years are worth an entire decade. Certainly 1963 was worth a decade.

- In June of that year, Medgar Evers, a field secretary for the NAACP, was shot and killed in front of his home in Jackson, Mississippi.
- In September a bomb exploded in the basement of the Fourteenth Street Baptist church in Birmingham, Alabama, killing four little girls in Sunday school.
- In November, John F. Kennedy, the president of the United States, was assassinated in Dallas.

At a time of great national moral crisis, Dr. King rose to the occasion and delivered one of the most compelling speeches in United States history. Dr. King's "I Have a Dream" speech resonated for decades. Everyone from white racists and black conservatives to liberals and black nationalists have used selective parts of the address to fit a multitude of agendas.

Six months before the march, an event of little note but great future consequence took place in Brooklyn, New York: On February 17, 1963, Michael Jeffrey Jordan was born.

Not even in his wildest dreams could Dr. King have imagined that thirty years after his address, a young black man would become the world's best-known athlete, the most recognizable American in the world, admired and revered from Shanghai to Saudi Arabia. He would be showered with the sort of acclaim, riches, and notoriety reserved for state officials. By the year 2000, Michael Jordan, basketball player, would be widely considered the greatest athlete of the twentieth century.

Three years after Jordan was born, Stokely Carmichael coined the phrase "Black Power." To some, Jordan in his prime became the embodiment of Black Power; to me he is the antithesis, however, the embodiment, if anything, of the destructive power of the Conveyor Belt and the perversion of the nobler goals of integration.

If his vast influence had combined with the vision of a Rube Foster, Jordan could have singlehandedly consolidated Black Power in sports and transformed the entire industry. Michael Jordan could have been a messiah who marshaled African American athletes into a strong, powerful collective. Had he said "jump," had he said "protest," most athletes would have jumped; most would have protested.

Instead, Jordan said, "Be like Mike."

Which raises the question: Who is Mike? What was the River Jordan? Was he Moses, leading us into the wilderness, or Judas, stranding us there? Jordan was in many ways the fruit of the Civil Rights movement, which reached its apex in the year of his birth. His right to remain silent is what we won. Jordan didn't have an obligation to speak up on racial injustices, but he had an unmatched opportunity.

Michael Jordan's story provides a revealing look into contemporary black culture in the wake of integration and the Conveyor Belt: fragmented, stratified as never before, stuck in a sprawling wilderness, but also more materially successful than ever. Jordan is a map of where African Americans have been, where they are, and where they might be headed.

Jordan is the one who fully exercises the won right to be publicly neutral, not to have to deal with quotas and segregation, and even to have the "black" elements of his style and image—bald head, baggy pants, soaring acrobatics—not just accepted by the mainstream, but revered, freeing him to be obsessed with wealth and image. Freed by the Civil Rights movement to be neutral, he's lightly shrugged off the historical mission of black athletes to push for progress and power.

But Jordan and his generation of African American athletes are merely a microcosm of the dilemma facing today's black community. The problem of the African American athlete is not an absence of resources—which are more abundant than ever—but an absence of vision and leadership to help define the next stage in the struggle.

As it is, black athletes like Jordan have abdicated their responsibility to the community with an apathy that borders on treason. He followed the most passive tradition of black sports heroes down a lucrative path, becoming a symbol of black prowess, but he could have been so much more. With the resources and possibilities at his disposal, simply being a paper tiger was really not enough.

★   ★   ★

For athletes born in the 1970s and 1980s, a disconnect has grown between their own experiences and the experiences of those who came before them; for many of them, the brutal struggle for freedom seems like fiction. Jordan attempted to explain his position of neutrality when he said, "I don't think I've experienced enough to voice so many opinions. . . . I think people want my opinion only because of the role model image that has been bestowed on me. But that doesn't mean I've experienced all those things."

Not only for Jordan, but for an entire generation of young African American athletes, the notion that they belong to a larger community with a shared history is a hazy concept, if it exists at all. The greatest distinction between Jordan's generation and those of Jack Johnson, Jesse Owens, Jackie Robinson, and even Muhammad Ali lies in those generations' connection and identification with "the black community." In many cases this was a forced identity—forced by crushing racism and suffocating segregation. But there was a collective identity nonetheless. That's changed.

Jordan didn't stand for a larger community; in fact, he stood for little beyond making money, hawking product. Jordan became the face of Nike in the 1980s and infamously refused to publicly support black Democrat Harvey Gant in his 1996 battle against former segregationist Jesse Helms for a United States Senate seat. During the final two weeks of the 1990 campaign, Helms went so far as to air the now infamous "white hands" TV commercial in which a pair of white hands crumples a letter that supposedly tells their owner that he has been passed over for a job because of affirmative action. But even this race-baiting didn't draw Jordan into the fray. His defense: "Republicans buy sneakers, too." Since then, Jordan supported the presidential candidacy of Bill Bradley and the senatorial campaign of Barack Obama.

Throughout his career, Jordan was criticized for being inactive in the fight for racial equality, but he stood silently by in other areas as well. When details emerged regarding Nike's use of Asian sweatshops, Jordan made no official statement. He said that he would "look into the problem." When children and teenagers began fighting and killing each other over his high-priced basketball shoes, he simply said that the victims should relinquish the items without a fight.

During his playing career, from 1984 to 2003, Jordan led the Chicago Bulls to six NBA titles. But his greatest gain came off the court. Jordan surpassed O. J. Simpson as the world's most marketable black man, becoming a major marketing tool and proof that a dark-skinned African American could be embraced as a pitchman for all. With Jordan at the forefront, the National Basketball Association became a global empire, a purveyor of American culture, with a black twist. The league would foreshadow trends in fashion, language, and music. The adoration of Jordan was phenomenal. He was described not only as one of the best players ever to grace the basketball court, but as one of the best humans to have graced the earth. His followers raised him to superhuman level. After the 1986 playoffs, for example, Boston Celtic superstar Larry Bird told reporters, "I think he's God disguised as Michael Jordan." Phil Jackson, who coached Jordan through all six of his championship seasons, said that Jordan "had somehow been transformed in the public mind from a great athlete to a sports deity." During a 1992 press conference for the Barcelona

Olympics, a Japanese correspondent asked, "Mr. Jordan, how does it feel to be God?"

Following his trailblazing path, African American athletes today are worth billions of dollars to the United States economy as marketers of all kinds of products, from sports gear to cars to deodorant. A handsome, strong, but harmless black man, Jordan would become the paradigm for the black star in a rising sports culture, setting the tone for others who aspired to commercial success.

In a 1998 column, Joan Ryan compared Jordan to the Shmoo, the creature in the Li'l Abner comic strip that could taste like any food you wanted. She wrote:

> Jordan is whatever we want him to be, according to our own values, dreams, and biases.
>
> He is the living embodiment of class, or hard work, or grace, or sportsmanship, or heroism. We have imbued him with all these qualities, even though—or rather, because— we know so little about him.
>
> Despite his global fame, Jordan has managed to give no clues about what issues he cares about, if any, or even what makes him tick. He has contributed little politically or socially, beyond the usual golf tournaments and chicken-dinner appearances. His public persona is like the perfect-looking man in the white dinner jacket in the board game Mystery Date, who was funny, caring, strong or rich, depending on the imagination of the twelve-year-old girl rolling the dice.

Some of the most useful insight into Jordan comes from the man who played a large part in inventing him: David Falk. Falk has described himself as apolitical and said Jordan was cut from the same cloth. The beauty of Jordan, Falk said, was that they didn't have to "indoctrinate him," work on him to be more neutral in his views. "People say that in order to market Michael we had to get him to back away from political issues," Falk said. "The truth is that Michael is apolitical by nature. That's who he is."

Largely because of Jordan, professional basketball became a hybrid sport, a cross between an ultimate team sport like baseball and an individual sport like tennis and golf.

But Jordan's singular importance—outside of his phenomenal ability—was knocking open the marketing doors that O. J. Simpson had broached in the 1970s.

With Falk pushing the agenda, Jordan broke corporate barriers in 1984. Falk said he wanted to prove to Madison Avenue that African American athletes could be sold to the public. This may be hard to recall, but in 1984 there were no million-dollar Nike deals, no lucrative Gatorade endorsement deals.

By 1984 the majority of Falk's clients were African American males, "and you had so much resistance in corporate America to accepting them off the court in business," Falk said during an interview.

Falk recalled that at this time there were "literally companies who would say, 'What are we going to do with the black basketball player in marketing?' "

It was like talking a foreign language. The challenge with Jordan was how to create access to corporate America with a really special raw diamond. Falk saw his job as opening doors and getting Jordan to market.

For Falk, 1984 was, along with 1492, a watershed year, proving the world wasn't flat and that black athletes could sell products. "People have no problems accepting Tiger Woods or a Ken Griffey, it's become commonplace, but thirteen short years ago it was heresy to believe that Michael Jordan could ever become as popular as Larry Bird.

"I'm not saying that it took a white person to do that," Falk added, "but it took someone who had corporate clout to do it."

Jordan became larger than black and white. You could look at him and really not see his color. Like O. J. Simpson, Jordan was racially and politically neutral.

Falk said he didn't coach Jordan to be racially neutral: "His parents had raised him to be color-blind," Falk said. "He's proud as an African American male, he's got a strong sense of black identity, but he's not exclusive. He's apolitical by nature, that's his personality."

Here's the problem with transcendence, however: The crossover black athlete often transcends his own race.

Falk said, "When players of color become stars they are no longer perceived as being of color. The color sort of vanishes.

"I don't think people look at Michael Jordan anymore and say he's a black superstar. They say he's a superstar. They totally accepted him into the mainstream. Before he got there he might have been African American, but once he arrived, he had such a high level of acceptance that I think that the description goes away."

Falk understood the mixed blessing of so-called racial transcendence. It's good because people accept an individual for accomplishments, independent of ethnicity.

"It's bad because if you are 'of color' you want that person to be a role model. It's like, you finally got a great role model and people take away his leadership by assimilating him into the general culture."

Depending on whom you speak with, Jordan's life mirrors the vision Dr. King laid out in his 1963 speech, his success determined by the content of his character, rather than the color of his skin. But Jordan was also a dream come true for the NBA. The challenge for the NBA as it went from a majority of white players to mostly black players was how to make a majority-black league palatable. How to take black style and showmanship, but somehow leave behind all of the more "inconvenient" features of blackness in America. How to make race visible and invisible simultaneously.

The answer was to have blacks act neutral, but perform spectacularly. Like Mike.

★   ★   ★

There was nothing in sports in 1963 that suggested this kind of breakthrough. In that year, an African presence in pro sports and big-time intercollegiate athletics was modest at best. Quotas at both levels were still in force. The African American presence in professional football, basketball, and baseball was modest. The rival American Football League had most of the black players, relying heavily on Historically Black Colleges for many of its players. African Americans, according to stereotype, lacked the endurance to run long distances in track; were not smart enough to play quarterback; did not have the guile to pitch. They could not manage or become head coaches.

Jordan's ascendance, viewed from this perspective, epitomizes the dramatic distance traveled by African American athletes from the beginning of the twentieth century to the end.

The twentieth century began with a bald-headed prizefighter named Jack Johnson stepping on white sensibilities and being hounded and demonized. The century ended with another bald-headed black man being idolized, even called a god.

Three years into a new century, however, Jordan was fired from his job as "God." In May 2003, hours after his extraordinary playing career ended with the Washington Wizards, Jordan was summoned to team owner Abe Pollin's office and dismissed.

★   ★   ★

What a fascinating and ironic twist at the end of a career. After retiring from basketball with the Chicago Bulls in 1999, Jordan had joined the Washington Wizards as team president. Soon after, he came out of retirement to rejoin the team on the court, playing his last two seasons with the Wizards on hobbled knees. After his final retirement at the end of the 2002–2003 season, Jordan planned to resume his front-office duties with the Wizards, learn the business, and eventually take over the franchise. That wasn't Pollin's vision, though. During their brief meeting, Pollin told Jordan, "As a gentleman, I appreciate everything you did. You're great. You've made a terrific contribution to the franchise. But I want to go in another direction in terms of direction and leadership." Pollin then offered to reward Jordan financially for his contributions.

The year before Jordan joined the team in January 2000, the Wizards had reportedly lost $40 million. With Jordan in uniform, the Wizards sold out eighty-two straight home games and made about $30 million in profits. But money was "not what I was looking for," Jordan said to Pollin. "I didn't do this for the money. I thought I was going to take over the franchise eventually."

Pollin replied, "That was never part of the arrangement. I've worked thirty-nine years to build this organization. I'm not giving it to you and I don't want you to be my partner, Michael."

The firing of Jordan marked the sudden end to perhaps the most remarkable career in sports history. Intentionally or not, the dismissal served as a warning shot that reverberated throughout the NBA. The greatest athlete of all time—"God," "the deity," His Airness—couldn't prevent his own firing. Jordan was effectively taken out into the yard and shot like a dog.

He was just another black athlete—albeit an extraordinary one—who had been put in his place. MJ had gotten too big for his britches. He had become larger than the game he helped promote. He was bigger than Bill Russell, Wilt Chamberlain, and all the rest. This was okay when he was promoting the NBA; the league used Jordan to become an even more lucrative, international business. But when Jordan threatened to take his skills and charisma and ambition over to the executive suite, he became a Negro who had to be reeled back in. Abe Pollin did the reeling.

John Thompson, the former Georgetown coach, said this was exploitation in its crudest, cruelest form. Thompson compared Jordan's dismissal to Pollin's sending Jordan back to the plantation after reaping profit from his labor. "They exploited this man," Thompson said. "The minute he was used up, they discarded him. There's something wrong with that."

A few days later, I was on the ESPN show *The Sports Reporters* with Len Elmore, the former All-American from the University of Maryland and now a television commentator and attorney. In his parting commentary, Elmore, who is African American, blasted Thompson for using the plantation analogy.

There was bad blood between Thompson and Elmore going back to Elmore's days as a player agent, when Elmore complained that Thompson steered all of his clients to David Falk, then the hottest sports attorney in the business. On the air, Elmore said Thompson's plantation comparison was stupid. Elmore was praised and applauded by the other panelists for his "strong" commentary; after he finished, the host reached over and patted him on his knee and said, "Beautiful."

I said to Elmore, before we went on the set, that he was wrong to associate money with slave status, because there were slaves who in fact made money.

For example, in the seventeenth century a slave economy emerged in the Chesapeake region. Many plantation owners, to defray the cost of operating a plantation and maintaining slaves during times of economic depression, entered into an agreement whereby slaves, in addition to their normal work, could work independently and earn their own money, with the understanding that they would feed and clothe themselves.

In *Many Thousands Gone,* historian Ira Berlin wrote: "Given time to attend to their own affairs in exchange for subsisting themselves, slaves gardened, tended to barnyard animals, and hunted and fished on their own. Occasionally, they manufactured small items and sold them to their owners, neighbors, or other slaves." Money was not the issue. The correlation to examine was between work and power. Jordan, for all the work he'd put in, had no power. Black athletes, for all the money they made, had no real power. Even the greatest athlete of all time was unable to keep himself from being fired.

But I also had a problem with Thompson's comment. My problem with Thompson's putting Jordan on a black plantation is that Jordan consistently, throughout his public life, has refused to identify with core African American values, issues, or problems. He was racially neutral; we learned to accept that—neutrality became his calling card. I'm sure he did things in private, working behind the scenes, as they say. What he did in public to inspire the multitudes—that core of black people estranged from power, the seemingly permanent underclass—beyond hitting game-winning jump shots, is hard to find. But to evoke the image of the plantation in Jordan's darkest hour—even when the analogy is correct—was disingenuous. The point is that he was always on the plantation, he just didn't know it or acknowledge it because he was flying too high to notice. Jordan supporters made the right argument, but in Michael Jordan, they were using the wrong model.

When Pollin slapped him down and put him in his place, Jordan suddenly recognized his surroundings.

What Pollin did to Jordan was a microcosm of what the NBA is doing to black athletes in general: phasing them out because they are no longer needed, as they once were. The global game is on the way, and the African American presence in the NBA, which was once almost stereotypically a black man's league, at least on the court, is in peril. Jordan was used for his muscle then discarded. Black athletes everywhere should see this as a cautionary tale: As long as black people don't take control of the industry that feeds them, they will always work at the pleasure of the white power structure, a structure that would like nothing more than to wean itself from its dependence on black muscle, to finally shake free of the Faustian pact of integration.

As neutral as he had been, as great as he had been, as much money as he had made for Pollin and NBA owners, Jordan was treated with the public disdain reserved for a menial worker. Ed Tapscott, now president of the black-owned Charlotte Bobcats, said, "Now Mike knows what it's like to be black."

★   ★   ★

I think Jordan knew all along. He made a conscious decision to stay neutral.

In the fall of 1997, I had a brief but illuminating conversation with Jordan. He was still His Airness at the time. The Bulls were coming off another NBA championship and Jordan had the veneer of invincibility.

I met Jordan at the Nike offices in Greenwich Village in New York. This was the first time I had spoken with him outside of locker-room chats. We talked a little pro football and the conversation segued into double standards—one standard for whites, the other for African Americans. This was around the time when the sports announcer Marv Albert was involved in his sexual misconduct scandal—the veteran broadcaster was on trial on felony charges of forcible sodomy, a case in which he'd been accused of repeatedly biting a woman. He'd eventually plead to a lesser charge but had already made the deals that would allow him to resume his lucrative career.★

"You know what they would have done if that was me?" Jordan said,

---

★ Albert was fired by NBC and resigned as the announcer for Madison Square Garden Network. In 1998 Albert's record of misdemeanor assault conviction was cleared. He was rehired by the MSG Network in 1998 and by Turner Sports in 1999 to announce NBA games for TNT and TBS.

referring to Albert's case. At that moment we became like two black men—Brothers—talking about the racism that most of us take for granted as part of life in the United States. We agreed that Albert should not be on the air—"at all," Jordan and I said in unison. They yanked O. J. Simpson out of the booth on suspicion.

I left the office with a far different view of Jordan than the one I'd brought in with me. He was not a Ward Connerly–Shelby Steele type of reactionary Negro, not one of those black people who, even in their private moments, mouth the notion of racism's being dead and worry over black people's complaining and blaming "the white man" for our problems. I was encouraged at least that Jordan was fully aware of double standards even at his level. He was like most African Americans: playing the game, seeing racism and sidestepping it, grumbling about it under his breath, but pushing it to one side in order to reap the full benefits of a multiracial society. At the same time, even if his attitude about race was familiar and defensible, his actions remained troubling.

★   ★   ★

The image of Jordan I had before that meeting was formed a few years earlier during a series of protests in 1992 that occurred at Jordan's alma mater, the University of North Carolina. There, at least a dozen black football players led approximately a thousand students on a march to the office of Chancellor Paul Hardin to ask for the construction of a black cultural center on the campus. A letter presented to Hardin said, "Failure to respond to this deadline will leave the people no other choice but to organize towards direct action," which some players speculated could include boycotts of games.

The march was the culmination of months of simmering frustration on the North Carolina campus over the issue of a separate center dedicated to the study of black culture. After the death in 1991 of

Sonja H. Stone, a popular black professor who had long supported the idea, a task force was formed to consider building such a center and naming it after Stone.

The idea attracted the attention and support of Dolores Jordan, the mother of Michael Jordan, and the task force proposed that, once built, the center contain the Michael Jordan Library, a library funded by Jordan and devoted to black culture.

The university was not receptive to the idea, especially if an entire building was constructed for the express purpose of studying black culture. Hardin, in an address to black students before school adjourned in June, said, "I favor a center that is by geography and program inviting and inclusive, a forum, not a fortress."

In subsequent weeks, though, the chancellor had softened his stance and asked students to submit architects' plans. But with school back in session, the university's not having committed itself to the center, and the football team now involved in the cause, the students' stance had turned militant. At one point a dozen black football players organized a march of four hundred students to Hardin's home in a peaceful demonstration that ended when police arrived and dispersed the crowd. The off-the-field leadership role of the football players represented a dramatic departure for black athletes on the UNC campus. Jordan, for example, was not a student leader as an undergraduate there and, along with other black athletes, was accused of a lack of community involvement after the riots in Los Angeles that same year. But the actions of the football players seemed to tap into an older, preintegration tradition—the tradition of Jack Johnson and Rube Foster, men unafraid to stir things up and to take action without waiting for a white man's approval.

"It's not common for athletes, black athletes, to be in this type of leadership role," noted Tim Smith, a junior defensive back and co-founder of the Black Awareness Council, a group founded by black athletes.

"Athletes feel they have a chance to make it, as the white man defines making it, in this society. You have a chance to go and make millions of dollars, and you don't want to jeopardize that by speaking out about injustice.

"We feel it's our responsibility to speak out and lead. That's what's surprising a lot of people. As athletes here, we have a lot of untapped power because we bring so much money into this university."

When Hardin attempted to read a prepared statement at one demonstration, Smith told the chancellor that the students wanted a meeting, not a prepared speech.

UNC had 23,000 undergraduates at the time, about 8 percent of whom were black. The university already had a black studies center, named for Sonja Stone, but it was housed in a renovated snack bar in the student center. The students wanted the symbolism and respect of a separate building.

"To me, when he says we want a forum, not a fortress, he's saying he doesn't want us to have any power," Smith said. "Having our own building would give us a unique sense of power. As long as you can have us in a glass-enclosed room where you can watch everything we do, every move we make—you can control us. We want our own building. He knows now we're willing to fight to get it. We're not going away."

There was a subsequent rally at the Dean Smith Center, where the film director Spike Lee spoke on behalf of the building project. Lee said he decided to become involved after learning that members of the North Carolina football team, with support from other UNC athletes, were in the forefront of the push for the center.

At the time Lee said, "I'm not getting involved just because Sonja was my cousin. I'm a big sports fan and I always longed for the day when black athletes would move to do something. Schools are making millions of dollars from TV contracts on basketball and football programs, and most of that money is being generated by great black athletes. Maybe black athletes are finally waking up and realizing how much power they have."

No doubt the events at North Carolina were monitored by presidents and athletic directors of large Division I schools with football and basketball teams composed predominantly of black athletes.

It is unusual for athletes to take an active role in anything that might threaten a scholarship or, as professionals, a contract. Activism is even rarer among black athletes, who often learn to see themselves differently as they find themselves treated differently from other black students.

"A lot of guys on the team were reluctant to get involved at first, until we explained how important it was and how it went beyond playing football," Smith said. "It's not about just having a building, it's about power, and building a monument to Dr. Stone and to all the black people who used to own the land this university was built on."

The big question was whether or not Michael Jordan would lend his voice to the students' struggle. After all, they had proposed that a Jordan library be a part of the project. Jordan's involvement would have been the tipping point. Here was a moment when black athletes—at his alma mater—had stepped off the field to lead a political movement, a model that could have been duplicated at universities all over the country, and even in the realm of professional sports. This could have been a pivot point, the moment when black athletes broke their chains and started speaking their own minds. Jordan, the world's megastar, could have helped ignite a sea change in the role of the black athlete in America.

He declined.

In the end, Jordan refrained from joining the movement. In fact, he favored the building of a library for family life that had his name on it. He wanted something for all students, of all races. This was his signature: the universal man.

Although eventually the Sonja Haynes Stone Center Building was constructed,* Jordan's lack of public support was telling. At a time when his voice would have strengthened the claims and resolve of the college athletes who'd put themselves on the line, he was silent—and if anything his comments worked against them. This little movement for a black cultural center may seem small, but it could have been the model for how athletes can leverage their power for the larger community. It was a chance for black athletes to show that they understood the difference between reaping the rewards of an unfair system and using their real power to change the system. Instead, Jordan, with one eye on his corporate masters, mouthed his mealy demurrals and stayed on the sidelines. A lion on the court, he was a lamb when his community needed him.

Jordan chose not to speak on the racial and power dynamics of the NBA and America at large because he does not relate to the struggle. Because life was not a struggle for him. Rather, he was whisked down the Conveyor Belt to massive success.

Young black athletes are essentially given two paths: the well-worn Conveyor Belt of the capitalist or the uncharted path of a leader who leads his people—or at least lends his strength—in struggle. Most choose the path of least resistance: Most choose to be like Mike, and why not? Unbridled hedonism is a lot more fun than marching with a tribe of malcontents and nonbelievers through the wilderness in search of an elusive Promised Land.

Mike was a multimillionaire who did not allow race, consciousness, or principle to get in the way of a making a dollar. He once told a friend not to deal with race "unless they slap you in the face." Of course, Abe Pollin eventually slapped Jordan in his face. Jordan was the carefully chosen prince of hype, the king of commercialism. He was

---

* In 1993, the university's board of trustees approved the site for the center, assuring the campus community that it would be integrated into the master construction plan for the university and serve as a resource for the entire campus.

the power structure's answer to Ralph Ellison's Invisible Man. Visible so omnipresent, virtually unreal.

Much of Jordan's commercial appeal was based on the fact that he was nonthreatening. But the condition for Jordan's global appeal was his racial and political neutrality. Jordan's neutrality is in the tradition of O. J. Simpson, who became the first African American athlete to have a major presence in the endorsement arena.

As Gordie Nye, a vice president at Reebok, stated, "It is very difficult to find someone who doesn't alienate part of your market. The thing about Jordan is that he doesn't alienate anybody."

"There's something very American about him," sociologist Shelby Steele has said. "He's the kind of figure who goes down easy with most of America." Simply in terms of his economic interests, staying silent on race was the smartest business move that Jordan could make. Remaining neutral was the only way he could continue to be marketed as "the embodiment of American virtue."

Almost singlehandedly, Jordan shaped the face of athletic and urban style: His bald head and long shorts became requirements to be considered "cool" both on and off the court. Whatever his promotion of choice—be it food, drinks, clothing, athletic equipment, cars, or restaurants—Jordan sold his playing ability and personality to sway public opinion in his favor.

As a competitor, Jordan's vim and vigor—his will to win, his willingness to criticize publicly and abrasively anyone he deemed counter to his cause—are legendary. No one was spared: coaches, teammates, front-office staff. He reveled in confrontation. Except when it came to confronting racism.

*   *   *

Some have used their platform and power to confront American racism and promote blacks' acquisition of true power in the sports industry. Paul Robeson, the Rutgers All-American, became a radical. Jim Brown organized African American athletes to support Muhammad Ali when Ali refused to step forward for the draft. In 1972, Jackie Robinson showed up at Yankee Stadium and said he would be contented only when there was an African American manager in the dugout. When Kellen Winslow Sr. was inducted into the Hall of Fame in 1995, he used the occasion to blast the NFL owners for closed-shop hiring practices. In 1996, Mahmoud Abdul-Rauf refused to stand for the National Anthem and was suspended.

John Thompson, then head coach at Georgetown University, walked off the court in 1999 in protest against NCAA legislation that he thought would limit opportunity for young African American athletes.

These are not easy models to follow; each made some sacrifice. Jackie Robinson was a national hero when he kept his eyes and mouth shut to injustices, but when he began to speak his mind, he was met with a backlash of negativity by whites. When Robinson criticized the baseball establishment for its persistent racism, his popularity plunged. "You owe a great deal to the game," *The Sporting News* instructed him in an editorial. "Put down your hammer, Jackie, and pick up a horn." Repay baseball, he was told, with "glad tidings."

During the Mexico City Olympics in 1968, two of the world's greatest sprinters, Tommie Smith and John Carlos, ran their race and then raised their fists on the victory stand after winning the gold and bronze medal, respectively. Here they were, running with USA emblazoned on their chests, and both wanting the watching world to know that everything was not cool in this fool's paradise. They protested the condition of inhumanity that this great democracy imposed upon African American citizens.

Smith and Carlos stood in black socks and black gloves. Afterward, Smith explained that the black socks symbolized the economic and social disenfranchisement of so many blacks in the United States. The gloves symbolized the mounting anger, frustration, and fury of so many

African Americans, impoverished, brutalized, and marginalized in the world's greatest democracy.

Twenty-four years later, Jordan made a "stand" of his own on the medal ceremony at an Olympics game. Jordan's "protest" underlined the thickness of his blinders and revealed where his heart lay.

I was in Barcelona in 1992 for the Summer Olympic Games. These games marked the ultimate triumph of the NBA push for a global presence. Barcelona was the NBA's Normandy. The 1992 games marked the debut of professional basketball players from the United States participating in Olympic competition. This was the so-called Dream Team, but some of the things that happened were a nightmare for Pan-African sentiment, as when Charles Barkley said an opponent from Africa was concealing a "spear" and told him to go hunting. The most telling part of the Dream Team's triumph came on the victory stand after the United States had crushed all competition. Rather than promote the team's official sweatsuit, designed by Nike competitor Reebok, Jordan instead draped himself in the American flag. Not out of patriotism or protest, but to hide the Reebok label. Refusing to disrespect Nike, Jordan emphatically declared that "I feel very strongly about loyalty to my own company."

Contemporary black athletes have ridden the coattails of protest movements, benefiting from the sacrifices of the Robesons and Robinsons and Jim Browns and Muhammad Alis, but have been content to be symbolic markers of progress rather than activists in their own right, pushing progress forward. They have been unwilling to collectively rock the money boat. Ironically, this new lack of interest in the larger world has occurred just at the moment in their evolution when black athletes have more economic muscle and cultural influence than ever. At a time when they could actually *own* the boat— rather than just rock it—the level of apathy is greater than ever before. The Jordan model has contributed greatly to this malaise.

Lusia Harris of Delta State was the first great star of women's basketball. She illustrates the paradox of the African American woman athlete: simultaneously overlooked by white women and marginalized by black men. *Used by permission of Delta State University.*

Ain't I a Woman?

The Dilemma of the Double Burden

LUSIA HARRIS WAS THE FIRST DOMINANT force in women's basketball. With her bruising inside play and intense sense of competition, Harris changed the face—and ultimately the complexion—of women's basketball in the United States.

"She broke ground for women's basketball and paved the way for so many other players who are playing today," Pat Summit, the legendary head coach at the University of Tennessee and a former Olympic teammate of Harris, said. "Without the success, the international success, that we enjoyed, without the college game growing and growing each year, there's not a WNBA, and so many times people forget about the pioneers in sports. Lucy as a player was a great pioneer."

One of the great cliché's in sports is that an athlete put a place on the map. Lusia Harris really did. She took a little known school like Delta State in Cleveland, Mississippi, and made it a household name. In 1975, Harris—a powerful, six-three center from Minter City, Mississippi—led unknown Delta State to the first of three consecutive national championships under the auspices of the Association for Intercollegiate Athletics for Women (AIAW).

Between 1974 and 1977, Harris's name was synonymous with power and dominance in the women's game.

"What changes the game?" asked Pat Summit. "Players change the game. But before we think about the changes, we have to think about who really laid the foundation. I mean, we've had a lot of wonderful coaches, and we've had a lot of great players, but one player that gave us international respect was Lucy Harris."

Harris and Summit were teammates on the 1976 women's Olympic basketball team that won the silver medal in Montreal. Those games marked the first year women's basketball became a medal sport. The American team included emerging stars like Ann Meyers and Nancy Lieberman. But Harris was the player of her generation. Fittingly, she made history in Montreal by scoring the first two points of women's basketball Olympic competition as the United States defeated Canada.

"Lucy Harris helped us win a silver medal. Without her, we don't win a silver medal. She was our anchor," Summit said.

Three decades later, Harris's name has been lost in time. A name that was synonymous with women's basketball is now largely unknown. While several of her Olympic teammates and players from her era made names for themselves in the sports industry—as coaches, broadcasters, and sports executives—Harris is largely unknown, and there has been no sustained effort to resuscitate her memory.

Before the 1999 Women's National Basketball League all-star game in New York, the league spent a week leading up to the game, heralding the dramatic strides women's basketball had made. On game day, the league celebrated the rich history of women's basketball by flashing a historical timeline of women's basketball. I was stunned as they showed a brief clip that began with Carol Blazejowski, the former Montclair State star; Nancy Lieberman of Old Dominion; Ann Meyers of UCLA; and Cheryl Miller of UCLA.

Lusia Harris's name was never mentioned. This was tantamount to talking baseball history and not mentioning Babe Ruth. It was as if the WNBA wanted to manufacture a false timeline that elevated the Blazejowskis and Liebermans at Harris's expense. And as it turned out, the league had never reached out to—or checked in on—Harris.

"It used to bother me, but not anymore," Harris said in 2005 during an interview at her home in Greenwood, Mississippi. "I still watch the games, there are some fantastic players. And it would have been nice to be a part of it."

Harris is the symbol of the dilemma facing women's sports as they continue to fight for space and respect in the United States. Her condition is a metaphor for how African American women have coped with and been crippled by the burdens of race, gender, and class in the sports arena.

★   ★   ★

Lusia Harris Stewart was born on February 10, 1955, in Minter City, Mississippi, the tenth of Willie and Ethel Harris's eleven children—six boys and five girls. She learned the game by being pummeled in the backyard by her older siblings. Harris attended Amanda Elzy High School in Greenwood, Mississippi, and although she starred on the team, she didn't have grand plans for playing college basketball. She planned to attend Alcorn State College, an Historically Black College in Lorman, Mississippi. Alcorn did not have a women's team, so Harris would earn her degree and teach.

But Melvin Hemphill, an admissions counselor at Delta Sate, came to Elzy High School to speak with Harris. He told her coach that Delta State was restarting its women's basketball program and that the school wanted Harris to be part of the rebuilding. Since Delta State, located in Cleveland, Mississippi, was only a few miles away from Minter City, her parents could come see Harris play.

Harris leaped at the chance: "I said, 'Yeah, I want to play basketball. I want to play a little basketball.'"

Margaret Wade was the legendary Delta State coach. During Harris's four years at DSU, she was the only African American player to make Wade's team. In fact, Harris was one of only a handful of African Americans at the entire school. "It was kind of scary—it wasn't very nice there—you know. I came from an all-black school—all-black high school—and there weren't many black students and no black teachers [at Delta State]. And it was a big adjustment, and I can remember walking into the cafeteria the very first time and everybody was staring because, you know, six-three was considered tall then. Girls are a lot taller now. But then, being six-three, that was almost like being a giant—in the seventies. And everybody would just stare, and I would say, 'Why is everybody staring at me?' And then they'd say, 'Oh that girl is tall.' So, uh, it was a big adjustment. But I adjusted."

She led Delta State to three consecutive AIAW championships. During Harris's four varsity seasons at Delta State, the Lady Statesmen compiled a remarkable 109–6 record. They were the dominant program of the era.

She competed in the Olympics after her junior year, returning to lead Delta State to the national championship. In 1977 she was graduated with a bachelor of science degree in physical education and after the season became the first woman player to be drafted by an NBA team when the New Orleans Jazz selected her in the seventh round.

She didn't go to camp, though. She felt that the NBA post players were too big and too good. "I really thought it was a publicity stunt because I'm six-three and a center," Harris said of being drafted. "And, in the NBA, players like Kareem—they're the centers for the teams you have to compete against, so I really thought it was a publicity thing."

Harris's decision reflects who she is and why she has been forgotten. She thought her being drafted was a PR stunt and refused to go, even if the novelty event would put her in the news and lead to other opportunities. By contrast, Blazejowski, Meyers, and Lieberman all played in men's leagues.

Harris may have had a better chance than she thought. "She was to me like Shaquille O'Neal," Pat Summit said. "Just so strong and physical, but great hands and great touch around the basket.

*   *   *

Harris played for the Houston Angels of the Women's Basketball League in 1980. When the team disbanded in that same year, she returned to Delta State and worked as an admissions counselor. In 1984 she completed a master's degree in health and physical education.

Harris served as one of Margaret Wade's assistants at Delta State from 1980 to 1984, and when the head job became available, she wanted to be considered. They hired a white man instead.

Harris was crushed. She *was* Delta State; she had put the program on the map and had helped bring students to the school. But consistent with her reticent manner, Harris never told the school how hurt she was by having been overlooked. "I guess it was just the idea of not being asked. Of all the accomplishments that I have made in women's basketball, I would have to say that it's a disappointment not to have been asked to be the head coach of the women's team," Harris said.

Harris left Delta State and accepted the head coaching job at Texas Southern, a Historically Black College in Houston. She moved there with her husband and their son on the basis of promises the school had made.

At the time she was pregnant with twin girls.

The experience there was brutal. The women's program, like so many at such black institutions, lacked much needed support. Harris did not have a full-time assistant coach and was docked pay when she missed a class in order to coach. After two seasons, Lusia Harris, college hoops legend, was dismissed.

"They didn't put a lot of emphasis on women's basketball," Harris said. "The men got a chance to fly places and we had to take the bus. We took the bus to Oklahoma from Texas. That was just unheard of, I didn't think that was fair. That was just one of the things that they would do. The women's program was just not important at that time."

She had three children, and a husband who wasn't working, and her marriage was falling apart. Filled with years of pent-up frustration and anger, Harris suffered a nervous breakdown and spent two months in a psychiatric hospital.

★   ★   ★

In 1992, Harris was inducted into the National Basketball Hall of Fame, and in 1999 she was one of the twenty-six inaugural inductees to the Women's Basketball Hall of Fame. But why is Harris so over-looked today?

One simple answer is that she was ahead of her time. Women's basketball came of age in the eighties, when Title IX—a law aimed at equalizing spending on women's and men's programs in educational institutions—began to have an effect. Title IX became the Emancipation Proclamation of Sports: Coaches' salaries improved, schedules became more competitive, equipment was upgraded, practice time grew more equitable, recruiting budgets increased, and transportation and accommodations on the road slowly began to improve. It was a boon to white women or black women who participated in so-called white sports.

But the more complex answer is that Harris's invisibility is a symbol of the race-tinged ambivalence African American women encounter within the women's sports movement. It's often been noted that women of color in sports have been rendered nearly invisible, a reflection of America's lingering association of femininity with whiteness.

Today the dilemma for black women athletes is played out graphically in a bourgeoning women's sports movement that has seen white women gain and black woman languish.

According to the NCAA, the four fastest-growing women's sports in the past fifteen years have been soccer, rowing, lacrosse, and golf, none of which have been successful in recruiting large numbers of minorities. While almost a third of the women playing basketball in Division I of the NCAA are black, only 2.7 percent of the women receiving scholarships to play all other sports in Division I universities are black.

As coaches, executives, and entrepreneurs, white women have also enjoyed enormous success in the sports industry—in Major League Baseball, the National Basketball Association, and the National Football League—while black women have lagged. And it's also true of the coaching ranks in collegiate sports: According to a study conducted by Northeastern University's Center for the Study of Sport in Society in 1995, of 6,881 coaching positions available in women's athletics, 1.5 percent were held by females of color.

Tina Sloan Green, a professor at Temple University and the director of the Black Women in Sport Foundation, says that although Title IX has eliminated gender bias in college sports, the law might have spawned a greater tilt in racial inequity.

"Title IX was for white women. I'm not going to say black women haven't benefited, but they have been left out. When you compare now that years have passed, and see who has moved up the ladder, white women have benefited more from Title IX than women of color," Green said. "Sometimes, women are fighting for individual rights against men, and they tend to forget there are other women in the mix."

Donna A. Lopiano, president of the Women's Sports Foundation, says Green has a point.

"The women's movement is so focused on so many gender issues that the plight of women of color, who are in double jeopardy, is often on the back burner," Lopiano, the former women's athletic director at the University of Texas, told *The Chronicle of Higher Education.*

The tragedy of the feminist movement in sports is that, in ignoring race and in many instances embracing the exclusionary practices of their male counterparts, the movement as a whole is weakened, though individuals may gain. The truth is that black and white women in the United States have historically been put in separate compartments of the same sexist trick bag, hence women of all races have been fighting an uphill struggle.

Black and white women are victims of parallel stereotypes designed to keep one imprisoned and one shackled in a gilded cage. While black women are considered aggressive, loud, and dominating, white women are seen as passive and nonassertive.

In 1923 the Conference on Athletic and Physical Recreation for Women and Girls discouraged track and field activities for women—white women—at the college level. This philosophy governed women's college sports competition until the 1950s. Physical educators and trainers agreed to "discourage athletic competitions that involved travel," as well as to "eliminate types and systems of competition which put the emphasis upon individual accomplishment and winning rather than upon stressing the enjoyment of the sport and development of sportsmanship among the masses."

On the other hand, in the early twentieth century, Olympic official Norman Cox proposed that in the case of black women, "the International Olympic Committee should create a special category of competition for them—the unfairly advantaged 'hermaphrodites' who regularly defeated 'normal women,' those less skilled 'child-bearing' types with 'largish breasts, wide hips [and] knocked knees.' "

★   ★   ★

When Althea Gibson became the first African American to win a major tennis championship, the white press took surprised note that she actually took a bath every afternoon. Gibson was even forced to take a test to see if she had an extra chromosome. The social stereotypes still exist.

Where do black women fit in on the great African American timeline of sports in the United States? African American male athletes benefited from the Civil Rights movement in sport, whose focus on integration and other boundary-breaking rights were extended to or symbolized by achievement and opportunity in mainstream, male-dominated sports. Black women have largely had to go it alone.

Lusia Harris is emblematic of that lonely journey. On the court, she was a punishing low post player; off the court, she was abandoned by a fractured women's movement that featured sex over race and a male-dominated Civil Rights movement that acknowledged race but not sex. As author Paula Giddings once wrote of black women, "We have been perceived as token women in black texts and token blacks in feminist texts."

African American women have not had an extended moment in the sun; the women's movement in sports has suffered as a result.

★   ★   ★

The plight of the African American woman was framed by Sojourner Truth in the summer of 1851 when, under some protest, she addressed a women's rights convention in Akron, Ohio. Truth—at six feet tall, much like Lusia Harris—was an imposing figure of her era.

The women had seethed as white male cleric after white male cleric attempted to justify white male dominance, claiming superior rights and privileges for men on the strength of superior intellect, on the strength of the manhood of Christ, or on the basis of the Edenic sin of Eve.

Despite the ministers' condescension, a number of women did not want to challenge them. There was even sentiment to keep Sojourner Truth from speaking, for fear that she would antagonize the ministers' racial and gender prejudices. One dissenter protested: "Every newspaper in the land will have our cause mixed with abolition and niggers, and we shall be utterly denounced."

Three years earlier at the 1848 Seneca Falls convention, pioneering feminist Susan B. Anthony had said, "I will cut off this right arm of mine before I will ask for the ballot for the Negro and not for the woman."

Truth was a leading exponent of liberty in both the abolitionist and feminist movements; she boldly represented oppressed women and enslaved African Americans. She was born into slavery and had been separated from her parents as a child. She was sold to a succession of owners who freely used her extraordinary strength in the fields and did not hesitate to issue beatings. She had five children in slavery and left her final master in 1826.

When it was her turn to speak, Truth spoke of the strength of woman in general but also testified to the extraordinary strength of black women, who had to survive as women and as African Americans in a society that devalued both. She outlined the complex dilemma of race and gender with powerful and simplicity:

> That man over there say that women needs to be helped into carriages and lifted over ditches, and to have the best places everywhere. Nobody ever helped me into carriages, or over mud puddles, or gives me any best place and ain't I a woman? I have plowed, and planted, and gathered into barns, and no man could head me—and ain't I a woman? I could work as much, and eat as much as a man (when I could get it), and bear the lash as well—and ain't I a woman? I have borne thirteen children and seen 'em most all sold off into slavery, and when I cried out with a mother's grief, none by Jesus heard me—and ain't I a woman?

Sojourner Truth made white feminists painfully aware that their movement, like the very Constitution they were challenging, failed to take into account the dilemma of African American women. Lusia Harris underlines the dilemma of the contemporary black women in sports and the conundrum faced by the feminist movement in sport. If the movement is to be complete—and successful—the leaders must deal with race and class in an ever-expanding sports world.

Lusia Harris could very well ask the same question as her legend fades into obscurity, even as the visibility of women's sports rises: "Ain't I a woman?"

New York Knick Larry Johnson surrounded by the media on June 22, 1999, during the Knicks' playoffs series against the San Antonio Spurs. Johnson had been fined repeatedly by the League for refusing to talk to the press; when he finally spoke his mind, his references to slavery touched a nerve and set off a national controversy. *AFP Photo/Jeff Haynes.*

The $40 Million Slave:

The Dilemma of Wealth Without Control

*Niggas are players. Niggers are players, are players. Niggas
play football, basketball and baseball while the white man is
cutting off their balls.*

—The Last Poets, circa 1969

CURT FLOOD WAS THE FIRST PERSON I ever heard use a plantation metaphor in connection with professional athletes. I'm sure
someone else had used the metaphor before him, but the first time the
comparison really resonated in my soul was when Flood invoked the
comparison in 1969. At the time he was probably the best centerfielder
in baseball. He was a three-time all-star and a seven-time Gold Glove
winner, with a career batting average of .293. Flood's brilliance went
beyond numbers. He had the effortless, gliding speed that I first saw in
Willie Mays. By 1969, Flood, in most minds, had replaced Mays as the
greatest centerfielder in baseball. Flood, like Mays, wasn't just great—
he was *cool* and great.

I had no idea just how cool Flood really was.

In the winter of 1969, he was traded from the St. Louis Cardinals,
where he had played since 1958, to Philadelphia. Flood was stunned; a

trade was the furthest thing from his mind. Flood had hit .285, knocked in 57 runs, and generally had another sound season. But Jim Tooney, the Cardinals' vice president, told Flood that he had been traded. Despite his time and stature in the game, Flood had not been given the courtesy of a call or a warning beforehand. Nothing. He was traded. That's how business was done. Athletes of his generation were powerless to determine their fate; they had limited options. Flood, who was making $92,500 at the time, exercised his option in the extreme: He refused to go to Philadelphia. In one of the most significant communications in sports labor history, Flood wrote to then baseball commissioner Bowie Kuhn that "after twelve years in the major leagues, I do not feel that I am a piece of property to be bought and sold irrespective of my wishes."

But that's exactly what he was; in fact, that's what all athletes were: so many pieces of property to be bought, sold, or discarded as their "owners" saw fit. This was—and still is—allowable in sports because athletes are supposed to be grateful for the opportunity. This mode of treatment was legitimized by the Reserve Clause in Major League Baseball.

The Reserve Clause allowed teams to hold on to players as long as they wanted but forbade the players from testing the market on their terms, an "iron fist" that Flood compared to sharecropping. "The reserve system was the same system used in the South where the plantation owner owned all the houses that you live in," Flood said. "And you worked for him and you shopped in his store and you never got over the hump." In Flood's mind a divide between players and owners was ingrained in their roles: "They're the ranchers, and we're the cattle."

The owners were given license to do this by the federal government. The Reserve Clause prevented players from moving to another team unless they were traded or sold. Flood challenged the fairness of a system that kept players in perpetual servitude to their teams at the owners' pleasure.

Flood's dramatic action took place in the middle of my sophomore year in college. I was just beginning to become aware of the brutal business side of sports, of how athletes were economic creatures in a peculiar entertainment industry. The sports industry ran on the fuel of strong bodies—black or white, from small colleges or large—and an overdeveloped sense of gratitude. Athletes generally were just happy to be there, whether they were on scholarship or under contract. But by 1969 the tide had been shifting, giving way to a more aggressive sense of self-worth on the part of black athletes.

In 1967, Muhammad Ali was stripped of his heavyweight boxing championship for refusing to be drafted for religious reasons. In 1968, Kareem Abdul-Jabbar, then known as Lew Alcindor, refused to join the United States Olympic basketball team. And, of course, at the 1968 Mexico City Games, Tommie Smith and John Carlos staged their historic protest.

Flood filed his suit in 1970. During a meeting with the union's executive board in December 1969, Tom Haller, a white player, asked Flood if his action, then pending, was his response to baseball's history of racial discrimination. Flood said that he believed he had suffered harder times than white players; the change in black consciousness in recent years had made him "more sensitive to injustice in every area of my life." There was so much social turbulence in the United States that political and social neutrality wasn't really an option, particularly for black athletes who were aware of the recent controversy as well as the larger dramas of the Civil Rights movement.

What made Flood's fight resonate is that at one level his battle went beyond race. Flood said he was filing this suit against a "situation" that was "improper" for all ballplayers. Many white players never thought of themselves as being on a plantation or as being only so much chattel. But the legacy of black people in sports had sensitized Flood; that history had tuned him in to a different frequency than white players had access to. He used the insight born of that legacy to help all players, black and white, fight a corrupt system. The executive board of the Players Association liked what it heard and voted unanimously to support Flood.

But Flood had committed the cardinal sin: He'd challenged baseball bosses, and they went on to destroy him—as a player—with the help of other players and the sports media.

Marvin Miller, the attorney for the players' union, warned Flood from the start of his battle with Major League Baseball that if he went forward with the suit, his life in baseball was over; he would not be elected to the Hall of Fame, he would never manage or be given any significant management position in baseball. Undaunted, Flood pressed on. He decided to sit out the 1970 season, rather than report to Philadelphia and accept the $100,000 salary the Phillies offered. Sitting out was the ultimate sacrifice for a veteran player with limited seasons left to play and desperately needing to play to keep his skills sharpened.

But Flood was committed to the fight. What makes one man stand on principle and others sit quietly by and accept what is being handed out? Most of Flood's peers were terrified. Fast and courageous on the field, star players of the day—like star players today—were terrified of taking on their owners. Maury Wills, the daring base runner who set a base-stealing record in 1962, admitted, "Most of us were not courageous enough to take that stand and challenge the owners. I know I wasn't."

But some were.

Flood's friend and teammate Bob Gibson came to Flood's trial. Jackie Robinson testified on Flood's behalf. In his autobiography, *The Way It Is,* Flood said that one of the most moving moments of the trial occurred when Robinson walked into the courthouse on the day he was scheduled to testify.

"As he and Rachel Robinson moved into the courtroom, you could hear a pin drop because he had a real presence about him."

Robinson sat close to Flood. Flood later recalled, "Then he looked at me. I said, 'I really appreciate your taking the time and effort to do this.' And he said, 'Well, you can't be out there by yourself.' I remember these words very well: 'You can't be out there by yourself and I would be remiss if I didn't share these burdens with you.' "

Robinson understood history—he *was* history—and he understood the continuity of struggle, both the black struggle and the struggle for human freedom, which in Robinson's mind were intertwined. A year earlier, Robinson had supported John Carlos and Tommie Smith in their protest at the 1968 Summer Olympic Games in Mexico City.

Once, while explaining why he had reluctantly supported Nixon over John F. Kennedy, Robinson explained that he had not felt Kennedy was committed to the black cause and thus the cause of humanity.

He said, "I am most interested in a candidate who I think will be best for the Black American because I am convinced that the black struggle and its solution are fundamental to the struggle to make America what it is supposed to be."

Robinson had long since stopped repaying baseball with "glad tidings," no matter what *The Sporting News* demanded.

While Curt Flood told the Major League Baseball executive board that his challenge was not coming out of the race-bag of the sixties, he also knew that he could not separate himself from the political and racial climate of the day.

"The sixties is an era that will never be forgotten. Being a child of those years between 1959 and 1969, America was coming apart at the seams and our boys were in Southeast Asia giving their lives, we were marching all over Berkeley. We lost Dr. King, we lost the Kennedys, we lost Medgar Evers, and true ugliness was happening to us as a people in the sixties. Little children were being shut out of education, and the mood of the sixties was dark and somber, and merely because you're a professional athlete does not defend you from that."

Flood said that the currents of world affairs had a direct impact on him as an athlete and baseball player because "all of the things that we were fighting for all over the world, we weren't getting in my profession. And from the time someone made me stay in the colored section while the white kids stayed on the beach in the white high-rise hotel, I felt like 'a nigger,' whatever that means. Those years between 1960 and 1969 really were growing years for me."

With the union executive board's support, Flood's case reached the Supreme Court two years later, in 1972.

He lost his case that year, in large part because no active players showed support.

Not only did Flood lose the case; he lost any chance he had to finish out his career with dignity. Joe Garagiola, a mediocre journeyman catcher, testified for baseball in the lawsuit. Years later Garagiola explained weakly, "I thought if the Reserve Clause went, baseball was going."

In 1973, when the owners agreed to federal arbitration of salary demands, the way was opened for the free agency that now makes players less the pieces of property they once were.

Flood was in Spain in 1975 when he learned that the Major League Baseball players had finally won free agency. Two white players, Dave McNally of Montreal and Andy Messersmith of Los Angeles, had brought a grievance against the owners, challenging the renewal clause in the basic player contract. The two pitchers won their case when the chairman of the arbitration panel ruled that they could bargain with other teams.

During a 1996 interview for a documentary I was writing for HBO, Flood said that he was happy for the victory, but that he felt the decisions had a tinge of racism. "It disappointed me that I didn't win," Flood said, "but I had to feel that somewhere in the equation, America was showing its racism again. They were just merely waiting for someone else to win that case."

As difficult as it was for even the most palatable African American to get a job in baseball after retirement, Flood's black mark made him untouchable. He was not welcomed back to the game. He played briefly for the Washington Senators in 1971, then, citing personal problems, left the Senators after thirteen games. He went to Majorca, Spain, for five years, where he painted and ran a café and struggled with alcoholism. He came back to the United States, went to Sweden, then came back home.

He returned to baseball briefly when he became a broadcaster for the Oakland A's in 1978. Later he operated a youth center in Los Angeles.

Flood died in January 1997, at the age of fifty-nine.

Thanks to Curt Flood, The Last Poets, and Fred Hampton, I emerged from 1969 much more aware, much less naïve. Flood put the sports industry in a whole new perspective—the new variation of the slave owner paradigm. He challenged the plantation mentality of big-time athletes, according to which the athlete was supposed to be grateful. Most athletes were and still are operating under that mentality: happy to be playing, not wanting to rock the boat.

★   ★   ★

In the antebellum South, the slave and the plantation described tangible circumstances; today the slave and the plantation describe a state of mind and the conditioning of the mind.

In an era of multimillion-dollar salaries, slavery remains the model for the power relationship between athletes and their owners.

A day before Game Four of the 1999 National Basketball Association's finals between the New York Knicks and the San Antonio Spurs, a throng of media crowded around Larry Johnson, the Knicks' veteran forward.

For months Johnson had refused to speak with reporters; two weeks earlier the NBA had fined him $10,000 for not talking to the media after a practice during the Eastern Conference finals against the Indiana Pacers. He'd been fined another $25,000 during the league finals for again declining the NBA's request to speak to reporters during a Sunday practice session. Johnson not only refused to comply, he cursed the media and a league official for hampering his ability to practice.

But now Johnson was ready to give the league what it wanted. The NBA wanted words; L.J. would give them words.

"I don't care if anybody likes me or not," he began. "I play basketball. I play for the New York Knicks. My main focus is to win. You guys, maybe you don't like me or not. Fine. I don't care. Ask my teammates. Ask my coach. Y'all can kiss my ass. I don't like you. That has been my motto my whole life growing up. I wear my heart on my sleeve. I make it known I don't like you. That way we don't have to communicate.

"Those guys out there are the main focus in my mind," Johnson continued, referring to his teammates. "What we have is a lot of rebellious slaves on this team."

Now everyone was all ears. In a nation that equates wealth with happiness, Johnson's equation of well-compensated athletes with largely uncompensated slave ancestors set off a maelstrom of angry criticism. Asked to explain what he meant by "rebellious slaves," Johnson snapped, "I have to explain that? We don't have a lot of mainstreamers. We don't go along with the masses. We're in a different stream on this team."

That year's playoffs culminated a strife-filled season in the NBA that in its own way underscored the meaning of Johnson's rebellious slave metaphor. David Stern, the NBA commissioner, acting on behalf of the league's owners, had bullied, beaten, and outmaneuvered the league's 350 players during a nasty, three-month-long lockout. The dispute exposed a lack of unity among players and revealed how unprepared the Players Association was to launch a sustained battle against the owners. The lockout revealed the extent to which lavish lifestyles had made many totally dependent on their owners. One poignant example was Kenny Anderson, a guard with the Boston Celtics.

Anderson complained that he had a fleet of cars to maintain, mortgages on two homes, and child-support payments, an admission that did little to win public sympathy for the players' cause. The lockout ended in near-complete victory for the owners.

This was the backdrop to Johnson's news conference.

*   *   *

The reaction to Johnson's comments was swift and unambiguous. Johnson was crucified by the sports media. Sam Smith of the *Chicago Sun-Times* wrote, "Larry Johnson is simply a jerk, perhaps the worst individual in the NBA."

Steve Bulpott of the *Boston Herald* called Johnson outrageous and said he was "like a car accident that you slowed to see."

Most of the criticism was aimed at Johnson's lack of gratitude. Here he was, a young, wealthy, black male who went from poverty in Dallas to making $11 million a season playing professional basketball, talking about slavery.

Speaking to a smaller group of media a day after his "rebellious slaves" remark, Johnson explained that money had little to do with his analogy of being like a slave on a plantation, but that he was really referring to relationships—namely between owner and worker.

Johnson followed his comments with an abysmal Game Four of the finals. After Johnson's 2-for-8 shooting performance, Bill Walton, the former counterculture basketball player at UCLA who had, over his years as a television analyst, morphed into a shrill defender of the mainstream, blasted the Knicks' twenty-nine-year-old forward: "Larry Johnson, who spent the last forty-eight hours railing against the world, what a pathetic performance by this sad human being. This is a disgrace to the game of basketball and to the NBA. He played like a disgrace tonight; he deserved it."

Johnson fired back. "Damn Bill Walton. Tell him to trace his history and see how many slaves his ancestors had. Y'all trace y'all history and see how many slaves y'all ancestors had. Come on, now. That's a touchy subject. But why does the truth always hurt?"

The criticism of Johnson boiled down to a recurring theme: How could an athlete making millions of dollars per season consider himself a common "slave"?

You can always count on a harsh reaction to any invocation of this unresolved Achilles' heel of American democracy. I wrote in my "Sports of The Times" column:

"Major intercollegiate sports functions like a plantation. The athletes perform in an economic atmosphere where everyone except them makes money off their labor. . . . In the revenue-producing sports of football and basketball, athletes are the gold, the oil, the natural resource that makes the NCAA engine run and its cash register ring."

But how can professional black athletes, who, as a group, have grown into one of the most identifiable presences in global culture, enjoying unprecedented wealth, still, in the end, feel as marginalized and joyless as slaves?

Far from being the "sad human being" that Walton and much of the mainstream press ridiculed him as after his comments, Johnson had up to that point lived a life that fit the sports media's ideal cast for the black athlete; his NBA career represented the classic rags-to-riches route in professional sports, from the ghetto to the gated community. The fact that he came credentialed with this Horatio Alger glow and still showed bitter dissatisfaction, refusing to play along, may be one reason the press turned on him with such viciousness.

Johnson and Curt Flood used the same language, speaking not about material poverty but about the ultimate powerlessness of their condition. For Johnson, the plantation was the NBA, where power was not shared fairly and players were bought, traded, and discarded when used up. This was, of course, no less true for white players. But Johnson found in his NBA experience surprising parallels with his upbringing in the inner city, which led to his belief that from the plantation to the ghetto to the NBA, the power hierarchy of slavery prevailed.

Johnson was born in Dallas, Texas, and was raised on Dixon Circle, a part of South Dallas he once described as the baddest part of town you'd ever want to see. His mother, Dortha Johnson, was born in Laneview, Texas, and moved to Dallas at age eighteen. She had her first child, a daughter, when she was twenty, and Larry when she was twenty-two. When it became apparent that her son's father would not be around, Dortha vowed to pour everything she had from that point on into raising her children. She worked as a cook at a Dallas country club, often from ten in the morning to ten at night.

"My mom was in the struggle," Johnson would later say. "I didn't realize it then, but she was part of the struggle."

Johnson, meanwhile, was involved in his share of mischief, from stolen fruit and stolen bikes to fights. He was an active participant, not a spectator, in the rough-and-tumble fabric of the community. "When I was fifteen, sixteen, it was all about having fun and trying to survive in my neighborhood, day to day. I used to run the streets, my mom used to be crying all the time, coming to get me out of the police station all the time. Sports took me off the street."

He discovered sports when he was twelve, beginning with boxing, and by age thirteen he had become immersed in them. At Hood Middle School, Johnson was the starting quarterback on the football team, the centerfielder on the baseball team, ran the second leg of the district championship relay team, and was the goalie on the soccer team.

Johnson said sports saved him from the streets; his mother told me that the source of his salvation ran deeper than that.

"Sports doesn't stop anything, basketball doesn't stop anything," she said. "The only thing that stops something is when a kid decides, 'This is what I want,' and stays away from the crime, gets his attitude together and stays away from drugs. As far as I'm concerned, all of those things are in sports. Larry wanted it so bad and he knew he couldn't get it if he was in the street. So it was a combination of his desire and my staying on him."

Throughout college and the NBA, Johnson remained connected to Dixon Circle. After his UNLV team won the national championship in 1990, friends took Johnson back to his favorite basketball court. "Three or four of the cats I used to play with had gone there after we won the championship and spray-painted my name, 'Big L, #4, Johnson,' everywhere," Johnson said, still smiling as he recalled it.

"It made me feel good to know that a lot of people live through you and a lot of people feel that way about you."

But he said that when he goes back to Dixon Circle, he is depressed as well. "I go back there and nothing's changed, I'm the only one who got out."

Fans and the sports press often deride athletes for not "getting involved," but at the same time they show extreme wariness when an athlete seems *too* willing to stay intimate with old friends and neighborhoods in a way that goes beyond league-sanctioned, drive-by volunteerism. When players continue to hang with homeys they've had since childhood, or find themselves getting caught up in neighborhood drama when by all rights they should be home asleep in the suburbs, the press squeals. Johnson's "rebellious slaves" comment suggested that he had made a rudimentary start to thinking of his own evolution and commitment to his community in broader terms than merely hanging out there or celebrating his "escape." He was asking more fundamental questions about whether, in some ways, he had "escaped" at all.

In Johnson's analysis, Dixon Circle was simply a latter-day plantation, an effective blockade of opportunities that reinforced the age-old power equation in America. The police were overseers to keep the residents in their places. The poorly stocked grocery stores, the bad schools, and the easily available drugs and guns kept the poor in their place as much as the old sharecropper system had. Johnson had made a fortune but maintained a focus that saw through his wealth. In a

comment that seemed revolutionary in the mouth of a pampered athlete, Johnson underlined his point: "No one man can rise above the
condition of the masses of his people. Understand that.

"So I am privileged and honored by the situation that I'm in, no
question. Here's the NBA, full of blacks, great opportunities, they made
beautiful strides," he said. "But what's the sense of that . . . when I go
back to my neighborhood and see the same thing? Everybody [else]
ended up dead, in jail, on drugs, selling drugs. So I'm supposed to be
honored and happy or whatever, by my success. Yes, I am. But I can't
deny the fact of what has happened to us over years and years and years
and we're still at the bottom of the totem pole.

"You know what I've come to find out in thirty years?" Johnson
said. "For a black man here in America, there is a struggle and you're
either in it, or you're not. You [can] go about your life like it's peaches
and cream, and not better the condition of black men and women
here, and better our lives and better our community here, or not. You're
trying to just do well by you."

This sense of disconnection from "struggle" among many athletes is
a common motif. Paul Silas, then head coach of the Cleveland
Cavaliers and a veteran of sixteen NBA seasons as a player, traced its
origins to the fact that young African American athletes are removed
from their communities at an early age.

"I don't envy these kids. They're in a quandary because they don't
really fit anywhere. They want to belong, they don't want to change
because they want to be like their 'bros.' But they're not. But they don't
fit in that other echelon either, in white society. They don't want that,
so they're just kind of neutral. They don't fit anywhere.

"It's hard. They've got to be leery of everybody. They have to look
at everybody for who they really are and for what they want from you.
Like I said, I don't envy any of these kids because they're trying to find
where they belong, and really they don't belong anywhere."

Don Chaney, the former New York Knicks head coach, said,

"There's a detachment when guys are making a ton of money. When you make a lot of money, you walk in a different circle. You're driving better cars, eating in better restaurants. You have a tendency to mingle with the upper class, and predominantly the upper class is non-black."

This was underlined by NBA star Grant Hill. Asked about the prospect of African American athletes moving in unison with a sense of righteous indignation, Hill said, "When you're making $200,000 every two weeks, it's hard to get angry about much of anything."

Asked about Hill's comment, Johnson said, "That's what I'm talking about, people saying, 'I got a good job,' that's it. People ask, 'What happened to the struggle?' Niggas got jobs."

Johnson said, "These people were saying I wasn't appreciative. Or I didn't appreciate where I came from. Who is it that I should be thankful to? Who is it that I should give thanks to for the blessings that have been bestowed upon me? That's the question."

For anyone who bothered to listen, Johnson's rough rhetoric came to a surprisingly pointed conclusion. His point was that in terms of his attitude and desire to maintain a connection to his brothers and sisters back on the plantation, he was essentially a runaway slave. But, rather than mixing in, "passing," or forgetting his roots, he decided to identify himself with the larger community and trumpet the corrupt replication of power relationships from the plantation to the ghetto to the NBA. He saw himself as still being heavily policed and clearly owned. For all the wealth he and his fellow players generated for the league in their comet-quick careers, his share would always be circumscribed— through bullying or forcible lockouts if necessary—by the dictates of the owners rather than by the widely praised American free-market system. All of his success, Johnson knew, would always be at the pleasure of the white men who signed the checks and the white media who told the stories. And rather than this unfair system provoking any sort of sympathy, it was endorsed by the average fan, who was typically already nursing resentment at the quick wealth these athletes attained and sometimes flaunted.

Larry Johnson saw his own life in the context of "the struggle," but even he seemed to come to his feelings more through intuition than anything else; he never quite articulated what exactly that struggle was, or what role he saw for himself in it. He never rooted his angst in the detailed history of his people—or even in the history of black athletes in this country. That context might have helped him make more sense of his discontent. As it was, it was too easy for others to dismiss it as the ranting of a frustrated player after a loss.

Near the end of the 2001 season, the Knicks were playing the Los Angeles Clippers in Los Angeles. During a time-out, a fan who had been heckling the Knicks from behind a bench yelled at Johnson, "You're nothing but a forty-million-dollar slave." Running down-court on his damaged knees, his career hobbling into its final act, Johnson might not have disagreed.

★   ★   ★

The story of the black athlete seemed to go from plantation to plantation, from Tom Molineaux fighting his way to freedom, to pampered millionaires still fighting to own their own labor. Throughout their history, African Americans in sports have broken through one dilemma only to see another emerge. In 2004 the dilemma of ownership seemed—at last—to be on its way to being solved when a black man became the majority owner of a major American sports franchise. But this seeming triumph only presented a fresh dilemma in the quest for power.

Entrepreneur Robert Johnson became the first majority owner of a professional sports franchise when he bought the expansion-team Bobcats in 2002. Despite the historic nature of the purchase, Johnson's move was met by ambivalence from the black community. © *Fred Prouser/Reuters/Corbis.*

The One Who Got Away?

The Dilemma of Ownership

ON DECEMBER 17, 2002, ROBERT JOHNSON, a black man, became the principal owner of the Charlotte Bobcats.

His successful bid to buy the National Basketball Association team was heralded as one of the most significant milestones since Jackie Robinson desegregated Major League Baseball. It seemed to be the ultimate triumph for black folk in the realm of sport, capping a history of continual struggle, from segregation to exploitation. Here, at last, was the final victory, catapulting the level of black participation beyond labor—no matter how glamorous—into the rare air of ownership.

Johnson wasn't, of course, a true original. With his purchase, he followed a line of black entrepreneurs in the sports industry. Rube Foster, "the Father of Black Baseball," had founded the Negro National League in 1920. Robert Douglas had founded the Harlem Rens, the first professional black-owned basketball team in the United States, in 1923. Fritz Pollard, the Brown University football All-American, had owned two professional black football teams in the 1930s. In 1989, Bertram Lee and Peter Bynoe were part of a group that purchased the Denver Nuggets, though Comsat Video actually owned 62.5 percent of the team.

Despite these precedents, Johnson's purchase meant a good deal more: He became the first black majority owner of a professional sports franchise in the high-stakes, multibillion-dollar era of the sports industry, an achievement signaling economic participation in the previously all-white club of modern sports owners.

Had Johnson bought the team a generation earlier, the purchase would have been met with unfettered celebration by the African American community as a breakthrough of monumental significance. "We need ownership!" was the cry in sports then, as it was in so many other areas of black life—an acute and chronic quest for a people born in slavery. Ownership was viewed as the logical culmination of the Struggle, the magic wand, the elixir to all of our sports woes.

At least that's what we thought, until it actually happened. The revolution had arrived, but, as has always been the case in the topsy-turvy, shape-shifting history of black athletes, the revolution didn't look like we thought it would. In fact, the announcement of Bob Johnson's ownership was greeted with mixed reviews. I was surprised by my own ambivalence. It quickly became clear that while black ownership in the abstract seemed like an unfettered good, the fact that the particular black owner would be Bob Johnson complicated matters.

The story of Johnson and BET, the television network he founded that became the source of his enormous wealth, is a cautionary tale about how the forces of race, capitalism, and entertainment can converge in unexpected ways. It also points to the fatal flaw in the theory that merely having black owners in sports would change the game.

Robert Johnson was born on April 8, 1946, in Hickory, Mississippi, the ninth of Edna and Archie Johnson's ten children. Johnson's father earned a living driving a pickup truck, cutting and hauling wood to the railroad yards. His mother, Edna, taught at an all-black one-room school in Good Hope, Mississippi. In 1963 the Johnsons moved north, to Freeport, Illinois, where they lived in a succession of old rental homes on the predominately black East Side. His father worked in a factory and continued to drive the pickup truck, salvaging junk around town. His mother worked at Burgess Battery and the MicroSwitch division of Honeywell. She also earned money as a hair stylist. Whereas his parents—like most black people of their generation—were severely limited economically because of their race, Johnson transformed his blackness into phenomenal wealth.

Black Entertainment Television was Johnson's baby, started with a $15,000 bank loan. It debuted on the USA Network on January 25, 1980, for two hours. Its first offering was *Visit to a Chief's Son* (1974), a safari movie that followed a father and son's travels through Africa. An odd start, yes, but the early programming of BET had not yet found its moneymaking formula. Johnson said of the fledgling BET: "It was uplifting and pro-social. The right kind of thing for us in the early days." Many black viewers thought so, too, and eagerly supported a network they believed was, at last, trying to serve their interests.

In the network's first year, Johnson set aside $1 million for airing basketball and football games of Historically Black Colleges. In the early 1980s, BET paid $500 to each school for a football game, whereas for the larger broadcast networks it wasn't unheard of to pay as much as $50,000 to schools for the rights to broadcast their football games. The black college games often featured spectacular halftime shows, another source of cheap entertainment for Johnson. Sunday morning gospel showcases and black music videos also offered Johnson cheap programming that he could use to maximize his profits and serve his niche. Despite his claim that in the early years his aim was to be "uplifting and pro-social," his underlying motive was always the same. From one of his white mentors, billionaire media mogul John C. Malone, Johnson learned a simple maxim that guided his approach to business: "Get your revenues up, and keep your costs down." There was room for little else in this narrow commercial ethic. BET was an outfit strictly out to make money.

On October 1, 1984, BET became a twenty-four-hour network, helping Johnson to extend his vision: "Our goal is to make BET the predominant source for advertisers to reach the black consumer." The limit of this vision is all too obvious: BET's focus was to be a dominant tool for advertisers, not a service for the black audience it was "delivering." During the mid-1980s, nearly 50 percent of BET programming was infomercials. In broadcasting hours and hours of crass infomercials, Johnson was clearly not using his tremendously powerful platform to inform or empower his audience.

Along with its infomercials, BET filled its programming time with hours of music videos, becoming an important player in the entertainment industry. Mega-artists of the era like Prince and Whitney Houston, as well as dozens of other black performers, could be seen on videos on BET at a time when they still struggled to be seen on MTV. Entertainment—in the form of black music videos and chitlin-circuit stand-up comics—came to be the network's prime identity, even though the videos were increasingly exploitative and the comics were systematically paid lower than their white counterparts.

Johnson took BET public on November 1, 1991, while retaining the majority of the company's voting shares. By 2000, BET's programming was 70 percent music videos, most of which featured the same set of predictable images of black life. Tommy Boy Records took out an ad that year in the *Hollywood Reporter* featuring a message that was all too revealing of the image of blackness BET perpetuated: "Congratulations BET! You keep on shakin' it, and we'll keep on smackin' it." The "it" is a black female derriere. This image—of the black woman's shakin', and occasionally smacked, rear end—is what remained of BET's blackness. And this is the image that the white-controlled Viacom would buy for $3 billion.

Ignoring calls of race betrayal, Johnson sold BET to Viacom and used the equity to fulfill his dream of buying a pro basketball franchise. He began BET with a $15,000 bank loan in 1979 and sold it to Viacom for $3 billion two decades later. As a businessman, clearly Johnson knew a thing or two. As a race man, his record was also established—and it wasn't pretty.

With his launching, development, and selling of BET, Bob Johnson proved that even though race was the means to his fortune, he was ultimately out for himself. Anyone who put any great hopes in him as a race man, or in his network as a force for change, was bitterly disappointed— and perhaps misguided from the start. High expectations were natural; as in sports, entertainment was a field in which black people had long toiled, but had never owned the fruits of their labor. And as much as any group of people, African Americans know the power of the media and the potency of images. From *Uncle Tom's Cabin* to *Birth of a Nation,* their destiny has often been closely tied to their projections in the American media—projections that have typically been controlled by white people and distorted beyond recognition. BET was the best shot yet for black people to own their own images in the most powerful medium of all: television. But black America was bamboozled by Black Entertainment Television. The images that BET brought to the screen were reminiscent of those described by James Weldon Johnson, when he wrote back in 1922 that "the Negro in the United States has achieved or been placed in a certain artistic niche. When he is thought of artistically, it is as a happy-go-lucky, singing, shuffling, banjo-picking being or as a more or less pathetic figure." Given a shot at reclaiming the black image from this history of distortion and insult, Bob Johnson only proved that a black man could put on a minstrel show as well as anybody.

To be fair, Johnson *did* create a successful business, at least as far as the balance sheet goes. He also helped groom a generation of black executive talent and did satisfy at least a portion of the black audience's demand for more black images on television. In fact, Johnson often proclaimed BET the network of black America. But then, when the time was right, Johnson sold out. He shopped black America's most important media outlet to white people.

All of this raises some unsettling questions for those of us who have always dreamed that black ownership in sports would represent a radical gain for black athletes and for black America as a whole. On the multibillion-dollar plantation of sports, will Johnson offer the black athlete, and black America, a sense of enfranchisement, or will he be just another businessman out to make a buck? Where is Johnson's true allegiance?

Is the core of his being black or green?

I wanted to get answers to these questions from the source. And Bob Johnson graciously took time to meet me one afternoon in New York for a stroll through the minefield of race and capitalism.

"I am a businessman first. That's the first foot on the ground," Johnson explained during our interview. "I come at it [owning an NBA franchise] as a business. That's where I initially come at it. I didn't invest $300 million just to say I'm an owner. I invested in it to say, 'I'm an owner with the chance to have a business proposition in sports.'" But herein lies the contradiction. For all of Johnson's "green first" orientation, he also stands ready to use race to his advantage whenever possible, especially in an industry dominated by African American players. Johnson believed that his black roots would give him a competitive edge, particularly when it came to the traditionally vexed relationship between owner and player.

"This *is* what I'm hoping," Johnson said. "I think if you're black and you believe in your blackness or the importance of racial pride, you will do something just a little bit harder working in a black organization, or for somebody black, if you respect that person. And it will show up just a little bit, because you'll think, 'We're in this together— as a black man out here trying to do something; I'm a black player playing for a black man. I can't let him down.' My hope is that it translates into a little bit more hustle, a little bit more aggressiveness, a little bit more behavior modification. If eight out of fourteen guys feel that way, then they have an impact on the city.

"If you get a balance of the players playing for the Charlotte Bobcats feeling that they're playing for racial pride, it might make a change."

Johnson also believes that race might offer a slight advantage when it comes to recruiting players.

"I think there are some who might say, 'Everything being equal, I'd love to work for him,' " Johnson said. "And maybe someone will do what Karl and Payton did, but they did it to get a ring." He meant basketball legends Karl Malone and Gary Payton, who took pay cuts to play for the Los Angeles Lakers in hopes of getting the championship ring that would crown their Hall of Fame careers. If Malone and Payton, prominent African American stars, would take less money to make a championship run, then what are the possibilities of star black basketball players coming to play with the Bobcats out of a deep sense of racial pride?

"One thing they are going to know when they come here: This team is owned by black people," Johnson said.

This potential—to get players to play for something other than their next check or personal pride, to believe they're playing for a higher cause—is what Bob Johnson brings to the table as a majority owner in the NBA. The idea that race can be a catalyzing force is very seductive, conjuring visions of a team that consciously represents the best of black America. This notion of athletes being driven by race is an old idea, one that stretches back through the history of sports in America, but one that normally applied to individual athletes, particularly boxers. From Jack Johnson to Joe Louis to Muhammad Ali, great black hopes took on the burden—sometimes willingly, sometimes not—of being symbols for the race. But this sort of symbolic representation would be particularly potent if applied to an entire organization, from the owner to the management to the players. It wouldn't just represent black individual prowess, which has been on display for hundreds of years, but the power of a black collective. Johnson clearly senses that it's an idea that some players might find desirable. But he never publicly embraces the idea, with all of its complicated ramifications. Instead he hints at it, in a savvy effort to exploit the potential desire of black players to play for a "black" team that represents black America. And he never suggests that a "black" team would orient or organize itself differently from a "white" team, never suggests that it offers a chance to overturn the exploitative model of professional sports.

Johnson also used race to persuade NBA owners to award him a franchise in the first place, choosing his bid over that of a group led by Larry Bird. The ownership council, during his presentation, asked Johnson if he felt diversity mattered. Naturally, he told them yes.

"Given the nature of your business," Johnson remembers telling the council, "if you're going to have any future, then you cannot ignore diversity as an issue." Johnson was here referring both to the racial makeup of the league and the potential for increasing the minority fan base of the league. He could also have been referring to the fact that the league's promotional idiom—its slogans and commercials, the musical soundtrack that accompanies the game at arenas and on television—is largely taken from contemporary urban black culture.

He went on, "If Bird had put up $300 million and I put up $300 million, they still would have had to pick me, under my definition, because otherwise they're saying, 'If there's going to be jump ball with white folks, then white folks will always get it, because we made the decision to give it to 'em.' [Our bids were the] same amount of money, and he's a basketball legend. Yeah, okay, but 75 percent of your players are black now."

In other words, Johnson used the racial makeup of the league—and of the country—to muscle his way into the owners' box of the NBA. He clearly leveraged not just his race as an individual, but a whole race of people, to get his franchise. And, as noted, he expects his race to give him some advantage in recruiting and getting the most out of his talent. So now, does Bob Johnson owe anything to those people—those 35 million—who helped him score a $300 million deal?

Apparently the answer is yes and no.

"One is you have to succeed at what you're doing," Johnson said. "I guess I'm saying the obligation you owe is to build up a dynamic of success to the point where the debate goes away. So it's no longer 'We got to give you the opportunity because you're black.' Now it's 'We have to give the opportunity to you because you're just good.' You got to get to the point where [American Express CEO] Ken Chenault can walk into American Express and there ain't no leverage point. You can't say, 'Well, gee, you know half our card users are black and we got to do this.' You got to say, 'We need the best guy, and the best guy is Ken Chenault.' "

Johnson seems caught up in his own nimble footwork here. In his bid for an NBA team, he essentially believed that the league should give him a team because of his blackness, while at the same time arguing that his ultimate goal was to help create a world that would award people based strictly on ability. Johnson has proven himself an able moneymaker, but that ability wasn't enough for him to gain admittance to the ownership level of the NBA. For that, he banked on his blackness. So the question remains, What can he do to pay back that debt in the short term?

One answer is that he could think about the franchise not merely as his possession, but as a joint possession, partly his, partly that of the black folks he leveraged to get the franchise. Of course, the same could've been said about his television network. So, when it came to BET, why did Johnson feel he had to sell to a white person, after having built up the company on the goodwill and economic power of black America? How could he have handled it differently and respected the equity that black people had in the business?

One possibility is that Johnson could have sold BET to a black investor for less money, for less of a profit, in order to satisfy the "debt" for leveraging the undocumented black masses. He leveraged black folks to help create a $3 billion asset. Of course, much of that value came from the work of Johnson and others. But how much of that was due to black leverage? Pick a number—say $600 million.

So that $600 million ain't Bob Johnson's, it's ours. Right?

"[What you're saying is that] I take the $600 million hit to keep it in black hands and that's the way I'm returning back to the undocumented investors—black people—their own assets, by keeping it back in black hands," Johnson responded. "You could then argue that you're passing on an asset that will then always be in the hands of black people. Berry Gordy could have done the same thing at Motown."

So far, so good. But black-built assets, assets leveraged on black culture and the legacy of the black experience, always seem to end up in white hands with no payback to the black people who supported the company. Why?

"The problem," Johnson says, "is that first you got to find somebody willing to pay. And you got to have confidence that they're going to run it almost like a trust, as a custodian for black people. That is very hard to do, and it's almost impossible to do if you have white investors in your business."

Of course, Johnson is right. He could have gone to John Malone of TCI with his idea to sell BET at a lower price for "the Cause." Malone would have told him to jump in the lake. And there isn't a gang of black investors ready to fill the gap to support black-owned organizations, a problem that stems, ironically, from the success of integration.

Integration weakened the collective resolve of African Americans and spawned a mentality—which Johnson mastered—of using blackness as a way to get a piece of the pie without necessarily feeling any reciprocal responsibility to sustain black institutions. This mentality was the natural outcome of a half-finished mission. Integration, while never truly complete, led to the splintering and tearing apart of black institutions and culture, making it difficult for African Americans to move in a concerted fashion. Without the collective spirit of institutions, black people are left wandering as individuals.

"You're preaching from my script," Johnson said in agreement. "The cost of integration can be measured in the decline of black economic power in some sense. Jackie Robinson, not to blame Jackie for this, but the fact that he went to say, 'I want to play for the white man,' that basically destroyed the Negro Leagues because everybody else said, 'The ice is colder over there'—which it was—'the water is good.' "

But the result was that black institutions were destroyed as each individual sought to improve his personal lot. Johnson claims he found himself in the same situation.

"Look at Motown," he went on. "Motown developed artists. When their contracts would come up, some of them would say, 'I love you, it's been good, but I'm going over here to take this big check.' Now, you can sit back and say, 'Can I blame a black person?' I got the same thing when I sold BET to Viacom. One columnist wrote, 'Bob Johnson sold BET to Viacom for $3 billion, and guess what, folks, he didn't even get money for it. He got paper stocks for it.' But the point was when I looked out, there was nobody out there to write a check for $3 billion."

This dilemma runs close to that expressed by James Semler, a black team owner in the original Negro Leagues, when he was forced to sell the New York Black Giants to Nat Strong, a white man. While many fans were disappointed, Selmer explained, "We needed cash and couldn't get it from any colored businessmen, so we borrowed it from Strong." That was 1933. Not much seems to have changed.

A businessman first, Johnson sometimes gives voice to his visionary side: "Before I sold BET to Viacom, I wanted to merge BET with Radio One—with the black radio company—and that to me would have been a major development that would have created overnight about an $8 billion, black-owned company with tremendous cash that would have been coming off the radio and the tremendous ability for a radio network to cross-promote the TV, the TV to cross-promote the radio—[a] tremendous footprint for entertainers to reach their audience, [a] tremendous footprint for politicians to reach their audience. The economic and political might of it would have been awesome. You could have said, 'Let's start a movie company 'cause we've got a way to promote and market it. Let's start our own record company because we got a way to promote and market it. Let's start our own black national newspaper because we got a way to promote and market it.' "

Johnson said the merger never took place.* "The young guy who owns the other business didn't want to see himself under my shadow It wasn't right for him."

It's clear that on some level Johnson understands the concept of "the debt," paying what you owe to a history of struggle that got you where you are today and to the struggling population that justifies your position. Now that he's entered into this new arena of sports, how will he respond to the debt? How will he repay a history of struggle?

⋆   ⋆   ⋆

Another answer is to offer opportunities to other black people that they might not have had at a white-run organization. And Johnson has done that, to some degree. Just as he did at BET, Johnson filled his executive ranks at the Bobcats with African Americans. His first significant hires were two black men with strong credentials, Ed Tapscott, the team president, and Bernie Bickerstaff, the general manager and head coach.

Bickerstaff grew up in Kentucky under strict segregation.

"When I got on the bus, I went straight to the back," he said. "I didn't even think about it, because that's what my grandparents did."

Bickerstaff entered the NBA in 1973 as an assistant to K. C. Jones with the Washington Bullets. He spent twelve years with Washington, and in 1985 he replaced Lenny Wilkens as coach in Seattle. Bickerstaff was eventually hired by Wes Unseld as coach of the Bullets and was soon thereafter fired by Unseld, who at the time was one of the league's few black general managers.

---

* Alfred C. Higgins III owns Radio One with his mother, Catherine L. Hughes.

At forty-six, the erudite Tapscott has credentials any corporation, especially a sports franchise, might covet: a bachelor's degree in political science from Tufts, a law degree from American University. Tapscott served as head coach at American for eight seasons, followed by eight seasons as a VP with the New York Knicks. He worked with general manager Ernie Grunfeld to recast the Knicks as a younger, more athletic team that came three victories short of a National Basketball Association championship. In a political shakeup that saw Grunfeld fired, Tapscott lost out and in 1999 found himself passed over as president of the New York Knicks in favor of Scott Layden, although Tapscott was thought to be the leading candidate. Three years later Bob Johnson gave Tapscott his second chance in the executive suite.

Johnson believes that the example of his ownership will provide "broader opportunity for people in the NBA." As Johnson has pointed out, his ownership has made him a role model: "You're seeing it now. Jay-Z wants to spend his money being part of the Nets, and you'll see more and more of those young Brothers who come up and want to be in sports because they like the feel of it, and that will have an impact over time. [Soon] you'll see younger guys coming in the league [as owners], and you've seen it already—the guys in Boston. They bring in Doc Rivers, no? And you see this guy Bruce Ratner is taking the Nets; he brings in Jay-Z—hip-hop guy. You know, they swirl around with black business folk and that's going to have an impact on the players, so that if Jay-Z sees other players and they're talking about ownership issues or player contracts, I guess they'll figure, 'You know, Jay-Z, y'all got to take care of us,' and to the extent Jay-Z can sense a reason [and] say, 'Look, we'll be reasonable and y'all be reasonable. Maybe you get a deal,' that to me is the most interesting dynamic."

To his great credit, Bob Johnson's rise to wealth has been characterized by his serving as a model for other entrepreneurs while also opening the doors for other black executives. This is progress and is one of the most commonly touted benefits of black ownership. But why doesn't it feel like enough? Why does Johnson's seizing control of an NBA franchise not feel like the exciting culmination of all these years of struggle?

★   ★   ★

The Bob Johnson story tells us something very important: Simply being black is not nearly enough to carry on that legacy. A black man can move the ball forward for himself—or even for a handful of others—but to become a genuine force for change, he has to act in the best tradition of that history, while seeking to learn from its mistakes.

The legacy of that historical search for power is perhaps a simple one, one that Tom Molineaux should've understood, standing in the squared circle in the center of a crowd howling for his blood on that winter's day over a century ago: Keep fighting till you win. At every juncture in the struggle, black athletes have fought hard and then let their guard down when they thought victory was in their grasp. Inevitably, that moment of lapsed vigilance was all the opening the opposition needed to strike back.

Black athletes have fallen prey to this again and again. When black athletes secured a toehold in the earliest versions of organized sports in America—in baseball and horse racing and cycling—they settled for individual success rather than trying to use what power they had to remake a system to ensure fairness and the possibility for future success. The Negro Leagues were undermined when Rube Foster died because he was the visionary who understood that temporary, individual successes weren't enough if they weren't accompanied by new institutions to ensure the perpetuation of that success. "Black style," for all of its revolutionary power, failed as a true revolutionary force, because no systems were put into place to make sure that style—the style created by a whole people—wouldn't simply be ripped off for the enrichment of a few. And integration ended up merely allowing black athletes to join in a corrupt, unfair system. Visionaries like Curt

Flood made the connection—Flood understood that it wasn't enough to be *allowed* to play the game, but that history and the legacy it offered demanded that he fight to change the system, not just buy into it.

And now we have a black owner. But without a full reckoning with history and its lessons, even a black owner is susceptible to the usual isolation and backlash. Buying in is only the beginning; the key is to transform, to make something newer, fairer, more just. Something that responds to the demands of the chorus of history to create something new, to change the game.

Soaring. Breaking free. *Image courtesy of Hank Willis Thomas.*

Epilogue: Making the Open Shot

For there is hope of a tree,
if it be cut down,
that it will sprout again,
and that the tender branch thereof
will not cease.

—JOB 14:7

ON SEPTEMBER 18, 2005, A GROUP of current and former players representing the National Basketball Association and the Women's National Basketball Association traveled to Mississippi to view the devastation of Hurricane Katrina. The trip was arranged by the NBA players union but initiated by the players themselves.

I drove from New York to Mississippi, not as part of any assignment for the *New York Times,* but to see the devastation firsthand and deliver some supplies. The caravan began in Jackson with a news conference. Afterward, players mixed easily with fans and posed for photos and signed autographs.

The next stop was Hattiesburg, where players held another press conference and helped unload trucks and distributed supplies.

It wasn't until the caravan headed toward Gulfport that the magnitude of Katrina began to hit home. The players slowly got off the bus and stared at what used to be a Las Vegas–like strip, once glitzy and glowing and crammed with tourists. The entire coast had been reconfigured. Casinos that had sat on barges had been lifted out of the water and slammed to shore. The back of one casino had been ripped off and blown two blocks away, and now sat in the middle of a highway.

Trucks that loaded and unloaded ships from ports across the highway were twisted in a heap a hundred yards from where they had been
parked. The most overriding sensation was the smell: The stench of
rotting carcasses was something that television images could not convey. The flood of 2005, which had called for, in the words of FEMA,
the "biggest single disaster response in our nation's history," was a
wake-up call for a global audience—those who were washed away as
well as those who watched. The disaster awakened us to the harsh realities of the widening gap between rich and poor. More than the event
itself, the reaction to the disaster became the focus of debate and controversy. Some victims complained of feeling like foreigners in their
own land.

Horrifying images underscored the reality that there are multiple
tiers of life in America. The images of death, desperation, hopelessness,
and poverty, flushed into full view, made many of us wonder where
this America had been hiding. We did not recognize it. Some of us did
not even realize this America existed.

The hurricane was also a wake-up call for this group of NBA athletes, because the hardest hit were black and poor, many of them having stayed behind because they could not evacuate—they lacked the
transportation and money needed to leave.

Many of the athletes were raised in Mississippi and other parts of
the South. They knew firsthand what it meant to live by a slender
thread. Justin Reed, a forward for the Boston Celtics, said he saw himself in the faces of young storm victims. "I come from a single-parent
home, and once upon a time we were homeless," he said. "I know how
hard it is to start from scratch, to have to build and build and wonder
if you're ever going to be able to live like you once lived. I feel what
they're going through because I come from a path like that."

As we stared out at the Gulf, for a split second I felt as though I
were standing on the banks of the Jordan River looking over the
Promised Land. Earlier in the afternoon, Shareef Abdur-Rahim of the

Sacramento Kings and Allan Houston, the former Knick, sat at a table discussing the crisis, as well as the dilemma of leadership among African American athletes. What was needed at this moment of crisis was a galvanizing figure who could lead athletes to mobilize, rally, and execute a collective plan of action.

But who might that be? Abdur-Rahim felt he was too young and didn't have the respect. They needed a Michael Jordan–type figure to captain the troops, to say, "This is the plan, I'll lead the way."

As deep and rich as their history has been, black athletes have failed to produce a leader who understood the potential of this black athletic nation to join in the larger push for freedom. That's because, in their own world, by their own definition, black athletes already were "free." Unfortunately the terms of liberation have always been defined by the white men who were responsible for their wealth.

When Pharaoh defines your Promised Land, you can bet you'll never reach it.

There was a flurry of individual initiatives—donations, contributions. Individual players performed good deeds in the wake of the storm. Most participated in a number of commendable initiatives, from buying books to buying groceries, through their various foundations. But no one could galvanize the collective power of African American professional athletes to create a more far-reaching initiative.

The question remains: Who will step up and take the shot?

What Katrina illustrated, quite graphically, was that the economic problems confronting communities from which many professional athletes come are too large for one foundation to solve. If players hope to make an impact, the principle they apply to basketball must also be applied to the arduous process of rebuilding communities: teamwork. "Much can be done when you pull together as a group rather than trying to do it as an individual," said Erick Dampier, the Dallas Maverick center. "Though this time, it's going to be very important for us to pull together as a group."

The Mississippi excursion was a good gesture, but by the end of the year, with the NBA and NFL seasons in full swing, the immediacy of the disaster, the sights, sounds, and smells of misery began to fade.

Where do we go from here?

The journey of black athletes has been an exercise in overcoming obstacles and confronting paradoxes. The obstacle part of the journey has been well documented. Less attention has been paid to the paradoxes.

The paradox for this contemporary tribe of black athletes is: How do I simultaneously move as an individual and move as part of a group?

A more fundamental question is: What constitutes "winning" for African American athletes in the twenty-first century? The question is as complicated as asking what constitutes being African American in the twenty-first century.

This was a simple question fifty years ago, when African Americans of all colors and at all levels of wealth and education were largely excluded, marginalized, not even allowed to compete on the same field as white men and women.

For my grandparents, born in the nineteenth century, "winning" meant survival. For my parents' generation—the generation of Jackie Robinson—"winning" was gaining access. After access came a fair chance and real opportunity.

"Winning" was Jackie Robinson's historic breakthrough on the grand stage of Major League Baseball. Winning was Althea Gibson's back-to-back victories at Wimbledon, Wilma Rudolph's three gold medals at the 1960 Rome Olympics.

For African Americans, the Promised Land has been a moveable goal that changes shape from decade to decade.

The Promised Land was a scholarship to a big white school and a fat pro contract. For those of us who make our living in athletics, the Promised Land, mistakenly, has become lifestyle, high-profile employment, and prestige.

The challenge of the first part of the twenty-first century is how to convert all of our accumulated wealth and presence into power. In the twenty-first century, "winning" for African Americans in the field of sport and play, from athletes and agents to journalists and executives, means extending the reach of power beyond the courts, fields, and diamonds. Winning means ownership: owning teams, owning networks, owning the means of communication, and owning our collective image.

The challenge for African American athletes in the twenty-first century, with unprecedented resources at their disposal, is building on the foundation, expanding, and—most difficult of all—working as a team to create a new Promised Land.

This, of course, is the question of the century—the question of every century for African Americans, in and out of sports: Where is the next Promised Land, and how do we reach it?

★   ★   ★

The first step toward harnessing the cultural and economic power of black athletes is forming a coherent association of professional African American athletes. There are organizations for every other type of black professional—physicians, accountants, journalists, attorneys—but there has never been a national organization of African American athletes.

An association would provide links and affiliations, set agendas, and define parameters. An association of professional African American athletes—like all professional organizations—would solidify a presence that has built over decades, framing issues, coordinating initiatives, and helping define what, in fact, it means to be a black athlete.

The late Arthur Ashe predicted that African American athletes would play a pivotal role in shaping a society in which they'd command an increasingly visible presence on the global landscape. Ashe constantly preached that African American athletes had to stop hiding from their responsibility to address hard social issues. He chided Michael Jordan for his neutrality on social issues and scoffed at the excuse that high-profile athletes who remained silent were actually working for change behind the scenes. Backstage isn't that large.

The Black Coaches Association was formed in the early 1980s by a handful of assistant basketball coaches. The BCA's original mission was to push African Americans for head coaching jobs in an industry where black men and women were dominant as players but nothing more.

After substantial growing pains, the BCA expanded to include every aspect of the intercollegiate sports industry: from coaching to administration to gender issues facing African American women.

An association of black professional athletes—whatever its mission—would potentially become one of the strongest associations in sports. Such a group would galvanize the power of a rich past and a prosperous present and figure out a plan for the future.

★   ★   ★

Historian John Hope Franklin doesn't think sports will ever be the Promised Land for African Americans. I spoke with Dr. Franklin in January 2005 on the eve of his ninetieth birthday. He has lived much of the history covered in this book. He was born in 1915, the year that Jack Johnson, the first black heavyweight champion, lost his title to Jess Willard.

Dr. Franklin was four years old in 1919 when Rube Foster founded the Negro National League, which gave black baseball players a home. He was thirty-three years old when Jackie Robinson integrated Major League Baseball with instructions from Branch Rickey to "turn the other cheek."

He was eighty-nine in November 2004 when black NBA players roared into the stands in Detroit and pummeled abusive white fans after a player was hit with a flying cup. He's seen black athletes go from pariahs to humble servants to outrageous millionaires.

This has been quite a remarkable arc, but Dr. Franklin doesn't think it marks progress. In fact Dr. Franklin, professor emeritus at Duke University, feels that sports has become something of a mirage, creating opportunity on the one hand but also creating the illusion that things are much better for black America than they really are. In fact, their prominence obscures the dire predicament of black Americans in the United States.

"There was always a time when society could absorb a select number, a small number, which would be the exception that proved the rule. You still have more black [men] in jail than you've got in college. Where are they in terms of income, where are they in terms of privilege, where are they in terms of just being able to 'make it' in our society? It's awful," he said. "It is distressing. So we have to put this in perspective. I know that blacks have risen in basketball, football, and so forth, but they still are the exception that proves the rule. I get more pessimistic the longer I live."

Still, Dr. Franklin ended on a note of hope. "In the end I have to be optimistic or else you can't get up in the morning and get through the day. "I have developed a capacity to make myself feel that things are going to be all right. Even if deep down I may have some doubts, I have to believe that they're going to be better."

In fact the element that links black athletes through time is the legacy of hope. This has been the black athlete's primary contribution to the journey of African Americans: providing a source of hope, a beacon of light. Jack Johnson gave the community joy in defiance. Joe Louis gave the community hope with knockout boxing victories. Jackie Robinson provided the metaphor of access and opportunity, Muhammad Ali provided inspiration with his conviction. The dominance of Venus and Serena Williams in tennis provided a glimpse into the power of self-definition.

Hope, that glimmer of faith in the new day, has been the thread that has guided African Americans through a journey of four hundred years. Historian Roger Wilkins eloquently spoke about hope and African Americans a few years ago when he was asked on what he based his own sense of hope.

"It's based in part on some of my black ancestors who never drew a free breath in their lives but who believed there was going to be a future, that it was going to be better," he said. "And they held themselves together and they passed on values even in slavery. And even while they were in slavery, they were doing things that created wealth and made this country better.

"In part I have a belief that the country can be better because I have seen that history, which shows it can become better, and I have lived through times when it has become better and I have participated in struggles that have helped make it better."

There is a glimmer of hope that the unity and sense of community that has escaped African Americans for so long will be recaptured by this small but influential band of professional athletes who occupy such a prominent position in contemporary culture, not merely in the United States but throughout the world.

There is hope that a new generation of athletes will use its popularity, wealth, and influence to help create a desperately needed economy for the vast majority of African Americans who sit on the periphery of society.

The evolution from being a Lost Tribe to $40 million slaves to completely free men and women is realizing that racism is more virulent and determined than ever before.

The reality is that, from Tom Molineaux to LeBron James, challenges have changed, but the struggle continues. There is no one Promised Land, but a succession of Promised Lands. And there's hope in that because, as every athlete knows, as long as you struggle, as long as you keep up a fight, no victory is impossible.

Notes

Prologue

x. *"I'm not quite sure making $12 million"*: Robert Johnson interview with the author.

xi. *"Do the players see themselves"*: Ibid.

xi. *"I knew that in [Ewing's] mind"*: David Falk interview with the author.

xi. *In 1988, the late Jimmy "The Greek" Snyder.* Snyder made the remarks to Ed Hotaling in February of that year; they were later picked up by a number of news outlets. For Hotaling's account of the comments, see his book *The Great Black Jockeys: The Lives and Times of the Men Who Dominated America's First National Sport.*

Introduction

1. *In 1895, Charles Dana, the editor of the* New York Sun: Fleischer, *Black Dynamite*, vol. I, p. 6.

Chapter 1: The Race Begins

14. *When Johnson defeated Jeffries on July 4, 1910*: David Porter, ed., *African American Sports Greats: A Biographical Dictionary* (Greenwood Press, 1995), p. 154.

15. *We were the "indecent others"*: Nasaw, *Going Out*, p. 47.

15. *"When I was out on a football field or in a classroom"*: LLoyd L. Brown, *The Young Paul Robeson: "On My Journey Now"* (Westview Press, 1998), p. 61.

16. *"A child of circumstances"*: Sammons, *Beyond the Ring*, p. 178.

16. *Even John F. Kennedy*: Ibid.

17. *Even Malcolm X, like Liston, a threat*: Ibid.

19. *Morgan won that 1945 meeting 35–0*: Morgan State University media guide.

20. *Two beer companies—Rheingold and Ballentine—were fighting*: Information regarding competition between Rheingold and Ballentine and other details of the Morgan-Grambling game were obtained from the author's interview with Collie Nicholson, Grambling's longtime sports information director. Nicholson, a former marine who began at Grambling in the late 1940s, was the architect of the Grambling mystique.

21. *Coach Robinson said, "Tank, this is a great opportunity"*: Eddie Robinson interview with the author.

21. *None of us was aware of it at the time*: *New York Times*, April 7, 1989, p. 4. In 1968, Herman Ferguson, an assistant principal in New York City, was indicted on charges of conspiracy to murder two moderate civil rights leaders. Two weeks after the Morgan-Grambling game an all-white jury convicted Ferguson of conspiring to murder Roy Wilkins, at the time the director of the National Association for the Advancement of Colored People, and Whitney Young, who led the Urban League.

22. *In fact, this game was a footnote to Dr. King's death*: Collie Nicholson interview with the author.

23. *Two years earlier, in his book*: Harold Cruse, *The Crisis of the Negro Intellectual*, reissue edition (Quill, 1984).

24. *In 1966 Stokely Carmichael*: Hamilton, *Black Power*.

25. *John "Frenchy" Fuqua, Morgan's star running back*: John Fuqua interview with the author.

26. *"What stood out in my mind"*: Frank Lewis interview with the author.

31. *The area is Sugar Hill, the building is "409"*: For a description of the building, see the *New York Times*, July 24, 1994, section 9, p. 7.

Chapter 2: The Plantation

35. *Tom Molineaux cursed under his breath*: For a full description of Molineaux's fight with Tom Cribb, see Pierce Egan's *Sketches of Pugilism* (1823).

35. *Molineaux, the impetuous black American challenger.* There is debate among scholars and boxing historians about Molineaux's roots, especially his slave roots. The International Boxing Hall of Fame inducted Molineaux in 1996, and the first line of his IBHOF entry reads: "Tom Molineaux was born a slave but fought his way to freedom and ultimately a shot at the heavyweight title."

36. *The British people were known throughout Europe for their rowdiness*: E. P. Thompson, *Making of the English Working Class* (Vintage, 1963).

36. *In an odd way*: For another description of Molineaux, see Peter Fryer, *Staying Power: The History of Black People in Britain*, reprint edition (Pluto Press, 1984), pp. 446–448.

36. *Most of the crowd had come here from London*: See Fleischer, *Black Dynamite*, vol. I, pp. 32–45, for a description of Molineaux's background.

37. *Molineaux had barreled into London*: In *Fights for the Championship: The Men and Their Times*, vol. II, Fred Henning writes that Molineaux won a series of matches in New York between 1798 and 1800 and declared himself champion of the United States.

38. *Molineaux's uncles were fighters as well*: See "Tom Molineaux" by Paul Magriel, *Phylon (1940–1956)*, vol. 12, no. 4 (4th Qtr., 1951), pp. 329–336; see also Fleischer, *Black Dynamite*, vol. I, p. 35.

38. *When the slave fight came*: Fleischer, *Black Dynamite*, vol. I, pp. 21–32.

40. *"Some persons feel alarmed at the bare idea"*: Egan, *Sketches of Pugilism*.

41. *"The affair excited the most extraordinary sensation"*: Ibid.

42. *Indeed, few had given Molineaux a chance . . . In the nineteenth round . . . "Molineaux astonished everyone that afternoon"*: Ibid.

46. *By 1810, free blacks in the United States*: John Hope Franklin and Alfred A. Moss, *From Slavery to Freedom: A History of African Americans*, 8th edition (Knopf, 2000), p. 218.

46. *Molineaux came of age near the end of an era*: Ibid.

47. *The Naturalization Act of 1790 was designed*: Paul Denice McClain and Joseph R. Stewart, *"Can We All Get Along?": Radical and Ethnic Minorities in American Politics*, 3rd edition (Westview Press, 2001), p. 211.

47. *Douglass did not like fêtes and festivals*: Frederick Douglass, *The Life and Times of Frederick Douglass* (Citadel Press, 1983), p. 186.

48. *"To make a contented slave"*: Ibid., p. 148.

48. *Douglass achieved his own liberation*: Ibid., p. 143.

51. *"It was a custom in those days"*: David Wiggins, "Sport and Popular Pastimes in the Plantation Community: The Slave Experience," dissertation, University of Maryland, 1979, p. 245.

51. *Another slave, William Mallory of Virginia, recalled*: Ibid., p. 244.

52. *"To any person apprehending and delivering at this place"*: *Maryland Gazette*, August 3, 1797.

52. *"It was common for planters to pit individual slaves against each other"*: Wiggins, "Sport and Popular Pastimes in the Plantation Community," p. 241.

52. *John Finnely, a former slave from Alabama . . . "The slaves' uncommon manner of performing"*: Ibid.

53. *In one narrative, Felix Haywood of Texas . . . Even Frederick Douglass, who frequently criticized*: Ibid.

55. *"The person who couldn't be broken"*: Ann Patton Malone interview with the author.

56. *In his dissertation*: Wiggins, "Sport and Popular Pastimes in the Plantation Community," p. 69.

56. *The point is not that slave children never fought each other*: Ibid.

57. *These included cotton picking, hog killing*: Roger D. Abrahams, *Singing the Master: The Emergence of African-American Culture in the Plantation South*, reprint edition (Penguin, 1994).

57. *In fact, in 1797 the city of Fayetteville, North Carolina*: Tom Gilbert, *Baseball and the Color Line*, reprint edition (Franklin Watts, 1995), p. 38.

58. *In England, beginning early in the seventeenth century*: Nancy Struna, *People of Prowess: Sport, Leisure, and Labor in Early Anglo-America* (University of Illinois Press, 1996), pp. 12–13.

58. *Eventually, in 1617*: Ibid.

59. *Sub-Saharan, non-Muslim Africans had a strong athletic tradition*: Baker and Mangan, *Sport in Africa*, p. 15.

59. *White planters judged an individual's worthiness*: Wiggins, "Sport and Popular Pastimes in the Plantation Community," p. 88.

60. *Their hearty physical presence prompted Theodore Roosevelt*: Dyer, *Theodore Roosevelt and the Idea of Race*, p. 95.

Chapter 3: The Jockey Syndrome

65. *Garrison was so acclaimed for his dramatic races and comebacks*: Hotaling, *The Great Black Jockeys*, p. 261.

65. *Likewise, the New York Tribune complained*: David Wiggins, *Glory Bound: Black Athletes in a White America* (Syracuse University Press, 1997), p. 23.

66. *Murphy's victory capped three years of escalating fame*: Hotaling, *The Great Black Jockeys*, p. 255.

67. *Even as the NBA actively grooms*: Steve Smith and Grant Hill interviews with the author.

68. *The black stronghold on the sport*: Arthur Ashe, *A Hard Road to Glory: A History of the African American Athlete*, reprint edition (Amistad, 1993), p. 50.

69. *This new sport was called quarter racing*: Hotaling, *The Great Black Jockeys*, p. 11.

70. *At a time when blacks were being demonized as beasts and rapists*: Ibid., p. 260.

70. *A year before Murphy's glorious Coney Island race*: Hotaling, *The Great Black Jockeys*, p. 259.

71. *Hawkins was the first to be lavished*: Ibid.
71. *"His sagacity is greatly relied on"*: Ibid., p. 183.
72. *According to historian David Wiggins*: Wiggins, "Sport and Popular Pastimes in the Plantation Community."
73. *Even after the Civil War, Hawkins remained loyal to his former owner*: Hotaling, *The Great Black Jockeys*, p. 196.
73. *The story of slave and trainer Charles Stewart*: Harper's New Monthly Magazine (vol. LXIX), June–November 1884.
74. *"I was just as free"*: Hotaling, *The Great Black Jockeys*, pp. 84–85.
74. *Before Hawkins and Stewart, there was Austin Curtis*: Ibid. p. 255.
76. *While Jimmie Lee, one of the last black jockeys to win a major sweepstakes races in 1908*: Ibid., p. 326.
77. *The proud Murphy was shattered*: Ibid., p. 271.
78. *"What made the colored boy drift away"*: Sam Lacy with Moses J. Newsom, *Fighting for Fairness: The Life Story of Hall of Fame Sportswriter Sam Lacy* (Cornell Maritime Press, 1998).
79. *By the mid 1800s, baseball was making*: David Quentin Voight, "The League That Failed," *American Baseball*, volume II, p. 106.
79. *Then as now, the media took a "they should be grateful" attitude*: Zang, *The Life of Baseball's First Black Major Leaguer: Fleet Walker's Divided Heart*.
80. *In 1883 William Voltz, a former sportswriter, hired*: Ibid pp. 43–44.
80. *In Toledo, Walker worked with a pitcher named Tony Mullane*: Ibid.
84. *Jack Johnson and Major Taylor stripped away*: For a full account of Major Taylor's life, see Randy Roberts's excellent biography, *Papa Jack: Jack Johnson and the Era of White Hopes* (Free Press, 1983).
85. *Taylor grew up on the farm of a well-to-do white family*: For a full account of Major Taylor's life, see Andrew Ritchie, *Major Taylor: The Extraordinary Career of a Champion Bicycle Racer* (Bicycle Books, 1998).
87. *The impetus for the vote*: Ibid., p. 37.
88. *"The crowds wanted action"*: Ibid., p. 165.
89. *"not one may be compared with [Taylor] in the matter of politeness"*: Ritchie, *Major Taylor*.
90. *"He was a racer"*: Sydney Taylor interview with the author.
90. *"I don't think he was proud"*: Ibid.
91. *"He had been a famous athlete"*: Ibid.

Chapter 4: The Negro Leagues

102. *Foster's vision extended beyond forming a league*: John Holway. *Black Diamonds*, (Mecklemedia, 1990), p. 75.
119. *Effa Manley, the co-owner of the Newark Eagles, said*: Overmyer, *Effa Manley: Queen of the Negro Leagues*, p. 269.
119. *"[Black fans] are stupid and gullible"*: Overmyer, *Effa Manley*, pp. 232–233.
120. *"Colored baseball has been acting"*: Sam Lacy, quoted in Overmyer, *Effa Manley: Queen of The Negro Leagues*, p. 297.
121. *"Organized baseball has practiced"*: Wendell Smith, ibid., pp. 231–32.
121. *The final blow for the Negro Leagues*: Bruce Adelson, *Brushing Back Jim Crow: The Integration of Minor-League Baseball in the American South* (University of Virginia Press, 1999), p. 8.
122. *Henry A. Scomp said that segregation*: George M. Frederickson, *The Black Image in the White Mind: The Debate on Afro-American Character and Destiny, 1817–1914* (Wesleyan Press, 1987), p. 267.
122. *Segregation helped maintain a social order . . . In white minds, the danger . . . In an 1899 article . . . Many of those who shared*: Ibid., p. 268.
123. *The impression was reinforced in 1949*: Account of Robeson's speech quoted in the *New York Times*, April 25, 1949, "Robeson As Speaker for Negroes Denied."
124. *Robinson told the committee*: *New York Times*, July 9, 1949, "Jackie Robinson Disputes Robeson."
124. *Near the end of his life, however, Robinson admitted*: Robinson, *I Never Had It Made*.

Chapter 5: Integration

127. *"Today, there are two organized leagues:"*: Epigraph by Wendell Smith from Joe Bostic column, quoted in Reisler, *Black Writers/Black Baseball*.
128. *A number of schools had multiple draftees*: Draft figures taken from *Total Football: Official Encyclopedia of the NFL* (Harper Resource, 1997).
129. *The irony of Cunningham's stardom*: Sam Cunningham interview with the author.
130. *"It was just one game"*: Ibid.

131. *"That's a myth"*: Ibid.
132. *"The powers that be who set the game up"*: Ibid.
133. *"I was excited"* . . . *She wanted to savor*: Maria Davis interview with the author
134. *"The black people were happy"*: Ibid.
137. *This created a family-like atmosphere*: Dana Brooks and Ron Althouse, eds., *Racism in College Athletics: The African American Experience,* 2nd revised edition (Fitness Information Technology, 1999), p. 29.
139. *But for black coaches and others*: History of Education Quarterly, Spring 2004 (vol. 44, No. 1). This article underlines the tenuous nature of faculty employment—including athletic personnel—in the midst of integration. In December 1950, the board of trustees of the University of Louisville wanted to close the segregated, all-black Louisville Municipal College, which it operated, and to integrate the two institutions' student bodies. Fourteen African-American faculty members and staff at Louisville Municipal College were informed that, despite tenure or contract status, they would be given two months of severance pay and were summarily dismissed. As the article notes: "In fact, for a period of approximately two decades, from the mid-1950s through the mid-1970s, African-American school staff at all levels—teachers, principals, coaches, counselors, band directors, even cafeteria workers—were fired, demoted, harassed, and bullied as white communities throughout the South reacted first to the prospect and then to the reality of court-ordered desegregation. No one was exempt."
140. *Black head coaches became assistant coaches*: For a broader analysis of the impact of integration on African American professionals at black institutions, see Robert Hooker, *Displacement of Black Teachers in the Eleven Southern States* (Race Relations Information Center, December 1970).
140. *In what would become a model*: An 1971 NEA amicus curiae brief argued that: "The impact of the displacement of Black educators is not fully depicted by a body count. Such displacement has a detrimental effect upon Black children. . . . Mistreatment of Black educators is a constant reminder to Black students of their own inferior status in desegregated schools. . . . Conversely, to the extent that Black educators are mistreated, attitudes of superiority among White children, teachers, and parents are reinforced, thus tending to undermine the desegregation process from each direction." (Taken from a reprint of the brief for the National Education Association in *Hearings Before the Select Committee on Equal Educational Opportunity of the U.S. Senate,* 5084–5085).
141. *The first all-black professional team*: See Charles K. Ross, *Outside the Lines: African Americans and the Integration of the National Football League* (New York University Press, 2001), p. 51.
141. *Wharton professor Kenneth L. Shropshire wrote*: Kenneth Shropshire, *In Black and White: Race and Sports in America,* reprint edition (New York University Press, 1998).
144. *"Without the presence of Negro American style"*: Ralph Ellison, *Time,* April 6, 1970.

Chapter 6: Style

149. *"When Jackie Robinson first started playing"*: Curt Flood interview for HBO documentary *Journey of the African American Athlete* (1996).
151. *Mays was the cornerstone of a second wave*: David Quentin Voight, *American Baseball,* vol. III.
157. *"People discovered that 'Hey, there's another level'"*: R. C. Owens interview with the author.
157. *"More of us came on the scene"*: Ibid.
159. *"Whatever you were doing"*: Ibid.
160. *Owens said that, for him*: Ibid.
161. *"There were quotas"*: Ibid.
162. *Owens has watched this evolution*: Ibid
163. *"In the past, the dominating big players"*: David Halberstam, *The Fifties* (Ballantine Books, 1999), pp. 697–698.
164. *"It's like, they made the free-throw lane wider"*: R. C. Owens interview with the author.
165. *On game day, Miami whipped the Longhorns*: William C. Rhoden, *New York Times,* January 2, 1991, section B, page 9.

Chapter 7: The Conveyor Belt

173. *"My, my, my"*: William C. Rhoden, *New York Times,* April 11, 1983, "School All Star Games Give Many Assists."
178. *"How tough is it to buy an inner city kid?"*: Alexander Wolff and Armen Keteyian, *Raw Recruits,* pp. 184–185.
179. *"Our membership is opposed to the games because"*: Warren Brown interview with the author, quoted in the *New York Times,* April 11, 1983, section C, p. 9.
179. *"That's not me anymore"*: Dennis Rodman, *Bad As I Wanna Be* . . .

179. *One egregious example*: Tates Locke and Ibach, *Caught in the Net* (Leisure Press, 1982), p. 42.
181. *"A lot of people put that pressure [on me]"*: Chris Webber interview with the author.
183. *"but we don't get too close"* . . . *"This is what the Belt teaches you"*: Ibid.
184. *Janet Hill, whose son Grant*: Janet Hill interview with the author.
185. *"And when he came back with the wrong decision"*: Kellen Winslow interview with the author.
187. *"I said no, no, no"*: Ibid.
189. *"Once an athlete begins to see him- or herself"*: Ibid.
190. *"He asked me a lot of questions"*: Ibid.
192. *"He understood the system"*: Ibid.

Chapter 8: The River Jordan

201. *His defense? "Republicans buy sneakers too"*: Guardian Newspapers Limited, March 2000.
201. *After the 1986 playoffs, Boston Celtic superstar Larry Bird told reporters*: LaFeber, *Michael Jordan and the New Global Capitalism*, p. 51.
201. *Phil Jackson, who coached Jordan through all six of his championship seasons*: Ibid., p. 27.
201. *"During a 1992 press conference"*: Ibid., p. 85.
202. *In a 1998 column, Joan Ryan compared Jordan to a Shmoo*: San Francisco Chronicle, July 5, 1998.
202. *Some of the most useful insight*: David Falk interview with the author
203. *By 1984 the majority . . . Falk recalled*: Ibid.
204. *"I'm not saying"* . . . *"His parents had raised him"* . . . *"I don't think"* . . . *"It's bad"*: Ibid.
204. *"It's like you finally get a great role model"*: Ibid.
205. *Three years into a new century*: For details of Jordan's dismissal, see the news stories by Mike Wise in the *New York Times* on May 6, May 8, and May 11, 2003.
206. *During their brief meeting, Pollin told Jordan . . . But money was "not what I was looking for" . . . Pollin replied*: Ibid.
206. *John Thompson, the former Georgetown coach*: John Thompson made the remarks on his WTEM radio show on May 12, 2003.
207. *"They exploited this man"*: Ibid.
208. *In Many Thousands Gone*: Ira Berlin, *Many Thousands Gone*, pp. 67–68.
211. *"It's not common for athletes, black athletes"*: Tim Smith interview with the author.
212. *"We feel it's our responsibility to speak out and lead"* . . . *"To me, when he says we want a forum, not a fortress"*: Ibid.
212. *At the time Lee said, "I'm not getting involved"*: Spike Lee interview with the author in September 1992; also in the *New York Times*, "Sports of The Times" September 19, 1992.
213. *"A lot of guys on the team were reluctant"*: Tim Smith interview with the author.
214. *He once told a friend not to deal with race*: LaFeber, *Michael Jordan and the New Global Capitalism*, p. 95.
215. *As Gordie Nye, a vice president at Reebok, stated*: Jim Naughton, *Taking to the Air* (Random House Value Publishing, 1993), p. 91.
216. *"You owe a great deal to the game"*: Editorial in *The Sporting News*, February 2, 1955.
217. *Refusing to disrespect Nike, Jordan emphatically declared*: LaFeber, *Michael Jordan and the New Global Capitalism*, p. 100.

Chapter 9: Ain't I a Woman

219. *"She broke ground for women's basketball"*: Pat Summit, quoted in an ESPN interview in February 2005.
219. *"Without the success, the international success"*: Ibid.
220. *"Lucy Harris helped us win a silver medal"*: Ibid.
220. *"It used to bother me, but not anymore"*: Lusia Harris interview with the author.
221. *Harris leaped at the chance*: Ibid.
222. *"She was to me like Shaquille O'Neal"*: Pat Summit, quoted in an ESPN interview in February 2005.
223. *"They didn't put a lot of emphasis on women's basketball"*: Lusia Harris interview with the author.
225. *while only 2.7 percent of the women receiving scholarships*: Welch Suggs, "Left Behind," *Chronicle of Higher Education*, April 2001.
225. *"Title IX was for white women"*: Tina Sloan Green interview with the author.
227. *"We have been perceived as token women in black texts and token blacks in feminist texts"*: Paula Giddings, *When and Where I Enter: The Impact of Black Women on Race and Sex in America*, 2nd edition (Amistad, 1996) p. 5.

228. *"That man over there say that women needs to be helped into carriages"*: Henry Louis Gates, ed., *The Norton Anthology of African American Literature,* 1st edition (W.W. Norton, 1996), pp. 198–199.

Chapter 10: The $40 Million Slave

231. *"Niggas are players"*: The Last Poets, "Scared of Revolution."
232. *"The reserve system was the same system"*: Curt Flood interview for HBO documentary *Journey of the African American Athlete* (1996).
234. *"Most of us were not courageous enough"*: Maury Wills interview for HBO documentary *Journey of the African American Athlete* (1996).
234. *"As he and Rachel Robinson moved"*: Curt Flood, *The Way It Is* (Trident Press, 1971).
235. He said, *"I am most interested in"*: Robinson, *I Never Had It Made.*
235. *"The sixties is an era"*: Curt Flood interview for HBO documentary *Journey of the African American Athlete* (1996).
236. *"And from the time someone made me stay"* . . . *"It disappointed me that I didn't win"*: Ibid.
238. *"I don't care if anybody likes me or not"*: *Chicago Tribune,* June 1999.
238. *"Those guys out there"*: Ibid.
239. *"Larry Johnson is simply a jerk"*: Sam Smith, *New York Daily News,* 1999.
239. Steve Bulpott of the Boston Herald: Steve Bulpott, *Boston Herald,* 1999.
240. *"Major intercollegiate sports"*: William C. Rhoden, *New York Times,* March 30, 1991, section 1, p. 31.
241. *"My mom was in the struggle"*: Larry Johnson interview with the author.
241. *"Sports doesn't stop anything"*: Dortha Johnson interview, *New York Times,* 1991.
242. *"It made me feel good"*: Larry Johnson interview, *New York Times.*
243. *"So I am privileged"*: Larry Johnson interview with the author.
243. *"I don't envy these kids"*: Paul Silas interview with the author.
244. *"There's a detachment when guys"*: Don Chaney interview with the author.
244. *"When you're making $200,000 every two weeks or so"*: Grant Hill interview with the author
244. Asked about Hill's comment, Johnson said: Larry Johnson interview with the author.

Chapter 11: The One Who Got Away?

248. Robert Johnson was born: See Brett Pulley's unauthorized biography of Robert Johnson, *The Billion Dollar BET* (Wiley, 2004).
249. *"It was uplifting and pro social"*: Ibid.
250. Along with its infomercials . . . Johnson took BET public . . . *"Congratulations BET"* . . . Ignoring calls of race betrayal: Ibid.
251. *"the Negro in the United States"*: From the preface of the original 1922 edition of James Weldon Johnson, ed., *The Book of American Negro Poetry* (IndyPublish.com, 2006).
252. *"I am a businessman first"*: Bob Johnson interview with the author
252. *"This is what I'm hoping"*: Ibid.
253. *"If you get a balance"* . . . *"One thing they are going to know"*: Ibid.
254. *"Given the nature of your business"* . . . He went on: Ibid.
255. *"One is you have to succeed"*: Ibid.
256. *"[What you're saying is that] I take"* . . . *"The problem,"* Johnson says . . . *"You're preaching from my script"*: Ibid.
257. *"Look at Motown"*: Ibid.
258. Johnson said the merger never took place: Ibid.
259. Johnson believes that the example: Ibid.

Epilogue

269. *"There was always a time"*: John Hope Franklin interview with the author.
269. Still, Dr. Franklin ended on a note: Ibid.

Bibliography

Anderson, Claud. *Black Labor, White Wealth: The Search for Power and Economic Justice.* Powernomics Corporation of America, 1994.

Baker, William J., and James A. Mangan. *Sport in Africa.* New York and London: Africana Publishing Company/Holmes and Meier, 1987.

Berlin, Ira. *Many Thousands Gone: The First Two Centuries of Slavery in North America.* Cambridge, Mass.: Belknap Press, 2000.

Hamilton, Charles V., et al. *Black Power: The Politics of Liberation in America.* New York: Vintage Books, 1967.

Dyer, Thomas G. *Theodore Roosevelt and the Idea of Race.* Baton Rouge, La., and London: Louisiana State University Press, 1980.

Ellison, Ralph. *Invisible Man.* New York: Vintage Books, 1952.

Fleischer, Nat. *Black Dynamite: The Story of the Negro in the Prize Ring from 1782 to 1938,* vol I. New York: C. J. O'Brien, Inc., 1938.

Gorn, Elliott J. *The Manly Art: The Lives and Times of the Great Bare-Knuckle Champions.* London: Robson Books, 1986.

Gottlieb, Robert. *Reading Jazz: A Gathering of Autobiography, Reportage, and Criticism from 1919 to Now.* New York: Pantheon Books, 1996.

Henderson, Edwin Bancroft. *The Negro in Sports,* Rev. ed., Washington, D.C.: The Associated Publishers, Inc., 1949.

Holway, John B. *Blackball Stars: Negro League Pioneers.* Westport, Conn.: Mecklermedia, 1988.

Hotaling, Edward. *The Great Black Jockeys: The Lives and Times of the Men Who Dominated America's First National Sport.* Rocklin, Calif.: Prima Lifestyles, 1999.

Hurd, Michael. *Black College Football 1892–1992.* Virginia Beach, Va.: Donning Company/Publishers, 1993.

King, Wilma. *Stolen Childhood: Slave Youth in Nineteenth-Century America.* Bloomington and Indianapolis: Indiana University Press, 1995.

LaFeber, Walter. *Michael Jordan and the New Global Capitalism.* New York and London: W. W. Norton and Company, 1999.

Life Application Study Bible. Wheaton, Ill.: Tyndale House Publishers, Inc., and Grand Rapids, Mich.: Zondervan Publishing House, 1991.

Malone, Ann Patton. *Slave Family and Household Structure in Nineteenth-Century Louisiana.* Chapel Hill, N.C.: University of North Carolina Press, 1992.

Marable, Manning. *Beyond Black and White.* London and New York: Verso, 1995.

Nasaw, David. *Going Out: The Rise and Fall of Public Amusements.* Cambridge, Mass., and London: Harvard University Press, 1993.

Overmyer, James. *Queen of the Negro Leagues: Effa Manley and the Newark Eagles.* Lanham, Md., and London: Scarecrow Press, Inc., 1998.

Reisler, Jim. *Black Writers/Black Baseball: An Anthology of Articles from Black Sportswriters Who Covered the Negro Leagues.* Jefferson, N.C., and London: McFarland and Company, 1994.

Ritchie, Andrew. *Major Taylor: The Extraordinary Career of a Champion Bicycle Racer.* San Francisco: Bicycle Books, 1988.

Roberts, James B., and Alexander G. Skutt. *The Boxing Register.* Ithaca, N.Y.: McBooks Press, 2002.

Robinson, Jackie. *I Never Had It Made.* Hopewell, N.J.: Ecco Press, 1995.

Rodriguez, Junius P. *The Historical Encyclopedia of World Slavery,* volumes I and II. Santa Barbara, Calif.: ABC–CLIO, Inc., 1997.

Sammons, Jeffrey T. *Beyond the Ring.* Urbana and Chicago: University of Illinois Press, 1990.

Sowell, Thomas. *Ethnic America: A History.* New York: Basic Books, 1981.

Wellman, David T. *Portraits of White Racism.* Cambridge, New York and Melbourne: Cambridge University Press, 1993.

Zang, David W. *The Life of Baseball's First Black Major Leaguer: Fleet Walker's Divided Heart.* Lincoln and London: University of Nebraska Press, 1995.

Acknowledgments

IN THE FALL OF 1996, I received a call from Elyse Cheney, a well respected and—as I would discover—tenacious literary agent who wanted to gauge my interest in writing a book about the African American experience in sports. Elyse and I met, discussed my perspective on race and sports, hammered out a proposal, and the journey began. This book, *$40 Million Slaves*, marks the end of that journey.

Endless love to my family: "Dad and Jan," "Lope," Sharon, Raisa; my sister Yaa Venson, whose spirit will always live in my heart; Adrienne, Kevin and Kyle; and my cousin Bob Gerrard for his unfailing faith and encouragement.

I owe a special thanks to Steve Ross, the senior vice president of Crown Publishers, who enthusiastically signed off on the project and allowed the journey to continue. I owe a debt of thanks to Arnold Rampersad, dean of humanities at Stanford University, whose critique of my initial manuscript illuminated the effort required to successfully complete a book with this reach. Thanks to Ayesha Pande, a Crown editor at the time and currently a literary agent, who helped keep the project breathing, and finally, thanks to "The Great" Chris Jackson, who brought the project home, and Bernice Bryant, my vice president and CEO, whose efficiency and dedication helps keep the ship afloat.

Deep appreciation to my friend Alex Bontemps for being a guiding light; and to my brother Girard, who provided insight from Germany. Thanks to George Smith and Mark Washington for being mentors and sounding boards and for assuring me that I was not seeing ghosts. A heartfelt note of gratitude for everyone at the Church of the Intercession, especially Canon Frederick Williams, Earl Koompercamp, and Dr. Ianthia Harris for making Intercession a haven and a blessing; and Shani Amana Moore for her invaluable research and insightful synopsis.

A special thanks to Sharon Howard at the Schomburg Center for Research in Black Culture for sending timely references that helped broaden and clarify. Thanks to Martha Biondi, professor of history at Northwestern University; to David K. Wiggins; Jeff Sammons; and to Urla Hill for her dedication and righteous consciousness.

Thanks to the irrepressible Joey Goldstein, who lent me his copy of Edwin Henderson's 1939 treasure, *The Negro in Sports*. My Morgan State University teammates, especially Mark Washington, Ed Hayes, Raymond Chester, John Frenchy Fuqua, Gary Merritt, and Vincent Robinson. To those Grambling Tigers, especially James Harris, Frank Lewis, Charlie Joiner, Coach Eddie Robinson, and Collie Nicholson. Gratitude to Dr. Phillip Butcher, Dr. John Hope Franklin, and the late Walter Fisher. Thanks to my colleagues at the *New York Times*, especially Jerry Eskenazi, Gary Bradford, Dave Anderson, George Vecsey, Bob Lipsyte, Laura Korbut, Neil Amdur, Joe Drape, Tom Jolly, and Bill Brink, who took time to listen and read. Thanks to all professional athletes, especially Allen Houston, Grant Hill, Steve Smith, and Larry Johnson; gratitude to John Carlos and Tommie Smith, Joe "The Jet" Perry, Lenny Moore, and R. C. Owens. Thanks to all of the "Sports Reporters," especially the late Dick Schaap and Joe Valerio for provocative Sunday mornings and never failing to ask, "How's the Book?" Janet and Calvin Hill; Wes, Nikki, and Joy Moore; John Thompson, Reginald Ballard, David Cummings, Delano Greenidge, and Eddie Mandeville. Mike Brown, Greg Simms, Sandra Jamison, the staff at Mechanics Library, and Pam Cash Menzies; David Cummings, Marissa Rosado, Bob Gerrard, Cornell West, R. C. Owens, Mark and Linda Washington, and Sherman Howard,

My neighbors at 409 Edgecombe Avenue—the spirits of those past and the vigor of those present; a thank you to Harlem U.S.A.—past and present—for providing the energy, the rhythm, and the reality.

Thanks finally to the memory of all of those who have fearlessly performed unrecorded acts of courage.

Index

About the Author

William C. Rhoden has been a sportswriter for the *New York Times* since 1983, and has written the "Sports of The Times" column for more than a decade. His work is distinguished by the breadth and scope of its subject matter, and also by the manner in which he manages to synthesize contemporary issues and sports into compelling commentary. Rhoden was the writer on the documentary *Journey of the African-American Athlete*, which won a Peabody Award for Broadcasting, and a consultant and guest on ESPN's *SportsCentury* series.